Feminist Debates

Feminist Debates

Issues of Theory and Political Practice

Valerie Bryson

Consultant Editor: Jo Campling

NEW YORK UNIVERSITY PRESS
Washington Square, New York

© Valerie Bryson 1999

All rights reserved

First published in the U.S.A. in 1999 by
NEW YORK UNIVERSITY PRESS
Washington Square
New York, N.Y. 10003

This book is printed on paper suitable for recycling and made from fully managed and sustained forest sources.

CIP data available from the Library of Congress

ISBN 0-8147-1347-5 (clothbound)
ISBN 0-8147-1348-3 (paperback)

Printed in Hong Kong

This book is dedicated to the memory of Kate Noel, bright and beautiful daughter of my friend Penny, who died on 12 August 1995, after being knocked down by a car. She was twenty three.

Contents

Acknowledgements		*ix*
A note on terminology		*x*

1 FEMINISM AND THE SITUATION OF WOMEN TODAY — 1
  Women today: the balance-sheet of change — 2
  Feminist debates — 5

2 FEMINIST THEORIES TODAY — 8
  Equal rights: the 'common sense' liberal approach — 9
  Capitalism and socialism: the oppression and liberation of women? — 16
  'Radical', women-centred approaches — 25
  Black feminism: from margin to centre? — 32
  The impact of post-modernism — 36
  Conclusions: feminist theory and political practice today — 43

3 GENDER, RACE AND CLASS — 45
  The language of 'gender', 'race' and 'class' — 45
  Feminism: a racist, class-based movement? — 59
  Who is the most oppressed?: from hierarchical to interdependent oppressions — 61
  Where do we go from here? — 66

4 FEMINISM AND THE LAW — 72
  A male-dominated profession — 72
  Equality with men: employment law — 74
  Equality with men: the criminal law — 78
  Gender and justice: women's 'different voice' — 81
  Law in a patriarchal society — 82
  Strategies for change — 84
  Conclusions — 89

5 POLITICS AND THE STATE — 90
  Feminist theory and political concepts — 90

viii *Feminist Debates*

    Recent political experience in Britain, the United States and
    Scandinavia   101
    Feminism and the political representation of women   112
    Conclusions: feminist political strategies today   121

6 THE FAMILY AND PAID EMPLOYMENT   **123**
    The family   123
    Paid employment   135
    Conclusions: towards a better balance in the
    interests of all   145

7 REPRODUCTION   **148**
    The situation today   149
    Competing perspectives on 'a woman's right to choose'   155
    Beyond rights: abortion and feminist debates   161
    Conclusions: feminism and the politics of reproduction   170

8 PORNOGRAPHY   **172**
    Background   173
    Feminists, pornography and the law: an overview
    of the debates   176
    What is pornography?   180
    Pornography, harm and the oppression of women   184
    Conclusions: debates and strategies for the
    21st century   192

9 THE PROBLEM OF MEN   **195**
    Theoretical starting-points   196
    Men and feminist theory today   203
    What is a nice man to do?   210
    Conclusions   213

10 CONCLUSIONS   **217**

Further reading   223
Bibliography   228
Index   256

Acknowledgements

I would like to thank my colleagues at Huddersfield University for enabling me to have a sabbatical semester to work on this book and for helpful feedback in the Politics Research Seminars. Special thanks to members of the Gender Research Group, to Andrew Taylor, Bill Stafford and Steve Brown for comments on early drafts of some sections, and to Peter Gurney for curbing my metaphors when they galloped out of control. Thanks too to many of the students in my Women, Politics and Society module for their hard work and enthusiasm.

Very special thanks are due to Ruth Lister and Elizabeth Meehan for their constructive comments on the draft manuscript, and to my editor, Jo Campling, for her confident support and patience when I needed to extend my deadlines. Thank you to Penny Noel for advice and references for Chapter 6, to Fran Thurling for the suggestion at the beginning of Chapter 9 and to Ben Enticknap for proof-reading much of the final draft.

Thanks to my friends, without whose practical, emotional and intellectual support this book could not have been written.

And thanks to Patrick and Lucy Bryson for keeping me in touch with reality.

A note on terminology

My use of the term *race* throughout this book refers to socially created identities and structures, not to biological categories. I have decided against putting the word into inverted commas to make this clear, because singling out this one term would seem to pre-judge feminist debates over whether *sex* and *gender* are also to be understood in societal rather than biological terms. For a fuller discussion of this, see Chapter 3.

1
Feminism and the situation of women today

As we enter a new millennium, many women throughout the world are campaigning, organising and working together to improve their lives. Their aims, methods and interests are diverse in the extreme. Some are working in women's refuges, others are establishing professional networks; some are campaigning against pornography, others are developing erotic writings for women; some are setting up women-only organisations, others are being elected into political office; some are demanding total legal equality with men, others want improved maternity leave; some are setting up literacy schemes for women, others are exposing the male bias of dominant forms of knowledge; some are campaigning for abortion on demand, others are insisting on the right of disabled women to have children. The list goes on.

These activities clearly do not constitute a united women's movement. Nevertheless, they all share an underlying concern with improving the situation or furthering the interests of women, or a particular group of women. As such, they have all at times been described as 'feminist' and all may in a sense be seen as a response to or continuation of the feminist movements which erupted in North America and western Europe during the 1960s and early 1970s. The status of feminism today is, however, highly ambivalent. On the one hand, it seems to be clearly a success story that has transformed both dominant ideologies and the material conditions of women's lives and that continues to inspire women throughout the world. On the other hand, its very successes have undermined its appeal to a new generation. In many countries of the world today, young women see legal, economic, political, social, sexual and reproductive rights and freedoms as obvious entitlements rather than feminist demands; for such women, feminism can seem at best out-dated and at worst a threat to loving relationships between men and women or an anti-male obstacle to genuine gender equality. Many other women who appear to be pursuing feminist goals reject the feminist label, which they see as elitist or racist, a form of political and cultural imperialism on the part of white, western women who are privileged in every way except for their gender.

Women today: the balance-sheet of change

The American feminist Naomi Wolf has argued that the 1990s should be seen as 'the era of the "genderquake", in which the meaning of being a woman is changed for ever' (Wolf, 1993, p. xiv). A subsequent study of the changing roles of young women and men in Britain adopted this term for its title, and argued that 'the cultural and economic enfranchisement of women is deep-seated and irreversible' (Wilkinson, 1994, p. 1). Such findings are not confined to industrialised societies; indeed, after the 1995 Beijing World Conference on Women, the Secretary-General of the United Nations declared that 'The movement for gender equality the world over has been one of the defining movements of our times' (Boutros-Ghali, 1996, p. 1).

The reasons for such optimism are not hard to find. Since the wave of feminist demands that began in the late 1960s, women in many parts of the world have gained a whole range of legal rights, opportunities and protections. There has been a near-global movement of women into paid employment: many of these women have moved into areas of work previously monopolised by men, many have achieved successful careers and full economic independence, and the earnings gap between women and men is generally in decline.

To a greater extent than ever before, women are able to control their own fertility through access to reliable contraception and legal abortion and to a range of new reproductive technologies. In some societies this has combined with a relaxation of restrictive sexual codes to increase women's freedom of sexual choice and expression. Violence against women, including sexual violence and domestic violence, is now widely recognised as a serious political issue rather than a joke or a natural state of affairs. In many nations, significant numbers of women have moved into positions of political power, and many women's pressure groups wield formidable resources. Women are also making their voices heard in the media and throughout cultural and academic life. Not only have they challenged the approaches and priorities of existing institutions and areas of study, but they are also being heard independently through the development of publishing initiatives and the growth of women's studies and feminist theory as serious academic disciplines. Above all, perhaps, there has been a widespread shift in attitudes both among ordinary women and men and at the level of national governments and international bodies such as the European Community and the United Nations. Increasingly, it seems that the goal of equality between women and men has been accepted, at least in principle, as an idea whose time has come.

These gains have, however, not been shared equally by all groups of women, and the lives of most women in the world bear testimony to the yawning gap between the political rhetoric of equal rights and opportunities and the political will and resources to translate this into action. In Britain, the Equal Opportunities Commission called its 1995 report 'The Lifecycle of Inequality', and national and international reports consistently highlight women's profound, continuing and, in some cases, increasing disadvantages.

In every country in the world, women retain the primary and frequently the exclusive responsibility for domestic and caring work; this is, however, largely unpaid and unrecognised in official statistics, as is much of women's work in subsistence agriculture. Significant gender gaps in earnings and career prospects remain universal, and all national workforces continue to be highly segregated along gender lines. The conditions of full-time employment still rarely take family responsibilities into account, while for many millions of women flexible employment practices have meant badly paid, insecure and unprotected part-time employment in a casualised labour force. These gendered disadvantages and a general increase in economic inequalities, both within many nations and between rich and poor areas of the world, have combined with a world-wide increase in female-headed households (25 per cent of all households in 1995 were economically headed by a woman) to produce an increasingly visible concentration of poverty among women: in 1995, 70 per cent of the world's poorest people were women (United Nations, 1996).

Despite the publicity attracted by individual women leaders, women remain grossly under-represented in decision-making positions. Key positions in the mass media, publishing houses and the universities continue to be dominated by men, as do those in the judiciary, national bureaucracies and the professions. Meanwhile, many women's lives continue to be restricted or brutalised by the fear or reality of male violence. As the United Nations Report to the Beijing Conference made clear, 'Violence against women is pervasive in all societies, cutting across boundaries of class, ethnicity, religion, age and a society's level of development' (United Nations, 1995, p. xii). In this context, sexual liberation has for many women meant little more than an increase in pornography and new forms of exploitation, while the double standard of sexual morality and hostility to lesbianism continue to restrict their sexual choices. Men's near-monopoly of decision-making positions means that they continue to regulate women's access to contraception, abortion and fertility treatment; women's reproductive choices are also frequently restricted by their lack of financial resources. In some parts of the world, women's ability to control their own bodies has been further restricted by the rise of religious fundamentalism and/or by nationalistic and ethnic conflicts in which women are of key symbolic and physical importance as reproducers and as sexualised bodies to be protected or raped.

More generally, official statements can often seem to be little more than political hot air and, even when these are the product of genuine goodwill rather than opportunism, they are seldom translated into effective and properly resourced programmes of action. At a more personal level, the shift in ideology often seems only skin deep, and has not produced any great changes in the attitudes and behaviour of men. The Platform for Action resulting from the Beijing Conference identified continued sexual stereotyping as a critical area of concern; it also noted that women's roles have changed much more rapidly and dramatically than men's. Even in Sweden, identified by a 1994 United Nations report as the country which had gone furthest in eliminating gender inequality, such stereotypes persist and feed into an economic and domestic division of labour which continues to disadvantage women (National Report by the Government of Sweden, 1994).

All this means that although women's roles and expectations may have changed dramatically in recent decades, the story is not one of simple progress, but one of confused, uneven, erratic and reversible changes through which many women have gained but many have also lost. It is therefore nonsense to suggest that we are living in a post-feminist world in which issues of gender inequality have been comfortably resolved. On the contrary, feminism remains critically important both as a political movement and as a political theory that can, by improving our understanding, enable us to develop effective forms of political action.

Feminist debates

Most women who call themselves feminists would probably accept Alison Jaggar's 'working definition' which 'identifies feminism with the various social movements dedicated to ending the subordination of women' (Jaggar, 1994b, p. 2). Many would also agree that 'feminist theories ultimately are tools designed for a purpose – the purpose of understanding women's subordination in order to end it (Jaggar and Rothenberg, 1993, p. xvii). This does not, however, mean that there is a united feminist movement; on the contrary, feminists are profoundly and at times bitterly divided, not only over political priorities and methods, but also over goals.

Given the complexity of the nature, causes and consequences of inequalities between women and men and their inter-relationships with other social divisions, political disagreements among feminists are hardly surprising. They are also the product of deep-seated theoretical differences. These involve competing arguments and assumptions about the very nature of politics, the meaning of equality, the significance of sexual difference and the possibility of social and economic change. They are, however, not always explicitly articulated, consciously recognised or consistently held. The result is often an inconsistent approach to political activity and analysis which confuses questions of style with those of substance and fails to distinguish between genuine political disputes and less significant differences of emphasis or priority.

The aim of this book is to contribute to feminist politics by clarifying key areas of current western feminist debate, analysing the theoretical assumptions underlying them, disentangling genuine disagreements from questions of political strategy and suggesting some possible ways forward. Although detailed discussion of non-western societies is beyond its scope, it recognises that women's movements in other parts of the world have never been simply a response to western feminist agendas. Rather, they have their own specific causes and independent histories; increasingly, they are also having an impact upon the perceptions and priorities of feminists in the west.

After an analysis of competing theoretical perspectives and assumptions in Chapter 2, I focus on seven key areas of debate. Chapter 3 explores the ways in which gender might be related to the social inequalities of race and class. It examines arguments over which is the most fundamental form of oppression, whether middle-class white feminists have wrongly claimed to speak on behalf of all women, whether such feminists are guilty of racism, and whether black women should organise separately.

Chapter 4 examines feminist approaches to law. It contrasts feminist demands for complete legal equality and gender-blind legislation with the insistence that women's gender-specific needs and interests should be recognised and protected by law, and with the demand for affirmative action in favour of women. It also questions whether the law can be used to achieve feminist goals, or whether it is inherently patriarchal.

Chapter 5 focuses upon political activity and organisation. It raises basic issues to do with the nature and definition of politics, the collective interests of women and whether feminists can achieve real change by working through the state. It asks whether quotas are the best way of improving women's representation in elected bodies, and what such increased representation might be expected to achieve.

Chapter 6 brings together different aspects of women's lives by exploring the inter-relationships between paid work and the family. It asks whether feminist demands for equal career opportunities are really what women want, whether equality within the workplace can be achieved without radical changes within the home, how the traditional family is being affected by the movement of women into paid employment, and whether women can expect men or the state to share their traditional domestic and caring responsibilities.

Reproduction is the topic of Chapter 7. An earlier general consensus that 'a woman's right to choose' is a central feminist demand has given way to feminist admissions of ambivalence around abortion, concern about the eugenic implications of fertility control and disagreements over whether new reproductive technologies represent an increase in women's choices or new forms of patriarchal control.

Chapter 8 focuses on pornography, linking debates over censorship with analyses of sexuality and the extent, significance and causes of male sexual violence against women. It questions whether sexual orientation and practices are purely personal matters, and whether heterosexuality is inherently oppressive for women.

Chapter 9 turns to 'the man question'. Many feminists have always argued that men, too, will benefit from a more egalitarian society; others, however, argue that they have too much to lose and that they are so advantaged by living in a patriarchal society that they will not pay more than lip-service to change. Others go further and argue that because men as a group systematically oppress women, they must be seen as 'the enemy'; some even argue that men's nature is inherently oppressive and aggressive, and that this is based in their biology. Disagreements here have clear implications for political strategy, women's personal lives and the possibility of a more harmonious society.

None of these debates is self-contained. Rather, each is interconnected with all the others, and common themes recur. It is my argument throughout this book that these political disputes among feminists frequently reflect underlying theoretical differences, and that it is essential to recognise and clarify these if feminist politics is to progress. The discussion in the next chapter is, therefore, not intended as an end in itself, but as an introductory guide which suggests some of the political implications of the different theoretical approaches.

2
Feminist theories today

Feminist theory has never been a united body of thought. Its many strands have evolved from a wide range of 'malestream' theoretical perspectives, and also from the diverse experiences of different groups of women. By the 1980s, many writers identified liberal, socialist/Marxist and radical feminism as its three main branches. Since then, many other categories have been identified: most frequently black and post-modern feminism, but also lesbian feminism, cultural feminism, standpoint feminism, global feminism, anti-racist feminism, disability feminism, power feminism, victim feminism and new feminism. Such classifications are to some extent artificial, and can represent an attempt to impose order upon fluid, interlocking and interactive ways of thinking which, by treating different approaches as competitive rather than complementary, restricts the free development of ideas. Nevertheless, a provisional identification of theoretical starting-points can help to clarify debates, disentangle arguments and expose contradictions. Although this chapter eschews definitive labels, it does, therefore, represent an attempt to identify key strands in terms of the organising principles and theoretical assumptions that underlie political debate.

This does not mean that any given feminist or campaigning group can necessarily be identified as an exponent of one particular theory. On the contrary, one of the central arguments of this book is that people frequently draw their ideas from more than one theoretical starting-point, although they are usually not aware that they have done so. These ideas will often reinforce each other, or interact to produce a deeper understanding than would otherwise be possible. At times, however, they can come into conflict, so that two contradictory sets of beliefs are often held simultaneously by one institution, group or individual. Failure to understand this can cause much political confusion; if we are to develop a more consistent and effective feminist politics, we need to acknowledge such conflicts and recognise their source in underlying theory.

Throughout this book, I attempt to provide a balanced discussion that will enable readers to judge for themselves the validity of competing arguments. It is not possible, however, to write as an outside observer clinically reporting facts and reaching objective conclusions; as a member of society who calls herself a feminist, I am inevitably a participant in the debates which I am examining. A few years ago, I would, if pushed for a label, have described myself as a socialist feminist whose ideas were informed by radical feminist analysis, and who was generally critical of much recent liberal and post-modern feminist writing. Since then, my perspectives have been altered by the writings of black feminists and disabled feminists; I have also found that, handled carefully, post-modernist insights can be helpful to feminist analysis. In the process of writing this book, I have had to question many of my own assumptions, and it seems clear that, in the real world, compromises have to be made and that the best strategies may vary with political circumstances: what is liberatory in one context may be regressive in another. My aim is, therefore, to provoke thought rather than to point to definitive solutions.

Equal rights: the 'common sense' liberal approach

In western democracies today, there is widespread agreement that women have as much right as men to be educated, to vote and to stand for political office; that women are entitled to work outside the home whether or not they are married; that men and women doing the same work should receive the same pay and that men are not entitled to use violence against their wives. Many also believe that the mothers of young children should be enabled or encouraged to enter paid employment, that women should be better represented in legislative assemblies and that a married woman has a right to refuse sex with her husband. Although none of these beliefs is uncontested, they have become increasingly accepted as common sense assumptions rather than controversial feminist demands.

This represents a profound shift since the 19th century, when it was generally accepted that women were incapable of benefiting from education or of exercising political judgement. It was also widely believed that women could have no respectable role outside the home, and that wives should be seen as the property of their husbands. These beliefs about women increasingly co-existed, however, with liberal and liberal democratic ideas about individual rights; these ideas provided a language through which women could articulate demands for change without challenging dominant political principles.

According to the liberal theories that developed from the 17th century onwards, individuals have a right to own property, sell their labour and go about their lives within a legal framework that protects them from arbitrary interference by governments or other individuals. Later, the assertion of these rights was combined with the democratic claim that individuals also have a right to choose their own representatives to govern them. It was argued that men have these rights because they are rational beings and therefore able and entitled to make their own choices and defend their own interests.

Most early liberal and liberal democratic theorists denied that these rights could be extended to women, indeed many argued that women were biologically incapable of the full development of reason. Nevertheless, from the early years of liberalism some women publicly argued that they were just as intelligent and rational as men, and that if they appeared inferior this was a result of their upbringing and lack of education rather than a quality inherent in their nature. If this basic point is conceded, others logically follow. Early feminists such as Mary Astell (1666–1731) therefore argued that women's ability to reason meant that they were of as much human worth as men, that they should be educated equally and that they should be enabled to live independently if they wished, rather than being forced by economic necessity to become the property of a man through marriage. As ideas of the 'rights of man' entered the political vocabulary more fully (most dramatically during the American struggle for independence from Britain and the French Revolution of 1879), Mary Wollstonecraft (1759–97) and other late 18th century feminists claimed that women's equal worth entitled them to the same rights as men in terms of education, employment, property and the protection of the civil law.

During the 19th century, men's demand for rights increasingly focused on the right to vote, which also became a key demand for feminists such as Elizabeth Cady Stanton (1815–1902) and Susan Anthony (1820–1906) in the United States, and Harriet Taylor (1807–58) and John Stuart Mill (1806–73) in Britain. Here, again, feminists could use existing arguments about individual rights to argue that if women are treated as autonomous, self-determining individuals, rather than simply as daughters, wives and mothers to be owned, controlled or protected by men, they can transcend the limitations of their 'womanly condition' and lay claim to citizenship rights on the same basis as men.

These ideas were further extended in the second half of the twentieth century, when feminists insisted that women were entitled to participate in the public worlds of politics and paid employment, whether or not they also chose to get married and have children. This approach was epitomised by Betty Friedan's *The Feminine Mystique*, first published in 1963. This best-selling book articulated the discontent experienced by many American housewives, and in 1996 it inspired the formation of the National Organisation for Women (NOW), which aimed at bringing women 'into full participation in the mainstream of American society *now*, exercising all the privileges and responsibilities thereof in truly equal partnership with men'. In 1993, Naomi Wolf's *Fire with Fire* updated this approach with the argument that women must refuse to see themselves as victims; rather, they must embrace what she calls 'power feminism', which demands that women realise their right to determine their own lives and teaches them to overcome their fear of success. Like the other writers and activists who come from a liberal perspective, Wolf argues that women's rights are a form of human rights, and that feminism must not be anti-men; male abuses of power must be resisted, but men, too, can learn the benefits of living in a sexually egalitarian society.

Ideas of autonomy and self-determination were also invoked in campaigns demanding access to abortion, and 'A Woman's Right to Choose' became a key rallying cry of the new feminist movement. From a liberal perspective, this, too, could seem to represent simply the consistent application of existing principles rather than any attempt to overturn them.

Feminist critiques (1): rejection of the male norm

Although none of these extensions of liberal principles to women was conceded readily or without a struggle, women in western democracies do today enjoy more or less the same legal rights as men. This does not of course mean that they are equal in practice. As we shall see in Chapter 4, feminists are now divided as to whether the law can be used to achieve more substantive equality. For some, a more consistent and strictly enforced application of the liberal principle of equality is required. For others, however, the whole liberal approach is flawed and inappropriate for feminist purposes. Precisely because it is an extension of existing principles that does not appear to require the abandonment of 'common sense' assumptions, the liberal approach is said to accept without criticism a set of values that are essentially male.

Such criticisms stem partly from liberalism's underlying assumptions about human nature. The independent individual who is entitled to rights is primarily a cerebral rather than a physical being and, critics argue, the whole tradition of liberal individualism is fundamentally flawed because it artificially abstracts people from both their physical bodies and their social relationships and treats them as autonomous, selfish and self-sufficient. Alison Jaggar has coined the term 'political solipsism' for such individualism which, she says, is based on a male perspective that cannot understand caring relationships and ignores the periods of physical and emotional dependency that are basic to the human condition (Jaggar, 1983).

Although liberal rights theorists have not all adopted such an atomistic approach as the critique suggests, highly individualistic approaches to rights have been politically very influential in recent years, particularly in the United States, where a culture of competitive individualism has always been strong. Such an approach can lose sight of the power relationships within which rights are exercised and choices made, and forget that social circumstances can restrict an individual's opportunities as effectively as legal prohibition.

The importance that liberalism attaches to rationality, self-determination and equal competition is also said to be the result of a male perspective which denies the value of qualities traditionally associated with women such as empathy, nurturing and co-operation. From this dominant perspective, much of the important domestic and caring work that has traditionally been done by women also becomes invisible. Society's reproductive and caring needs will however not simply 'go away' once it is recognised that women have a right to fulfil themselves in other roles. The goal of liberation from domesticity therefore begs the question of who is to clean the house and provide care for children and others who need it, if this is no longer the responsibility of women. This question is particularly difficult to answer from a liberal perspective, which sees the family as an essential foundation of a civilised society and would not favour collectivist or state-sponsored solutions.

An uncritical acceptance of male norms is also reflected in the assumption that women's aim should be to become like men and to seek success within existing structures and according to existing rules, rather than seeking to change them. This approach assumes that if women are not actually discriminated against, then they are free to compete with men and have only themselves to blame if they do not succeed. Some feminists, however, would prefer to challenge such factors as the confrontational and macho style of party politics, or working practices which deny men as well as women the opportunity to combine a career with family responsibilities. Some would also argue that although it seems to be a matter of 'common sense' that women should have the rights that a liberal agenda demands, it is also obvious that women are not in all respects the same as men, that their social situation and reproductive role may give rise to particular needs and interests, and that society will suffer if their traditional work is no longer done.

Male values and interests are also said to be behind liberalism's traditional distinction between public and private life and its insistence that the latter cannot be a matter of political concern. Critics say that this is an artificial distinction which denies the existence of structured power relationships within the family and conceals the ways in which inequalities within the home restrict women's ability to compete with men in politics or employment.

Feminist critiques (2): the role of the state

During the 1980s, the influence of New Right ideas, expressed in Britain as Thatcherism and in the United States as Reaganomics, brought to the fore those strands in liberal thought that stress individual self-reliance and freedom from state intervention. There is a clear tension between these and feminist demands for active policies to eliminate discrimination against women or to provide childcare, maternity leave and adequate welfare services. The individualistic assumptions of women like Margaret Thatcher, who always insisted that she had succeeded on merit and that women should expect no special favours or treatment, also make it difficult to see the ways in which the structures, norms and reward systems of society continue systematically to disadvantage women. They would, therefore, appear to rule out most forms of affirmative action.

During the 1990s, attempts to 'roll back the state' have continued in most western democracies, and many women have been hit by cuts in welfare provision that have increased their caring responsibilities for children and elderly or disabled family members at the same time as insisting that they themselves become more self-reliant. In the de-regulated economies of post-communist eastern Europe, women have fared particularly badly. State nurseries have been closed, the gender gap in pay has widened and there is overt discrimination of a kind now illegal in the west (Corrin, 1992; Einhorn, 1993); meanwhile pornography and prostitution have been increasingly freed from restriction, and there is a profitable sex trade in east European women with western societies (Khodyreva, 1996).

In the past, the principles of liberal democracy have proved more compatible both with Keynsian ideas about the need to regulate the free market economy and with the development of welfare states aimed at providing at least a minimum standard of physical security for all citizens. Such provision has gone furthest in the Scandinavian nations, where liberal principles of individual rights have merged with more collectivist ideas about social responsibility. The resulting form of social democracy has incorporated both industry and trade unions into political decision-making, developed the most extensive welfare systems in the west and adopted systematic approaches to the elimination of inequality, including inequalities of gender. As a result, the sexes are probably more equal here than anywhere else in the world. Nevertheless, some critics claim that full equality will never be achieved within existing frameworks, for these continue to reflect liberal beliefs in the impartiality of the law and the state. In reality, such critics claim, women are still having to live in a world in which the rules were written by men; although they may have freed themselves from dependence upon individual men, they have become dependent upon the patriarchal state (see Chapter 5). From this critical perspective, even interventionist approaches share liberalism's failure to understand the gendered and/or class nature of state power and the interests men have in maintaining their privileges. It suggests that once again feminists must challenge the key assumptions of liberal thought if they are to achieve effective change.

The demand for equality also raises the question of 'equality with whom?'. Here feminists are often accused of reflecting only the concerns of middle-class white women who aspire to the privileges of the most successful men. For such critics, the liberal approach does not reflect the values of all men, but only the most privileged. It therefore leads women to ignore the oppression experienced by many men, and accepts uncritically the values of an economic system based on the pursuit of profit rather than the satisfaction of human need, and a competitive and hierarchical society in which most women and men can only be losers.

Feminism and liberalism today

As Imelda Whelehan has said, feminists coming from a liberal perspective 'tend not to identify their position as "political" but rather as a sensible, moderate and reasonable claim for formal sexual equality' (Whelehan, 1995, p. 27). Such a claim has been in many ways successful, so that liberalism has historically proved to be a powerful liberatory force, and the acquisition of formal rights has opened up unprecedented opportunities and provided protection for many women.

Today few feminists would want to abandon the gains that have been made or to argue that they should not be vigorously defended. However, the above criticisms suggest that the principles of liberalism have been pushed to the limit by feminist demands, which have revealed the gendered nature of many of its most basic beliefs and exposed the self-contradictory nature of its implications for women. Many also argue that it is impossible to isolate issues of gender equality from the class society in which they occur, and look to socialist rather than liberal ideas for feminist solutions.

Capitalism and socialism: the oppression and liberation of women?

Socialism covers a huge range of political theories and practices from reformist social democracy to revolutionary Marxist communism. Despite their profound differences, these share a general belief that unrestricted capitalism is oppressive for most men and women, and that greater economic equality in a less exploitative system is both possible and desirable. They also tend to see collective class interests rather than individual rights as the primary focus of political concern.

Historically, many socialist writers and activists, including Karl Marx, have failed to address the issue of women's subordination in any detail. Others, such as the British 'utopian' socialist William Thompson (1775–1834), the German Marxist Clara Zetkin (1857–1933), the Russian Bolshevik Alexandra Kollontai (1873–1952) and the American socialist Charlotte Perkins Gilman (1860–1935) prioritised it as a central concern. Many have claimed that a systematic application of Marx's theory holds the key to ending women's oppression, and the attempt to utilise Marxism for feminist ends has been an important strand in recent feminist thought. Such thinking has been less influential in the United States than in Europe, and today socialism in general is on the defensive. Nevertheless, some feminists continue to claim that the goals of feminism cannot be separated from those of socialism, and that Marxist theory can contribute to feminist understanding.

The theoretical attractiveness of socialism

Socialist approaches appeal to some feminists in a number of interconnected ways. In the first place, socialism, like liberalism, promises equal rights and opportunities to all individuals; unlike liberalism, however, it stresses economic and social rights and freedom from exploitation, and prioritises the interests of working class people. As such, some would say it is of more relevance to 'ordinary people' than the formal legal rights offered by liberalism, and many feminists have argued that it is only in the context of a general movement to economic equality that the needs of all groups of women, rather than those of an elite minority, can be met. For some, these egalitarian goals require the kind of mixed economy and welfare provision that were introduced in Britain after the Second World War and accepted by both the main political parties until the 1970s. For others, women's oppression can only be ended by the total abolition of a capitalist economy based on private ownership, and its replacement by a communist system in which the economy would be driven by the satisfaction of human needs rather than the pursuit of profit.

Socialism's collectivist approach may also be helpful for feminists. In contrast to approaches based on liberal individualism, this makes it easier to recognise that gender disadvantages are, like those of class, structural and built into the very fabric of society, and not simply the result of personal shortcomings or misfortunes. Such understanding can lead to collective policies to challenge disadvantages, as in the Scandinavian societies where state policies have been deliberately formulated to combat both class and gender inequalities. The collectivist approach is also said by some to be more in tune with women's experiences and approaches than liberal individualism, as is the whole goal of a more co-operative society, rather than the kind of rampantly individualistic competition that characterises some forms of liberal thought, and that has been particularly influential in the United States.

A third possible point of appeal stems from a strand in socialist and Marxist thought that is concerned with abolishing or reducing the division of labour. Here it is argued that, rather than specialising in one limited task, workers should be enabled to express themselves in a whole range of ways, so that work becomes a form of human fulfilment rather than alienation and degradation. In some early socialist thought, although not in Marx's, the attack on the division of labour included that between women and men. This general idea ties in with much recent feminist analysis, which argues both that women must be enabled to do 'men's work' and that men should develop their caring and nurturing qualities through participation in family life and childrearing; demands made by some feminists that sexuality be liberated from gender stereotypes and polarities can also be seen as the demand for an end to ascribed and limited gender roles.

Finally, socialism can appeal to those who dislike the anti-male approach of some forms of feminism. It allows women to recognise the ways in which many men are also oppressed, and to work with them to achieve a more equitable society in the interests of all. This need not rule out women-only activities and organisations in the short run; in the long run, however, it suggests that the goals of women and men are not opposed.

Anti-socialist critics

All but the last point are rejected by liberal opponents of socialism, who see them as based on muddled economic thinking and a naively optimistic view of human nature, and who argue that the pursuit of socialism inevitably entails both economic failure and a loss of individual freedom: at best, a bureaucratic 'nanny state' that stifles initiative by penalising success or at worst the nightmare of Stalinist dictatorship.

The final point is also questioned by those feminists who argue that although most socialists claim to support the ending of women's oppression in principle, many socialist men have, through their personal and political behaviour, contributed to that oppression in practice. At the turn of the century, Hannah Mitchell (a working-class socialist and suffrage campaigner from the north of England) found that 'a lot of the Socialist talk about freedom was only talk, and... Socialist young men expected Sunday dinners and huge teas with home-made cakes, potted meat and pies, exactly like their reactionary brothers' (Mitchell, 1977, p. 96). By the 1960s, women in left-wing groups found that little had changed, and that men treated them as housewives, secretaries or sex objects rather than as equal partners in struggle (Evans, 1980; Sargent, 1986).

Women have also fared particularly badly in so-called communist societies, despite the official Soviet line that the 'Woman Question' was a product of capitalist society which had therefore been solved. Women in these countries shared with most men a lack of social and political freedom, and their absence from powerful decision-making bodies was even more striking than in the west. They were expected to contribute as workers in industry and agriculture as well as retaining the responsibility for domestic work; in economies which provided far less by way of household facilities and appliances than the west, this often constituted a huge burden (Buckley, 1989; Voronina, 1989). Women were also frequently on the receiving end of coercive population policies, aimed in eastern Europe at increasing the birth rate and in China at drastically reducing it.

Few western Marxists or socialists would want to defend the repression of the former communist societies; instead most argue that these did not represent genuine socialism, but distorted versions of theories and movements aimed at increasing human freedom. For many feminists, therefore, the unhappy experience of women in so-called communist societies does not invalidate socialism in principle as a means of liberating women. Similarly, the sexism of some men in socialist organisations in the west is condemned and resisted, rather than being seen as the inevitable result of a patriarchal political theory.

By the 1970s, however, many feminists who had been attracted by socialism's liberatory promises and Marxism's claim to universal understanding were arguing that these problems were not accidental, but were an inevitable product of socialist approaches. In particular, feminists argued that Marxism's insistence on the primacy of economic and class issues made it unable to conceptualise gender inequality, or to see that even working-class men can benefit from the oppression of women. Many therefore agreed with Heidi Hartmann's critique of the 'unhappy marriage' of Marxism and feminism: she claimed that this was based on the same kind of subordination as the marriage of husband and wife in English common law, through which the wife loses her independent legal position which is incorporated into that of her husband. To avoid this secondary status for feminism, she argued, 'either we need a healthier marriage or we need a divorce' (Hartmann, 1986, p. 2). Since then, a more generally hostile political and philosophical climate has further discredited Marxism's claims to provide universal understanding and solutions. Some feminists, however, continue to argue that Marxist theory can provide insights into women's situation and the possibility of changing it. The arguments are complex, so it is necessary to discuss them in some detail.

Marxism and feminism: can the 'unhappy marriage' be saved?

Marx's original theory is extraordinarily rich and complex, and has been interpreted in many ways. In its simplest form, it argues that the key to understanding human society and history lies in the development of production – that is, in technology and the economy rather than in ideas or the actions of outstanding individuals. This implies that the family and sexual relationships are, like other forms of social organisation, the product of a particular stage of economic development; as such, they cannot be altered at will or on their own, but only as a result of more fundamental socio-economic change.

As applied by Engels and other early Marxists, this meant that women's situation was to be understood as a by-product of economic activity and class struggle, and the possibility that gender relations might have an independent dynamic of their own was ruled out of order. Although few feminists today would accept such crude economic reductionism, more would agree with the related claims that gender relations are historically produced rather than naturally given, that any analysis of the causes and possible cures of women's subordination has to be related to its socio-economic context, and that it is not possible to give women meaningful equality while leaving the economic system untouched.

By the 1960s, less rigid forms of Marxism had developed in the west. These were combined with new feminist analyses of patriarchy to produce more sophisticated theories that attempted to explore the historical development of patriarchy and its complex relationship to the capitalist economy. Some of these attempts used Marxist economic concepts to analyse women's work both in the home and in paid employment. The arguments involved were often highly technical and involved some fierce debates. There was, however, a general consensus that women's domestic labour does not simply represent a personal service to individual men, but is of critical importance to the capitalist economy. This led some to argue that the home can be seen as a potential site of anti-capitalist struggle and that socialist women should therefore be demanding 'wages for housework', rather than joining the paid workforce (for critical discussion of the 'domestic labour debate', see Molyneux, 1979; Bubeck, 1995; Gardiner, 1997). It was also argued that women's gender-specific oppression in the workplace is central to the maintenance of capitalism. Such arguments made women's work and economic situation visible; they also implied that attempts to change or improve women's role either within the home or in the paid economy are likely to be opposed by powerful economic interests, even if 'common sense' suggests that they are just.

The above arguments are based on economic analysis. Other attempts since the 1960s to extend Marxist ideas to analyse women's role in the family have involved the use of psychoanalytic theory and an exploration of the role of ideology in maintaining oppression (see in particular Mitchell, 1971, 1974, 1984; Barrett, 1988). However, even the loosest forms of Marxism have seemed to suggest that 'in the last analysis' class and capitalism are more fundamental than gender and patriarchy; hence the criticisms of writers such as Hartmann who reject such apparent economic determinism and the relegation to secondary status of feminist concerns (Hartmann, 1986).

In contrast to those who argue that what we have is a unified system of capitalist patriarchy, Hartmann has argued that there are two dynamic forces at work in history, which must be understood in terms of both class and gender struggle. Although modern society is both capitalist and patriarchal, neither of these 'dual systems' can, she says, be reduced to the other, and although at times they are mutually reinforcing, they may also come into conflict. Marxist analysis, she says, forgets that men as well as capitalism benefit from present arrangements, so that women's oppression both predates capitalism and may continue beyond it. As in the domestic labour debate, the arguments involved here are complex and can seem remote from everyday concerns. They do, however, have practical political implications, for if patriarchy exists independently rather than as an integral part of capitalism, it may be possible and necessary to challenge it directly, and for women to organise separately in defence of their own interests.

The idea that gender relations can develop independently from class seems to be supported by those writers who argue that the concept of *social reproduction*, which has foundations in classic Marxism, can be developed by feminists. This approach conceptualises sexual relationships, fertility control and the family as part of the material basis of society rather than its product. From this perspective, changes in sexual behaviour, changes in the role of women and men within the family and the development of new methods of contraception or reproductive technology can all be seen as real material changes that cannot simply be explained in terms of the needs of the economy. This means that efforts to change practices in these areas are as important as attempts to change conditions of paid employment. If, therefore, women demand the same sexual freedom as men, or insist that men contribute more to family life or campaign for affordable and legal abortions, these can be seen as basic material demands as well as political and ideological struggles. From this perspective, Marxism's focus on work is not essentially incompatible with a focus on sexuality, reproduction and the family, for all are part of the real material conditions in which we produce and reproduce.

Some recent feminist theories suggest that the complex interrelationship between the family and the paid economy can be further explored by using Marx's concept of *alienation*. This analyses man's loss of control over the productive process and the unsatisfying nature of work under conditions of capitalist factory production. It provides a powerful moral critique of capitalism which has helped explain why even well-paid workers may be dissatisfied with their situation. Foreman and Jaggar have both argued that for women this alienation is not confined to the world of paid employment, and that it is experienced within the family and private life (Foreman, 1978; Jaggar, 1983). Here it involves a loss of control over reproduction and sexuality and the provision of emotional and material support to men in a form that denies women's own needs. Although neither Foreman nor Jaggar explores the point, this might help us understand the strength of the 'discontented housewife syndrome' articulated by Betty Friedan in the early days of the modern women's movement (see above).

A Marxist perspective, however, does not simply identify such problems, but gives them a historical context. It argues that the ending of women's alienation will only be possible in a technologically advanced society in which the animal-like struggle for physical survival can be transformed into conscious and freely chosen human activity. The ending of women's alienation will, therefore, never be achieved on its own, as other perspectives might suggest, for it is integrally bound up with the struggle to end alienation in all its forms.

Finally, some writers have also suggested that, along with the kinds of radical feminism discussed in the next section, a Marxist approach can help us to see the ways in which feminist ideas may themselves be rooted in women's daily lives. Like Marx, many feminists have argued that good theory cannot be deduced from abstract speculation or outside observation, but can result only from concrete experience and political practice, which it both reflects and informs. Nancy Harstock (1985) uses Marxist concepts to explore this idea and to argue for the development of a 'feminist standpoint' based on the material reality of women's lives and leading to a form of knowledge superior to that available to men. The superiority of this knowledge stems in part, she says, from women's subordinate position; this gives them a material interest in understanding gender relations, while men's interests lie in ignoring or concealing them. It is also partly a consequence of the nature of women's work, which she says grounds their ideas in physical reality, and means that women would never develop the kind of abstract, disembodied theories that characterise male philosophy. In support of this point she quotes from Marilyn French's feminist novel *The Women's Room*:

> Washing the toilet used by three males, and the floor and walls around it, is, Myra thought, coming face to face with necessity. And that is why women were saner than men, did not come up with the mad, absurd schemes men developed: they were in touch with necessity, they had to wash the toilet bowl and floor. (Harstock, 1985, p. 236)

Such ideas may have an intuitive appeal. They have however been heavily criticised, not least for their failure to recognise that women may be divided as well as united by their experiences: at an obvious level, not every woman does have to clean the toilet, and for the black cleaning woman employed by a wealthy white woman, the experiences of racism and class exploitation may appear more salient than her gender. Here the logic of Harstock's own approach suggests that it is her situation as a white woman privileged by a racist system that has made it difficult for her to see this point.

As standpoint theory has developed, writers such as Sandra Harding have attempted to move beyond such criticisms by recognising the diversity of women's situations at the same time as arguing that their shared experience of subordination and marginality can provide the basis for an 'oppositional consciousness' and for forms of knowledge that are both different from and superior to the narrow and unreflective standpoints of the dominant male elite (Harding, 1986, 1991). Although Harding now says that such knowledge may in principle be accessible to men, standpoint theory remains prone to essentialising generalisations; to the extent that it avoids this by recognising a multiplicity of partial and specific viewpoints, it becomes increasingly indistinguishable from some of the ideas of post-modernism discussed below.

The failure to analyse the significance of racism is a common failing in white feminist thought from which feminists using Marxist concepts have certainly not been immune. Nevertheless, a more systematic application of Marxist principles can perhaps provide a corrective, for these principles point to the historical specificity of women's experiences, rather than claiming to identify universal, trans-historical truths. This means that the experiences of different groups of women must be related to the context of colonialism, imperialism and nationalistic struggles for independence; in the case of African-American women, the legacy of slavery, both economic and psychological, is clearly of pivotal importance.

Feminism, socialism and Marxism today

Today, few feminists want to turn to a Victorian patriarch for inspiration, few talk in terms of class struggle and the overthrow of capitalism, and even moderate forms of socialism are on the defensive in a political environment that has moved sharply to the right in most of the western world. Nevertheless, issues of economic inequality are now part of mainstream feminist politics and debate, and the general socialist perception that feminist issues cannot be isolated from their socio-economic context remains an important starting-point for an effective feminist politics. More specifically, an investigation of the ways in which powerful capitalist interests may benefit from inequality helps us to understand the opposition to apparently 'reasonable' demands. Marxism adds to these general socialist understandings the perception that feminist issues have a history, and an insistence on recognising the historical specificity of any situation and the political possibilities to which it gives rise. Used with caution, Marxist feminism can therefore provide a useful guard against the kind of individualism that finds it difficult to see collective interests and structured inequalities, the elitism that fails to recognise inequalities of class and race as well as gender, the optimism that thinks that if a cause can be shown to be just it will necessarily be successful and the ahistorical belief that all women are the victims of unchanging male oppression.

Nevertheless, many of the writers discussed in the next section argue that socialism, like liberalism, is inevitably limited by its masculinist assumptions, and that it represents a source of patriarchal control rather than liberation for women. Instead of attempting to extend or adapt male theories to feminist ends, they therefore argue that women must develop their own.

'Radical', women-centred approaches

From the earliest written records of western feminism, we can find some women insisting on the validity and centrality of women's experience and rejecting a scale of values that makes man the measure and judge of women's worth. By the 19th century, we can also find a well-developed analysis of the ways in which women's subordination extends beyond a lack of legal, political and economic rights and is rooted in family life and personal relationships. For example, the American Elizabeth Cady Stanton (1815–1902) not only campaigned for women's right to vote, to own property, to be educated and to work outside the home, she also asserted their right to dress for comfort rather than to please men, insisted on retaining her own given names (rather than becoming 'Mrs. John Stanton'), attacked the ways in which men had mis-used religion to legitimise female subordination, condemned the double standard of sexual morality, and identified a married woman's lack of right to deny her husband sexual access to her own body as a root cause of women's oppression. Men's power over women, she argued, is both oppressive and all-pervasive:

> Society as organised today under the man power, is one general rape of womanhood, on the highways, in our jails, prisons, asylums, in our homes, alike in the worlds of fashion and of work. (quoted in Dubois, 1981, p. 123)

This kind of analysis continued as an important strand in the campaign for women's suffrage, which had by the early 20th century become a mass movement in both Britain and the United States. Some campaigners did not simply see the vote as an end in itself, but as a weapon that could be used by women in their struggle for economic independence. Economically independent women, it was argued, would no longer have to sell themselves either as prostitutes or as wives. Because they could set their own terms for relationships with men, they could also, by insisting that men curb their sexual appetites, save the nation from the scourge of venereal disease:

hence the slogan 'Votes for women; chastity for men'. Some also argued that women should be entitled to vote not because they were the same or as good as men, but because they were different and, in important respects, better. From this perspective, giving women the vote would enable their 'womanly qualities', such as temperance and pacifism, to elevate political debate and improve the quality of public life.

After the vote was won, such analyses became much less influential. In the late 1960s, however, they become an important strand of the new women's movement known as 'radical feminism' because, its proponents claimed, it went to the roots of women's oppression. In contrast to Betty Friedan's appeal to suburban housewives (see above), the main constituency for this kind of feminism initially lay with a somewhat younger group of women, still predominantly white, who had been radicalised by their involvement in the movements to give civil rights to black Americans and oppose American involvement in Vietnam, and in New Left and student politics. Such women were rapidly disillusioned by the sexist behaviour of many men in these movements and by the dawning realisation that the language of freedom and equality were not seriously intended to apply to them. As attempts to get their concerns discussed were met with ridicule or contempt, many applied the rhetoric of the movements to their own situation. They therefore argued that women, like black people and workers, were an oppressed group who had to struggle for their own liberation against their oppressors – that is, against men. Some, such as Germaine Greer in *The Female Eunuch* (first published in 1970) argued further that the roots of this oppression lay in men's control over women's sexuality.

Consciousness-raising, the politics of personal life and patriarchy

Although Greer herself is very much an individualist, the confidence to make such claims frequently stemmed from a sense of shared experience gained through 'consciousness-raising' groups. The original aim of these was to enable women to express and share personal experiences in a small and supportive group, so as to bring out their political implications and develop a strategy for change. Through such groups, many women found that their own bad emotional, sexual or family experiences were not simply personal misfortunes, but seemed both to be widely shared with other women and to build up into a general pattern of male use and abuse of power. From this new perspective, the trauma of a woman who had been raped or who had had to resort to an illegal abortion seemed to be linked to the experiences of the wife whose husband refused to do his share of housework, appeared never to have heard of the female orgasm or sulked if she went out for the evening; the secretary whose boss insisted that she wear short skirts, expected her to 'be nice' to important clients or failed to acknowledge that she was effectively running his office; and the female student whose teachers expected less of the 'girls', refused requests to study female writers or even traded grades for sexual favours. This new understanding gave rise to the key slogan 'the personal is political', and to the idea that all women could unite in a common sisterhood; it also provided the foundation for a theoretical analysis of male power which focused on the concept of *patriarchy*.

The feminist concept of patriarchy (a term which has an earlier and very different usage in conventional political theory) was first systematically set out by Kate Millett in *Sexual Politics* (originally published in 1970); it is now widely employed by feminists as a shorthand for a social system based on male domination and female subordination. Millett argued that in all known societies, the relationship between the sexes has been based on men's power over women; it is therefore political. Men's power, she says, goes deeper than the power based on class or race, and it is so universal, so ubiquitous and so complete that it appears 'natural' and, until named by feminists, invisible. It is maintained by a process of socialisation which begins in the family and is reinforced by education, literature and religion; it also rests upon economic exploitation, state power and, ultimately, force (particularly sexual violence and rape).

This kind of approach seemed to many to offer a powerful new way of seeing the world that took women as its starting-point and made sense of their diverse experiences. It also implied new forms of political action, for if women's oppression is rooted in personal life, it is not enough to challenge unjust laws, campaign for better political representation or blame the capitalist economy; instead, women must recognise that it is men who oppress them, and that politics has to be re-defined to include the family and personal relationships. While some feminists have attempted to analyse the patriarchal bases of state power or the relationship of patriarchy to class exploitation under capitalism, others have, therefore, focused upon the family, reproduction and sexuality (particularly pornography and rape). This has led some women to confront the men in their lives or to make radical changes in their own life-style; it has also produced a wide range of collective activities, including campaigns for stricter controls over pornography, for adequate funding for women's refuges, for free access to abortion, for changes in the law on rape and domestic violence, and for an end to discrimination against lesbians.

Feminist criticisms

The core beliefs of the radical feminist approach have been attacked by other feminists on a number of grounds. First, some argue that to say that 'the personal is political' has dangerously totalitarian implications, for it implies that no area of life can be free from political scrutiny and that feminists are to be held accountable to their 'sisters' for every aspect of their behaviour. Women must therefore be aware of the political consequences of how they dress, who they sleep with and who they cook for and should regulate their activities accordingly; if they do not, then the feminist thought police is both entitled and obliged to point out the errors of their ways, or to condemn them for betraying the cause by collaboration with the enemy.

A second line of criticism, paradoxically, argues that the insistence that the personal is political is effectively *de-politicising*, as it can suggest that conventional political activity by feminists represents a futile engagement with man-made structures, and is therefore a waste of time. From this perspective, women's political priority might be to put their own emotional and sexual house in order rather than attempting to change the world outside. This can seem to legitimise a privatised and self-indulgent retreat from collective struggle and into the seductive world of open-ended therapy, counselling and 'alternative' healing. Such a retreat may also take the form of attempts to validate and develop a 'women's culture' that explores new forms of expression through art, music, drama and poetry. This kind of 'cultural feminism', critics say, may make the women involved feel good, but they leave the dominant culture unchanged and unchallenged, and they are relevant only to a privileged few.

Third, the concept of patriarchy is said to be descriptive and ahistorical rather than analytical. As such, it is unable to explain the origins of patriarchy or to provide a coherent strategy for ending it. Moreover, by universalising from the experiences of white, middle-class western women, it ignores oppression based upon race and class and, in the name of a spurious sisterhood, trivialises the suffering of women for whom oppression is literally a matter of life and death.

Fourth, the radical feminist approach is said to encourage women to identify only with their bad experiences with men, so that women who have suffered abuse will be listened to with reverence, while the experiences of happily married women are dismissed as 'false consciousness'. This produces a view of women as helpless victims, rather than celebrating their collective resistance and potential power. Such a view, critics say, is politically counter-productive and, in an era when women have made tangible gains, it is largely responsible for the popular view of feminism as a complaining, whining and negative creed, irrelevant to the lives of go-ahead young women. Such critics argue that women must learn to take responsibility for their own lives and combat injustice, rather than wallowing in the masochistic pleasures of shared victimhood.

Finally, the stress on women's status as victims is said to feed into a false and politically dangerous view of women as essentially good and men as essentially bad. Such a division is said to fly in the face of both historical and contemporary evidence. It ignores the fact that many women do have a significant amount of political and economic power and that many men are oppressed, and it falsely attributes virtues to women and vices to men despite innumerable examples of aggressive women and caring men. This produces an inaccurate and unworkable view of men as 'the enemy', which suggests that they cannot be trusted as fathers, friends, sexual partners or political allies; lesbian separatism therefore becomes the only feasible option for feminists both as political strategy and as a life-style choice. Such a view is unacceptable to those feminists who argue that many men have done great service to the feminist cause and that many more have always treated the women in their lives with the greatest love and respect. Thus the American feminist Naomi Wolf writes:

Don't tell me that the best friends of my body and heart are undifferentiated predators, who think of their genitals as if they were guns. My joyful life experiences with men are neither politically invalid nor so aberrant. Let us give the love of men, too, its legitimate feminist weight. (Wolf, 1993, p. 200)

Recent developments

The above criticisms may be true of some of radical feminism's early exponents. However, they have at times rested upon misunderstandings, and in 1996 a new international collection of essays by 68 self-proclaimed radical feminists provided a robust defence against alleged misinterpretations of their core beliefs (*Radically Speaking* (Bell and Klein, 1996)). These feminists are not demanding that private life *becomes* political, but claiming that it *already is*, and they see the identification of oppression as a first step towards confronting it, rather than as an end in itself. Several contributors insist that their goal is not individual therapy or the development of women's culture; rather, their aim is to change the world, with the ultimate goal of ending the oppression of women in the interest of all humanity. Several also explicitly refuse to see gender characteristics as biologically given rather than socially produced and amenable to change. They do not claim that every man is more advantaged than every woman, but they maintain that women throughout the world are vulnerable because of their sex, and that male domination is, therefore, a basic structure in all societies.

Other writers have also in recent years developed increasingly sophisticated approaches, which have attempted to analyse changes in the nature of patriarchy over time and between cultures, and the ways in which it interacts with other forms of oppression. Such developments can enable us to see the ways in which gender inequalities are built into the fabric of society without treating all women as a homogeneous, victimised mass. They therefore allow us to see the specificities of women's situations and the ways in which oppressions can and have been challenged.

Such approaches suggest that there is no one 'correct' form of feminist political activity. Robin Morgan, indeed, has argued that the very diversity of approaches and interests within radical feminism is a source of strength for feminist politics. She argues that this must be seen as:

> A means, not an end; a process, not a dogma. Consequently, what a radical feminist in Brazil might consider her cutting-edge issue (the nation's debt, for example), need not be the same as that considered a priority by a radical feminist in Thailand (combating sex tourism) or in Kuwait (winning women's suffrage) or in Sudan (ending the practice of female genital mutilation) or Nepal (gaining inheritance rights) or the Pacific Island nations (halting French nuclear testing, the fallout of which creates 'jellyfish babies' – children born with no spines), and so on – and so on, and on (Morgan, 1996, pp. 6–7)

From a radical perspective, these activities do not represent isolated struggles. Rather, they are connected by their opposition to different manifestations of male power, and they can both feed into and draw strength from the wider women's movement.

Despite such an open-ended approach, critical disagreements remain between many feminist activists and others who argue that any conventional political activity, any attempt to change the law, and indeed any attempt to work either with men or in man-made institutions must be doomed to failure. There is also a split between the minority who believe that there are essential and irremovable biological differences that shape men's and women's nature and those who argue that gender differences are socially produced, and who insist on distinguishing between structures of domination on the one hand and individual men on the other. For the former, women and the values associated with them are inherently better than men, with whom there can be no compromise. For the latter, male patriarchal power is analytically distinct from male persons; although some women may choose to live without men and women should at times organise collectively to defend their own interests, extreme forms of separatism will not be necessary.

Today, the influence of the ideas discussed in this section extends well beyond those who would accept any kind of 'radical feminist' label. At the same time, radical feminism's core assumptions have been profoundly challenged in recent years by the development of both black feminism and post-modernism, discussed in the following sections and in Chapter 3.

Black feminism: from margin to centre?

Feminism's marginalisation of black women

The approaches discussed so far claim to be relevant to all women, whether they are conceptualised as human beings entitled to the same rights as men, workers whose labour is exploited inside and outside the home, or sisters united by a shared oppression and the struggle to end it. Many critics have however said that feminism in general has ignored the experiences of women of colour and that, by failing to recognise or analyse racial oppression, it has served to support and perpetuate the inequalities of a racist society. The result, according to the African-American writer bell hooks, has been that

> Black women have felt forced to choose between a black movement that primarily serves the interests of black male patriarchs, and a white women's movement which primarily serves the interests of racist white women. (hooks, 1981, p. 9)

Today, the very fact that we can talk of 'feminism' and 'black feminism' is an indictment of a body of thought that treats the partial standpoint of a particular group of women as universal, and marginalises the experiences of women of colour as an optional extra in much the same way that male ideologies have marginalised all women.

To some white women, the claim that the women's movement is inherently racist may seem odd, for many white feminists were initially politicised by their involvement in campaigns against racial subordination, particularly the anti-slavery movement in the 19th century and the civil rights movement of the 1950s and 60s. For such women, there seemed to be clear parallels between the situation of black people and that of women, for both groups were denied the rights of white men. Thus the title of Gayle Rubin's 1970 essay 'Woman as Nigger' gained widespread popular currency, and echoed the words of Elizabeth Cady Stanton a century earlier: 'the black man and the woman are born to shame. The badge of degradation is the skin and the sex – the "scarlet letter" so sadly worn upon the breast' (quoted in Dubois, 1981, p. 83). However, such comparison between blacks and women ignores the specific situation of *black women*: because of their colour they disappear as women, and because of their sex they are largely invisible as black people (see Spelman, 1988).

In recent years, women of colour in North America and Europe have begun to rediscover their own history, and can now see their own foremothers as independent actors, rather than as victims or as adjuncts of the white women's movement or the male anti-racist struggle. However, such women have always had less access than white women to mainstream channels of political influence and communication, and are still under-represented in the academic and publishing circles in which much feminist theory is expressed. This means that while women of colour can find out what many middle-class white feminists are thinking and doing by watching television, reading newspapers, going into bookshops or enrolling on a women's studies course, their own activities and consciousness are largely invisible to other groups. Throughout the history of feminism, many white women writers and activists have therefore simply failed to 'see' women of colour. As a result, they have felt able to generalise from their own experiences to make universal claims on behalf of their sex which for many women are irrelevant, inappropriate or false. For example, the feminist complaint that women are stereotyped as weak creatures in need of male protection and unfit for any work outside the home, contradicts the experience of most black (and many working-class white) women whose labour has been exploited in the factories and fields. Even when women from a range of backgrounds and cultures are included in feminist discussion, critics say that they are fitted into a framework which has already been established according to the priorities of white women, so that 'differences are treated as local variations on a universal theme' (Liu, 1994, p. 574). Such an approach cannot see women of colour as independent actors or understand the ways in which the experience of sex oppression is mediated through race.

In 1851, Sojourner Truth (1795–1883), a former slave and campaigner for women's rights, reminded a convention audience of the strength and trials of those like herself:

> That man over there says that women need to be helped into carriages, and lifted over ditches, and to have the best place everywhere. Nobody ever helps me into carriages, or over mud-puddles, or gives me any best place! And ain't I a woman?... I have ploughed and planted, and gathered into barns, and no man could head me! And ain't I a woman? I could work as much and eat as much as a man – when I could get it – and bear the lash as well! And ain't I a woman? I have borne 13 children, and seen

them most all sold off to slavery, and when I cried out with my mother's grief, none but Jesus heard me! And ain't I a woman? (extract in Schneir, 1972, pp. 94–5)

Nearly a century and a half later, the tendency of many white women to treat their particular experiences as universal means that her refrain is still highly relevant.

Black women's centrality to feminism

A key initial demand for black feminists has been the insistence that their experiences are not simply added to feminist analysis as an optional extra, but that they should be included on an equal basis. Some writers go further, and argue that they must be the central starting-point. The arguments here take a number of forms. First, Angela Davis has argued that a feminist movement which begins with middle class white women will only change their position at the top of the social pyramid, leaving the lives of other women untouched. If however we aim at improving the situation of those at the bottom – that is, working-class black women – then the entire oppressive structure of society will have to be transformed; she therefore argues that 'The forward advance of women of colour almost always indicates progressive change for all women' (Davis, 1990, p. 31).

Second, in line with the standpoint theory discussed above, others have argued that those who are on the receiving end of oppression are more able to see it than those who are advantaged by it. This means that, precisely because they are the most disadvantaged group in society, with no institutionalised inferiors, black women have a special vantage point and a particularly clear understanding of the world from which we can all learn.

Third, it is argued that a focus on the experience of women of colour enables us to see the interconnecting and interactive nature of different forms of oppression, which opens up feminist analysis to other previously marginalised or excluded groups, such as disabled women or lesbians. According to Patricia Collins, if we take the real situation of black women as the starting-point, we necessarily take a multifaceted approach which understands that different systems of oppression are not independent, but support each other. This enables us, she says, to think inclusively about other systems of oppression, and to understand that any one individual is likely to be a member of both subordinate and privileged groups rather than simply either a victim or an oppressor. Such a stance is, she argues, in tune with an Afrocentric way of understanding, which insists that knowledge is rooted in concrete experience and assesses knowledge claims through dialogue rather than the assertion of absolute abstract principles (Collins, 1989, 1990, 1995).

This approach has been further developed in recent black feminist thought which argues that black women's situation should not be understood as the sum of cumulative disadvantages (gender plus race plus class), but as the *product* of multiple oppressions (gender *times* race *times* class). As discussed in more detail in Chapter 3, this 'multiplier' approach enables us to see that different forms of oppression interact to mean that gender oppression is experienced by different groups of women in qualitatively different ways. It also alerts us to the fact that *all* women, not only women of colour, have a racial identity.

Finally, the claim that different forms of oppression are interconnected and that they reinforce each other suggests that members of different oppressed groups can have a shared interest in social change. From this perspective, the struggles of all women are interconnected, although they are not all the same. bell hooks has therefore argued that the idea of *sisterhood*, which implies an oppression shared by all women, should make way for that of *solidarity*. This enables different groups of women to support each other without insisting that their situation is identical; it also enables women to form alliances with oppressed groups of men (hooks, 1984).

The implications of these arguments will be further explored in the next chapter, which analyses the inter-relationships between gender, race and class. It is however already clear that some exponents of black feminism do not simply see it as a theory of and for feminists who happen to be black, but a self-conscious epistemological standpoint. This does not argue simply that black women's perspectives should be included in feminist analysis as a matter of justice. Rather, it is claiming that if this is not done, then feminist understandings of the oppression experienced by white women will also be seriously flawed.

However, not all black feminists accept this analysis, and the British writer Heidi Mirza has rejected the view that black women have a superior standpoint, claiming that this is based upon 'a naïve essentialist universal notion of homogeneous black womanhood' (Mirza, 1997, p. 5). Rather, she argues that it is through the insights provided by post-modernism that the hitherto marginalised voices of minority group women can be expressed and differences among women understood. It is to post-modernism, therefore, that we now turn.

The impact of post-modernism

'Post-modernism' has had a profound effect upon the study of politics and academic feminist theory. It is, however, extraordinarily difficult to pin down. A feminist student attempting to discover its meaning is likely to find herself rapidly embroiled in a discussion of architecture, psycho-linguistic theory or literary criticism; bemused by an impenetrable jargon of shifting signifiers, decentred subjects and meanings endlessly deferred; and mystified by the paradoxically confident assertion that 'there is no truth'. If she perseveres, she may find post-modernism to be seductive, liberating and exciting. If so, she will be in the company of many academic feminists. She will, however, probably be accused by others of being elitist, and of peddling a theory which is not simply irrelevant to the lives of women, but which undermines the possibility of collective feminist action.

Post-modernism is not a clearly defined theory, but a loose body of thought which draws on interconnected ideas around language, knowledge, reason, power, identity and resistance. The term is sometimes loosely equated with post-structuralism; it is also sometimes used to identify the 'condition' of late 20th century post-industrial societies. Cynics might see it simply as a symptom of pre-millennial angst. I will focus here on those elements which have had most impact on feminist thought. It will be clear that some of these reinforce earlier feminist ideas; others however seem to challenge feminism's most basic assumptions.

An overview of themes

An important starting-point stems from post-structuralist ideas about the ways in which language mediates our relationship with the material world. According to this analysis, the meaning of an object, action or social institution is not inherent in it, but is called into being by words. For example, you may say that what you are now looking at is a page of a book on feminism. It might, however, also be described as a sheet of white paper with black markings on it, a cure for insomnia, a piece of smoothed-out dried wood pulp, or potential fuel for the fire. According to post-structuralists, none of these meanings is 'wrong', but none is simply 'true': meaning, they say, is not fixed and waiting to be discovered, but can be endlessly constructed and reconstructed through words, which themselves have meaning only in relation to other words. This analysis undermines the dualistic nature of western thought, which depends upon such fixed binary oppositions as truth/falsehood, public/private or man/woman, and therefore assumes a stability of meanings. It makes objective knowledge impossible, both because this has no constant object and because our perceptions are inevitably constrained by the language available to us. This means that our understanding can never be final and never complete, and our knowledge is always limited and partial; any theory claiming to know 'the truth' is therefore ruled out of order.

Words, meanings and claims to knowledge are not however free-floating and indiscriminately available, but form patterns or discourses, which organise our understanding and which are intimately connected to the exercise of power in society. The postmodernist analysis of power, following that of the French writer Michel Foucault (1980), does not see this as centralised or possessed by a ruler, government or state. Rather, it is increasingly fragmented and dispersed throughout society, and exercised at micro-level within such apparently non-political institutions as families, schools or hospitals. Claims to knowledge, particularly 'scientific' knowledge, are an important part of this exercise of power and can be used to justify existing inequalities and patterns of control. However, although some discourses are more powerful than others, there is always scope for resistance by subjugated and marginalised groups. Dominant discourses or ways of viewing the world can therefore be contested by subordinate groups which can offer rival interpretations of reality: for example, the competing discourses of liberal individualism and socialism may understand poverty as the product of personal shortcomings or of an exploitative economic system. This means that an understanding of the ways in which knowledge and culture are produced is both an important part of political analysis and a source of resistance to the existing exercise of power. Such resistance can, however, never be total or final, merely marginal and provisional; to think otherwise is to embrace out-dated 'modernist' assumptions about power, progress and certainty.

Ideas around the instability of meaning and its relationship with power have also combined with post-Freudian psychoanalytic theory to produce arguments about the essentially precarious nature of adult identity. According to these, the irrational and the unconscious are as important as the conscious, and ideas of autonomy and self-determinism lose their meaning; far from having a fixed identity, the individual can only be the unstable site of shifting meanings. At a fairly obvious level, one individual person may today be identified as a student, a potential mother, a pretty girl, a vegetarian, a non-voter, someone born exactly 20 years ago, Patrick's younger sister and so on. Tomorrow, she will be many things, but not exactly the same person she is today. At a deeper level, she is also said by the psychoanalyst Jacques Lacan and his followers to have acquired her identity, including her gender identity, via a resolution of the Oedipal complex and entry into the 'Symbolic Order' of adult masculine language – an order which is at the basis of binary, either/or thinking and which by the very nature of its 'phallic discourse' is unable to express the feminine. The ideas involved here are complex and disputed. The important point to note in this and related approaches is that it is not only the object of knowing that has been dissolved as a stable entity, but also its knowing subject, for both are 'discursively constructed'. In other words, although an object and an individual may both have a material existence, this gains meaning only when named – and the process of naming is inherently open-ended rather than closed.

All of this means that post-modernism represents a profound attack on the core assumptions of western philosophy and 'common sense'. Because it denies the very possibility of coherent knowledge in an incoherent world, it seems to attack the very foundations of reason and scientific understanding. It is hostile to the kind of 'grand theory' or 'meta-narrative' which Marxism claimed to provide; it denies the existence of both the rational individual of liberal thought and stable social categories such as 'class'; it also seems to reject any idea that justice, liberty or equality can be seen as universal human goals. Instead, it analyses the ways in which philosophy, knowledge and morality are constructed, seeing this as a fundamental form of political activity. Many find its claims fascinating and exhilarating. For its opponents, however, post-modernism is at best an irritating and pretentious irrelevance and at worst a reactionary, divisive and politically dangerous approach which denies the reality of human suffering and is incapable of making a moral distinction between freedom and slavery.

Feminist reactions

The relevance of post-modernism

Feminists are divided. For some, post-modernism's insistence on diversity and provisionality can seem in line with liberal defences of pluralism and free speech. Many erstwhile Marxists see it as a way forward after the challenge to earlier certainties produced by the world-wide collapse of communism, and a logical development from looser forms of Marxism which have been developing since the Second World War.

Post-modernism also seems to support many of the radical feminist ideas discussed earlier in this chapter. Its analysis of the ubiquity of power looks at first sight very like the claim that patriarchal power is exercised in personal life as well as through formal political institutions. The identification of culture and language as key sources of power and resistance is also familiar. In 1970, Kate Millett's *Sexual Politics* exposed the patriarchal assumptions of literary texts, and helped spawn a whole new field of feminist literary and cultural criticism; attempts to develop and celebrate women's cultural activities might also seem to be in line with Foucauldian notions of resistance by marginalised groups. Feminists such as Dale Spender and Mary Daly have long written about the power of words in maintaining and resisting patriarchy. Such analysis has taken a practical form in attempts to introduce non-sexist language. A feminist understanding of the power of words to construct reality also underpins attempts to challenge both legal and popular perceptions of rape, and the insistence that unwanted sexual attention should be understood as 'sexual harassment' rather than 'harmless fun'.

Post-modernism's critique of objectivity also seems to reinforce the radical argument that what passes for dispassionate knowledge is only a partial and limited male perspective, and the claim by some that female forms of knowing based on emotion and intuition can provide clearer understanding than reason and logic. Its rejection of 'grand theory' and 'universal goals' similarly reflects the feminist assertion that such theories and goals have been used to conceal particular male interests. This has combined with post-modernism's stress on 'difference' to reinforce the impact of black feminist critiques of a women's movement in which the easy rhetoric of 'sisterhood' all too often reflected the narrow interests of middle-class white women. The black British feminist Heidi Mirza has therefore argued that post-modernism 'has allowed the celebration of difference, the recognition of otherness, the presence of multiple and changeable subjectivities' (Mirza, 1997, p. 19).

Feminist criticisms

All this might seem to suggest that feminism's own logic has been pushing it in a post-modernist direction. Many feminists, however, reject the idea that good feminist understanding, gained through women's own experience, should be dressed up in inaccessible philosophical clothes, particularly when these have been designed by misogynistic men. Many are deeply and instinctively hostile to an approach which seems only to mystify what we think we already understand. They also reject an approach which, although it may politicise the study of literature, film and art, de-politicises the study of politics, and can seem to suggest that textual analysis is a more important form of political activity than setting up a women's refuge or campaigning for better pay.

More fundamentally, post-modernism seems incompatible with the identification and analysis of patriarchy and therefore with feminist struggles against it. Although recent theoretical developments within radical feminism recognise the specificity and variability of women's experiences, they do also insist that these are interconnected, and that society is fundamentally structured around men's domination over women. Post-modernism however questions not only the concept of patriarchy as a stable category, but also the very terms 'man' and 'woman'. The suggestion that the term 'woman' derives its meaning from discourse rather than physical reality has been greeted with outrage by those who experience or observe the reality of female oppression and exploitation and who see post-modernism as a ploy to deny women's collective identity just at a time when they were learning to recognise their shared experiences and act together politically. Such critics argue that post-modernism is 'apolitical, ahistorical, irresponsible, and self-contradictory' and insist that 'Stubbornly, defiantly, we hold on to that truth. There is such a thing as woman' (Bell and Klein, 1996, p. xviii).

Post-modern feminism

Post-modern feminists do not deny that 'real', flesh and blood women are going about their daily lives, nor that they may be systematically disadvantaged because of their sex. They have however used post-modern ideas to argue that the very process of sex identification and classification is socially produced rather than an inevitable and unchanging outcome of biology. They therefore reject the sex/gender distinction made by many earlier feminists, for this saw sex as natural and only gender as the artificial product of society. In contrast, post-modern feminists argue that it is society that creates the category 'woman' by attaching overwhelming significance to particular anatomical arrangements. These arrangements exist in nature, as do other variable human attributes such as skin colour or the ability to curl one's tongue. It is however society that makes them significant and gives them changing meanings; in this sense, it is society that creates sex as well as gender.

Although post-modernism has concentrated on discourse, some writers see social practices as important in constructing meaning and gender identity. Others have argued that gender is not a stable identity but an *act* that requires repeated performances of gender-appropriate behaviour, and which can never be fully internalised (see Butler, 1990).

These ideas can be seen as liberating, for they suggest that the meanings which society attaches to sex/gender can be challenged. They open up in principle the possibility of a much more open society that is no longer divided into the binary opposites of male and female. In such a society, gender identities could be multiple, fluid and freely chosen; as such, they would no longer constitute an organising principle of society (Lorber, 1991). According to some writers, they might even disappear; thus Judith Grant has argued that:

> The aim of feminist politics is the end of gender and the creation of new human beings who are self-determining and fully participate in the devel-

opment of their own constantly evolving subjectivity. We could think of this position as a feminist humanist position. (Grant, 1993, p. 183)

Rejection of 'woman' as a fixed category implies that we can intervene in the processes through which sex/gender is constructed. This may be done through cultural criticism; or through legal strategies which recognise the law as a particularly powerful form of discourse (see Chapter 4); or through deliberately de-stabilising gender codes so that, for example, transvestism becomes a subversive political strategy (see Butler, 1990). Such strategies allow scope for collective action. This scope is widened if we take a broader view which says that it is not simply discourse that creates sex/gender, but also a wide range of social practices. This could enable feminists to engage in conventional politics, while retaining a self-conscious awareness of the gendered implications of their activity. Thus a feminist seeking to become a member of parliament could see the ways in which dominant practices make it difficult for her to operate politically as a (currently defined) woman: she could, for example, understand the nature of political debate as the product of a particular kind of masculinity which perceives her contributions as ineffective if she speaks 'like a woman' and unfeminine if she speaks 'like a man'. She would also be aware that, even if she did not appear to be pursuing feminist goals, her very presence would challenge current meanings of what it is to be a woman and what it is to be a politician.

Broader alliances among women are also possible from a post-modernist perspective, provided that these are provisional and tactical, and that they do not lose sight of the historical and cultural specificity of women's experiences. Post-modernism is not therefore as inevitably hostile to the idea of a united women's movement as critics suggest, and can be seen as compatible with the black feminist idea of 'solidarity'.

It would, however, be naive to think that post-modernism's rejection of 'woman' as a self-evident, unchanging category and its stress on differences among women, could not be politically useful to those who hope to deflect attention from the very real consequences of living in societies that remain profoundly structured by the inequalities of gender. There is also a danger that the post-modern preoccupation with discourse can become a self-referential end in itself. As such, it can dilute feminist energies and contribute to what Diana Coole has described as an increasingly problematic gap between:

> Academics/intellectuals who embrace a post-modernism which has obvious appeals to them in privileging the sort of symbolic practices they are engaged in... and activists who struggle with the everyday exigencies of women's oppression. (Coole, 1993, p. 226)

Conclusions: feminist theory and political practice today

As we have seen, the feminist claim that women should have the same rights and freedoms as men has been largely conceded in western society. The more radical argument that private life can be oppressive for women has also become widely accepted in recent years. Issues such as abortion, sexual harassment, domestic violence, childcare and parental leave have entered the mainstream of political debate rather than being seen as purely personal concerns. The importance of women's unpaid work has become increasingly visible in official economic statistics.

However, feminist analyses of the structural and collective nature of gender inequalities and interests are much less widely accepted or even heard. Similarly, although there is a greater awareness that black, working class and/or disabled women face particular problems, there has been little public debate over the full implications of this, or of the ways in which different forms of inequality relate either to each other or to wider social and economic conditions.

This is partly a reflection of the extent to which the terms of public debate have been set by the assumptions of liberal individualism and by an elite minority of women. Because liberalism provides the 'common sense' political assumptions of western democracies, even those feminists who argue that its liberatory potential for women has been largely exhausted can find themselves sucked into its frameworks and using its language. At the same time, those who gain a public voice can forget that this itself may be a sign of privilege, and that the majority of the world's women are neither white nor middle class. A critical awareness of the theoretical assumptions underlying feminist politics can help guard against an inappropriate narrowing of its frame of reference and help ensure a more inclusive political practice.

It should by now also be clear that although many of the ideas discussed in this chapter can complement each other, they can at times seem to point in opposite directions. Particular tensions can arise between demands for individual rights and more collectivist and/or contextualised approaches, and between those that stress women's shared experiences and those that insist on the importance of difference and diversity. Even if these disagreements are ultimately reconcilable, this means that feminist theory is not some kind of lucky dip from which we can pick and mix at will. A more self-conscious awareness of its underlying starting-points can however enable us to think more clearly about these disagreements and about the feminists debates which form the subject of this book.

3
Gender, race and class

In Chapter 1, I provisionally identified feminism with movements and theories aimed at ending women's subordination. Such a definition, however, begs many important questions concerning the relationship between inequalities of gender and other forms of oppression. These include the question of whether differences and divisions among women are more important than their common identity; whether the women's movement has been based on the priorities of middle-class white women; whether women of colour should organise separately; whether gender, race or class constitutes the most basic form of oppression; and whether black and working-class white men should be viewed as allies or oppressors.

This chapter draws on writings by feminist women of colour and white feminists to explore these difficult questions. It should be noted that I am writing it as a white university lecturer (albeit in a 'new' university with students from a wide range of class and ethnic backgrounds). As in other chapters, my understanding is filtered by my personal experiences and by the priorities of academic institutions, publishers and the mass media, which enable some women's voices to be heard more readily than others.

The language of 'gender', 'race' and 'class'

The meaning of the terms 'gender', 'race' and 'class' cannot be established by a single act of definition, for they are deeply contested and fraught with theoretical and political implications. They are also linked with a number of other terms whose usage is constantly shifting and equally disputed. The following discussion is therefore intended to clarify analysis, rather than to identify 'correct' meaning or usage.

Sex and gender

The sex/gender distinction

Although gender is sometimes used as the more 'polite' term (much as 'lady dog' is sometimes used as a euphemism for 'bitch'), the terms 'sex' and 'gender' are frequently used interchangeably in everyday conversation. However, many feminists have insisted on making a clear distinction. According to this, sex is equated with the biological characteristics of males and females, and contrasted with gender, which refers to the socially produced attributes of masculinity and femininity and the social arrangements based upon them. This distinction leads to the argument that although there are some fixed biological differences between men and women, many other observable differences are the manifestations of gender; as such, they are amenable to change.

Since the 17th century, this kind of analysis has underpinned claims for women's rights based on the insistence that women's bodies do not limit their ability to reason or warrant their exclusion from the rights of man. Today, such liberal arguments are still used to claim that women's nature does not make them unfit to enter male-dominated occupations such as politics or the combat branches of the armed services: it is said that even if women appear to lack the necessary qualities (such as aggression), this is not an unchanging fact of nature, but the product of their upbringing. Such arguments have tended to treat femininity as an artificial product, while regarding masculinity as 'normal'; from this perspective, the goal is to enable women to become like men. In principle, however, the analysis throws masculinity open to scrutiny as well, and recent years have seen the development of studies in this area and a growing recognition that 'gender is not a synonym for women' (Carver, 1996). This suggests that change need not be one way, and that attributes traditionally associated with women, such as empathy, nurturing and caring, can also be learned by men.

Gender is not simply about individual attributes; radical feminist analysis has shown that it is also a basic principle of social organisation. In societies as they exist today, this means that it is about power: to learn masculinity or femininity is therefore to learn about subordination and domination; it may also entail learning about resistance. These power relations do not disappear when attributes cross sex lines, as they frequently do. This means that a man will generally lose status through 'feminine' behaviour, while a woman's exercise of 'masculine' qualities may represent a claim to authority (it was, for example, often said that Margaret Thatcher was the only 'real man' in her cabinet). Such masculinity is not however a guarantee of success, for in displaying the personal qualities deemed necessary to authority, a woman is also transgressing her gender role; if she succeeds as an individual, she will therefore fail as a woman, and it is as a woman as well as an individual that she is likely to be judged.

As the opening chapter showed, we live in a world in which our life chances and experiences seem in many ways to be determined by our sex; the analysis of gender suggests however that many current roles and rewards are not the inevitable outcome of biology, but of social arrangements which can be changed. For example, the obvious biological fact that it is women rather than men who give birth is in our society a source of economic disadvantage for women; in another society this reproductive ability could attract high status and financial reward, or it could be made more compatible with paid employment (through good maternity leave, public childcare provision and/or the sharing of childcare responsibilities with men). Similarly, men's physical ability to rape is a biological fact; the extent to which rape actually occurs and fear of sexual violence restricts women's lives is, however, socially variable.

The sex/gender distinction assessed

The idea that gender differences, divisions and oppressions are not fixed by nature is inherently optimistic and suggests that human society is not inevitably patriarchal. The question of where the line between sex and gender is to be drawn is however hotly disputed. There are also two strands within feminism which, for opposing reasons, argue that it cannot be made: the first insists that gender differences are based in biology, the second draws on postmodernist arguments to claim that even biology does not provide the basis for classifying the human race into two fixed and mutually exclusive sexes.

'Difference feminism' is a strand within radical feminism which agrees with some anti-feminists that women and men are essentially different in ways that go well beyond their physical attributes. Rather than seeing difference as a sign of women's inferiority, however, this approach claims that women are superior, and that 'womanly qualities' are better than those possessed by men. Such ideas have been expressed at popular as well as academic level, and have been justified by reference to 'natural' sex differences in hormones, brain structure and psychology. Thus it has been claimed that men are naturally aggressive, sexually predatory and inclined to rape (all that testosterone, and they've got the equipment); that women are naturally better than men at communicating (the left side of their brain is bigger); that women can express themselves in ways unimaginable to the pedestrian understandings of male logic (their diffuse sexuality enables them to transcend the boundaries of phallocentric discourse); that women are loving, nurturing and peaceful (because they are mothers); and that their ethical thinking is more caring and responsible than men's (again because they are mothers, or potential mothers).

Such essentialist ideas would seem to rule out the possibility of reforming men, or even of peaceful coexistence between the sexes (for a fuller discussion of such problems, see Evans, 1995). They are, however, also extremely difficult to prove. Even if there are such observable differences between the sexes, environmental causes cannot readily be disentangled from natural ones (for example, if baby girls learn to speak earlier than boys, this may be because their mothers talk to them more; if men have greater spatial awareness than women, this may be because they were given construction toys as children). It is also clear that both men and women display a whole range of behaviours and attributes, and that differences within each sex are frequently greater than those between individual men and women. Even if there are natural differences in character, it seems therefore that these take the form of tendencies, dispositions and averages rather than any kind of predetermination, and that what we have is a continuum in which environment plays a significant part, rather than a binary division based in nature (for a summary of the evidence, see Renzetti and Curran, 1992).

Even at the level of biological difference, the basis for a binary division between men and women does not exist. There is no criterion which allows the human race to be divided into two exclusive sexes, and the common sense arguments behind the division collapse on examination. The idea that women can be identified with the ability to give birth is clearly false: not all women can have babies, and even those who do are not fertile for the whole of their lives. Nor can women be defined in terms of their sexual relationships with men, for some women are attracted to other women, some are celibate and some are bisexual. We all possess a fluctuating mix of hormones, rather than exclusively male or female ones. Neither genitalia nor genes provide a clear-cut basis for sexual identity: although the vast majority of people who are classified as female have vaginas and XX chromosomes, a few have indeterminate sexual organs, and about 500 people in Britain have XY chromosomes but female bodies (that is, they are physically female but genetically male. See D'Silva, 1996). The vast majority of people feel that they have been classified correctly; a minority, however, believe that an error has been made, and that, despite the bodily evidence, they are 'really' of the 'opposite' sex; some such transsexuals have had 'corrective' surgery.

All this might seem to support the post-modernist arguments discussed in the previous chapter. These suggest not only that gender identity is much more fluid than commonly supposed, but also that the sex/gender distinction is untenable, because biological differences are not significant in themselves, but only if society makes them so. In reality of course society *does* treat certain biological differences as highly significant: every individual is legally classified at birth as a biological male or female, and a whole set of gender expectations are mapped onto this primary sex distinction. In this context, the sex/gender distinction is politically useful, because it enables us to identify and contest expectations, opportunities and forms of oppression experienced by people who happen to be female, and to show that these are not a product of biological necessity. In other words, we need to be able to see ourselves as women if we are to resist our current construction as women (for further arguments in favour of retaining the distinction, see Assiter, 1996; Oakley, 1997).

Although middle-class white feminists have tended to equate their own experiences with femininity in general, the sex/gender distinction does in principle enable us to see that gender roles and attributes are not an inevitable result of sex, but are highly variable both over time and among different groups within the same society. For example, the 19th-century idea that 'a woman' is someone who is frail, pure and in need of male protection applied only to middle-class white women. The economic situation of such women depended upon the exploitation of the labour of working-class or slave women who were perceived very differently; the denial of the sexuality of 'ladies' also coexisted with a perception by European men of working class and black women as sexually rapacious and available. Some feminists today would therefore argue that gender should be understood as a racialised category, for 'Social conditions of Black womanhood and manhood are inextricably linked to racial hierarchy, meaning systems and institutionalization' (Brewer, 1993, p. 17) and 'It is not simply that race, class, sexual identity and other factors generate contention among women, but that gender itself is a source of difference' (Smith, 1995).

This analysis means that although it is usually meaningful to talk about two sexes, we should perhaps insist on talking about a multiplicity of genders. Such an approach would recognise that the dominant models of masculinity and femininity are not the only ones at work in our society, and allow us to see that factors such as class, race, sexual orientation and (dis)ability all interact and profoundly affect the meaning of what it is to be a man or a woman (for a similar argument, see Spelman, 1988. See also Carver, 1996). This does not, however, preclude the possibility that all or most women have important experiences in common, and that they are systematically disadvantaged because of their sex. It need not, therefore, necessarily deny the existence of patriarchy as a system of oppression.

Ethnicity and race

The social construction of 'race'

There is widespread agreement among feminists that 'race' is not a meaningful biological category, and many avoid the term, or choose to place it in inverted commas, to distance themselves from those who believe that people can be classified into a number of distinct races, with particular attributes and abilities. Factors such as skin colour have no more inherent social significance than the colour of our hair. They have, however, acquired meaning in society, and race does therefore exist as a social construct which has a profound effect both on the lives of individuals and on the workings of society as a whole. Margaret Anderson's definition brings out particularly well its multilayered nature: 'Race is a social structure, constructed through social interaction and manifested in the institutions of society, interpersonal interactions, and the minds and identities of those living in racially based social orders' (Anderson, 1996, p. ix). It is in this sense, and not as a biological category that I use the term throughout this book.

Because it is socially constructed rather than inherently meaningful, race is also a highly unstable category which certainly cannot be reduced to the colour of an individual's skin. Terms such as 'coloured', 'non-white', 'black' or 'people of colour' can be the product of an unreflecting white perspective which labels all such groups as undifferentiatedly 'other', and leaves white identities unquestioned and unexplored. Inclusive use of the term 'black' has also been resisted by some Hispanic, Native American and Asian people in the United States and by Asian people in Britain who wish to preserve their own identity, and who feel that 'black' should be restricted to those identified as of African or Afro-Caribbean descent. Even a term such as 'British Asian' conceals the differences between peoples whose families originated in India, Pakistan or Bangladesh, or who were expelled from Kenya or Uganda during the 1970s; it also conceals cultural, religious and class differences within these groups. 'Black' has however also been used as a political term to identify groups which are on the receiving end of white racism and/or imperialism; in Britain it has, therefore, sometimes been extended to Jewish or Irish people.

There are no easy answers to the problems of terminology. I would therefore agree with Margaret Anderson and Patricia Hill Collins who write of such terms as White, Black, Women of Colour and Hispanic: 'Unfortunately, describing groups in this way reinforces basic categories of oppression. We do not know how to resolve this problem, but we want readers to be aware of the limitations and significance of language as they try to think more inclusively about diverse group experiences' (Anderson and Collins, 1995, p. xix).

It is also important to see that race, like gender, is not simply a matter of individual attributes or identity, but that it is a source of social identity and power which involves relations of domination and oppression. Such relations are often invisible to white people, who may be reluctant to recognise racial differences lest this be seen as a form of 'prejudice'. Thus a recent study of white American women found that many insisted that they personally were not racist, and that skin colour could therefore have no significance for them: a frequently used phrase was 'I don't care if he's Black, brown, yellow or green' (Frankenberg, 1993b, p. 149). Such a perspective is, however, one of privilege, for those who are racially oppressed know that their skin colour is often of profound significance. Even when white people can see the racial disadvantages experienced by black people, they are frequently unable to see that this also means that they themselves are privileged by their whiteness, and that racial advantage is not simply the product of individual racist acts, but of a whole system of racial hierarchy. A number of white feminists are, however, now self-consciously analysing their own racial situation. Such analysis suggests that whiteness can be understood as a location of structural advantage and race privilege, a 'standpoint' from which white people view the world and a set of cultural practices which are usually unmarked and unnamed.

The term 'ethnicity' is sometimes distinguished from 'race' and held to apply to cultural, religious or linguistic groups, or groups with a shared history or social customs. In Britain, this usage could see Poles, Muslims or Scots as ethnic groups, and some critics argue that the term therefore loses sight of the power relations and oppression that are involved in the production and exercise of racial identities. There is, however, a frequent slippage of terminology, and the term 'ethnic group' is often equated with racial identity and skin colour; because of the invisibility of whiteness, this in turn usually becomes 'non-white racial minority'.

Racism, nationalism and the oppression of women

Men and women both suffer from racism and from ethnic and nationalistic conflict. Their experiences are, however, also differentiated by gender; indeed such conflicts may create or reinforce specifically gendered forms of oppression. This oppression can arise from women's roles as symbols of the purity and integrity of their community and as its physical reproducers. These can combine to make the control of women's sexuality central to group identity, as it is both a matter of honour and a way of ensuring that the 'pure blood' of the community is not contaminated by alien males. This means that rape becomes a 'natural' weapon in racist, ethnic or nationalistic conflict (Zartov, 1995). To rape an enemy woman is to express contempt and inflict humiliation upon an opposing group; it is also a way of diluting the 'purity' of its stock. From the enemy's perspective, such acts legitimise continued aggression against the violators of a nation or community's honour. They may also be used to justify keeping women soldiers away from front line duties where they can fall into the enemy's hands; this in turn may reinforce gender hierarchies in political life, where women may be seen as unsuited to make policies on foreign policy or defence issues.

Women's bodies may also be used sexually to maintain racist institutions and practices. This was particularly clear in the United States in the era of slavery, when white men's sexual exploitation of female slaves was not only an abuse of the women involved, but a way of controlling and humiliating black people as a whole. As discussed in the previous section, the sexual availability of black women and the accompanying belief that they were naturally sensual and promiscuous, made possible the construction of privileged white women as frail and unsexual. Racial stereotypings also involved a fear of black male sexuality, which was used both to inflame racial hatred and to justify restrictions on the freedom of white women. Such stereotypings continue today (see Brah, 1993; Liu, 1994).

Demographic competition can also mean that women are denied the right to control their own fertility, as their bodies become a weapon in racial, ethnic and nationalistic conflicts. This is dramatically explicit in the case of Israel, where the respective birth rates of Israeli Jewish and Arab women are central military and political issues for both Jewish and Palestinian nationalists. Pregnant Jewish woman used to be congratulated with the words 'I see you are going to bring a small soldier into the world!' (Yuval-Davis, 1985, p. 669) while Palestinian slogans proclaimed that 'The Israelis beat us at the borders but we beat them at the bedrooms' (Yuval-Davis, 1989, p. 96) and 'Victory will come not on the battlefield but in the delivery room' (Grossman, 1993, p. 27. See also Najjar, 1992;

Abdo, 1994; Bryson, 1998). Similar demographic pressures have been brought to bear on women in eastern Europe both under communism and since its collapse. The most notorious example remains President Ceaucesco's 'five child' policy in Romania: not only were abortion and contraception outlawed, but an edict of 1984 subjected all women between the ages of 16 and 45 to regular gynaecological examination; those suspected of using contraception had to pay extra taxes (this policy was not only barbaric but counter-productive: in the last year of his dictatorship, it is estimated that 1.2 million illegal abortions were carried out, in contrast to only 300,000 live births. Seal, 1990, p. 35). In the United States and Britain, demographic pressures today take the form of policy pronouncements and policies about the dangers of feckless breeding by the 'wrong' kind of women. Questions of class, race, economics and morality have become hopelessly entangled, but it is clear that black fertility is seen as a welfare problem, and that black women have been sterilised or given long-term contraceptive injections without informed consent (see Chapter 7). At the same time, women in minority groups may be under pressure from their own communities to produce large families. In this context, the problems facing lesbians may be particularly acute; Cherrie Moraga has written that as a lesbian Chicano woman, she was not only seen as dividing her own community by rejecting male authority, she was also accused of contributing to the 'genocide' of her race (Moraga, 1993).

Other forms of cultural control over women may become particularly important in minority communities which are vulnerable in a racist society. In such communities, women may be seen as the embodiment of cultural values which have become ossified under outside threat, so that attempts to assert women's rights are seen as the product of corrupting, alien and feminist influences (Ali, 1996). Any attempt to discuss such issues as arranged marriage, codes of dress or infibulation (also known as female circumcision or genital mutilation) may therefore be seen as an act of betrayal. Attempts to confront issues of male violence against women are particularly difficult for communities in which the police and law courts are seen as violently racist, and in which issues of gender and community loyalty can seem to conflict.

Class

Definition

The language of 'class' often seems to be the language of confusion. Popular, academic and political usages of the term change over time and frequently merge, and discussions can easily drift from precisely agreed definitions into much looser meanings. At a popular level, class is often understood to refer to groups of people who share a common social and economic position, identified through such factors as occupation, income, education, accent or life-style. This can involve the idea of a social hierarchy, in which an individual has a particular location, but may move upwards or downwards to another class position. It may also be used to refer to a sense of identity, common interests or class consciousness; as such it involves a relation to other classes, which may take the form of aspiration, competition or conflict.

For Marxists, class is more strictly and technically defined in terms of relationship to the means of production and the extraction of surplus value. This means that capitalist society is basically divided into the workers, who have to sell their labour power in order to earn a living, and the owners of the means of production who exploit them; there is however a debate as to whether all workers from company executives to factory workers can usefully all be understood as members of the same class (see, for example, Miliband, 1977). From a Marxist perspective, the relationship between classes is one of conflict; classes in this sense are not, however, a permanent feature of human society, but could disappear when an increasingly inefficient capitalist system has been replaced by a socialist or communist society (for a recent re-statement of this position, see Wood, 1995).

This range of meanings complicates feminist debates on such issues as whether women constitute a class, whether the women's movement is narrowly middle class, and whether the divisions of class are more important than those of gender or race. It is also unclear how women fit into any of the above understandings of the term. In the past, it has usually been assumed that a woman derives her class position from her father or husband, rather than earning it in her own right. As feminists have argued, this assumption makes women's own subjective experiences invisible, and ignores the unequal distribution of economic resources within the family (see Chapter 6).

A feminist approach also reveals the inadequacies of stratification categories designed for men. These categories have tended to take the distinction between manual and non-manual occupations as the key indicator of working- or middle-class identity. Such categorisation, however, loses its meaning in the context of female employment, for poorly paid and low status clerical workers lack the rewards associated with middle-class occupations, and frequently identify with a working-class life-style (see Phillips, 1987a).

Are women a class?

The difficulty of fitting women into conventional class analysis has been partly responsible for the claim that women themselves constitute a class. This claim has been made by feminists in a number of ways. For some, it refers very generally to women's common position as a group oppressed by men. The New York Redstockings' manifesto of 1969 represents an extreme statement of this kind of position: 'Women are an oppressed class. Our oppression is total, affecting every facet of our lives. We are exploited as sex objects, breeders, domestic servants, and cheap labour... We identify the agents of our oppression as men' (quoted in Morgan, 1970, p. 598). Others have been more specific. In *The Dialectic of Sex*, first published in 1970, Shulamith Firestone attempted to use Marxist concepts to argue that sex–class is the most basic division in society, and that it arises from sex roles in reproduction; she also famously argued that this class division could be ended by the development of reproductive technology, as this could liberate women from the need to give birth.

In an influential analysis, Christine Delphy has argued that sex classes exist alongside social classes in a Marxist sense, and that they have an economic base. She argues that women's sex class is a product of their common role as unpaid workers exploited by their husbands in the patriarchal system of domestic production; although they may experience very different living standards and perform very different household duties, she says that housewives are all dependent upon their husbands for the maintenance which they receive in return for running the home (Delphy, 1984; Delphy and Leonard, 1992). This means that there are two class systems in society, and that married women who go out to work are oppressed in both. Delphy has been criticised for wrongly generalising from housewives to all women (Walby, 1986a) and for a dated, ahistorical and ethnocentric view of the family (Pollert, 1996. See also Jackson, 1996). Diemet Bubeck has further accused her of conflating the Marxist concept of *exploitation* (which involves the appropriation of surplus value) with the feminist concept of *oppression*; she argues against Delphy that the leisured wife of a wealthy man may be dependent, but that she is not in fact exploited (Bubeck, 1995). For Bubeck, gender norms and economic pressures combine to make women particularly vulnerable to exploitation as carers rather than as domestic workers; the beneficiaries are, however, not only men but also those women who have successfully opted out of caring work.

This debate merges with Marxist feminist arguments about the nature of housework under capitalism and analyses of social reproduction as part of the material basis of society. The claim that women constitute a sex class also has clear links with standpoint theory and its belief that women's common material situation can give rise to a particular understanding of society (see above). However, the logic of the standpoint position seems to imply that women will also have a standpoint based upon a more conventional understanding of their class situation in the capitalist system of production; although the material bases are less clear, they may also have a standpoint based upon other socially divisive factors such as ethnic identity, sexual orientation and (dis)ability.

The claim that women constitute a sex class in an economic sense has also been strongly disputed. Caroline Ramazanoglu, for example, forcefully rejects the idea that we can understand as a united sex class a group which includes 'Saudi Arabian princesses... British "immigrant" public toilet cleaners... African peasants... Wall Street executives... Turkish bank managers... white South African housewives... [and] Filipino servants'. On the contrary, she argues, women are profoundly divided by their class situation in a world capitalist system in which 'Some are worked to death, some are directly exploited, some are much less clearly exploited, and some clearly benefit at the expense of other women' (Ramazanoglu, 1989, pp. 112 and 104). It remains true that women still face discrimination in the labour market, and there is a sense in which they constitute a 'super-exploited' group of low paid and marginalised workers

(Davis, 1995). Nevertheless, increasing numbers of women are achieving economic success as well-paid employees or as entrepreneurs, and young middle-class women generally have greater economic independence and resources than ever before. As Ramazanoglu says, some of these women may be economic exploiters in their own right.

Partly for this reason, it is also increasingly clear that women are not all united by economic dependence on a male breadwinner; although only a few achieve full financial independence, an increasing number have at least some resources of their own. The traditional idea that marriage provides women with financial security in return for domestic labour also has little meaning in communities where men are badly paid and where unemployment is high; even for middle-income groups, reliance on a sole male breadwinner may seem financially unfeasible.

It remains true that women have primary responsibility for domestic work and childcare, whether or not they are in paid employment. There is however a huge difference between cleaning the house for one's own family, being paid to clean someone else's and supervising the employment of a cleaner. The gulf in female power and experience is even clearer if a well-paid career woman pays a surrogate mother to incubate her baby (this is legal in parts of the United States, although not in Britain). This means that even if the system of social reproduction produces relations of domination and subordination akin to the class relations produced in the mode of production, all women do not occupy the same situation within these relations. Rather, their situation is a product of both their gender and their command of economic resources; the latter may represent their own independent role in relation to employment and property, or it may be mediated by a partner (not necessarily male).

The above discussions suggest that women do not constitute an economic group united by their role in social production or reproduction and that it is not therefore appropriate to conceptualise them as a class. Their relationship to the paid labour market (either directly or as mediated through their male partners) may at times over-ride their shared responsibility for social reproduction, and it is clear that the meaning of being a 'housewife' or a 'woman worker' is highly variable. In other words, economic class as more conventionally understood can cut across 'womanly experiences'. This does not mean that women do not ever have common interests; it does mean that these interests cannot be assumed and that women can also have interests that divide them.

Feminism: a racist, class-based movement?

Although they have often been written out of history, some women of colour and working-class white women have always been politically active in a whole range of formal and informal groups and organisations aimed at improving the lives of themselves, their families and their community, or at achieving more general social change. Some have campaigned on specifically women's issues and seen themselves as part of a wider women's movement. Nevertheless, opponents of feminism have frequently portrayed it as the self-seeking politics of middle-class white women seeking to further their careers, indulge in the exploration of their sexuality or pursue esoteric theories of cultural representation. As such, critics say that it is irrelevant to the experiences, needs and wishes of 'ordinary' women and that it ignores the ways in which men as well as women are oppressed by racism, poverty and violence. It therefore weakens and divides exploited groups and may even contribute to their oppression.

At times, feminism's racism and its defence of economically advantaged women's class interests against those of other groups has been explicit and overt. The campaign for women's suffrage provides a particularly clear example of this. Although some women demanded the vote for all adults as a step towards a more equitable society, others wanted a limited franchise as a way of defending class and race privilege. They therefore demanded that white, educated, middle-class women be given the vote rather than former male slaves or male workers – a view encapsulated in a leading American suffragist's demand to 'cut off the vote from the slums and give it to women' (quoted in Evans, 1977, p. 204). Overt racism and hostility to the working class have also surfaced repeatedly among campaigners for birth control and abortion, as the claim that women should be enabled to control their own fertility has merged with eugenicist arguments about the need to limit 'feckless breeding' by 'undesirable' groups.

Less deliberately, feminists have sometimes used racist and class-based assumptions and invoked the power of racist institutions and attitudes in their fight against sexism. The race and class privileges of middle-class white women are particularly likely to be used against men in oppressed groups when issues of sexuality and sexual violence are involved. At a very basic level, it seems that even women who consciously oppose racism, nationalism and the inequalities of class tend to construct images of home/foreigner, self/other and safety/danger in such a way that men outside their own community or class are seen as a threat; women from privileged groups may also be able and prepared to use the power of the state to control or expel such apparently threatening men (see Rathzel, 1995).

Black feminists have been particularly angered by Reclaim the Night marches. Intended to assert women's right to walk through cities free from the threat of sexual assault, these have frequently taken the form of white women marching through minority and/or working-class neighbourhoods. Critics argue that they reinforce false stereotypes about black and working-class sexuality. In reality, they argue, women are at far more risk of violence within the home than from a stranger on the streets. Angela Davis has further claimed that although official figures in the United States show a disproportionate number of rapes by black men, it is white men who are the group most likely to rape; official figures simply reflect women's knowledge that they will not be believed if they report assaults by 'respectable' white men, while a white woman reporting a rape by a black man will benefit from the racism of the police and the law courts (Davis, 1982).

While some white feminists have exploited racist fears, others have been so anxious to remove themselves from accusations of racism that they have sought to deny the existence of sexist behaviour within the black community, or to excuse it as a response to deprivation. In left-wing circles, similar defences are sometimes made of men in working-class communities. Such thinking marginalises the experiences of many women, and stems from a failure to see that oppressions are not one-dimensional, and that 'poor and lower class men are as able to oppress and brutalise women as any other group of men in… society' (hooks, 1981, p. 86).

Affluent white feminists have also been accused of exploiting other women's labour. When Betty Friedan exhorted American women in the 1960s to work outside the home (see above), she saw this as a means of fulfilment rather than the result of economic necessity, and argued that it was worthwhile even if the former housewife had to spend most of her earnings on a cleaning woman

(Friedan, 1986, p. 303). The needs of the cleaning woman, along with those of all the other women who have always had to work in monotonous, badly paid jobs rather than interesting careers, were, however, completely ignored. Today, the ability of a minority of women to achieve successful careers is dependent upon an army of badly paid nursery nurses, cleaners and child-minders, and the lifestyle of most successful women is as much the product of exploitation as is that of middle-class men. As feminism becomes institutionalised, an increasing number of feminists are able to maintain a middle-class life-style by analysing the oppression of their sex; however, women's studies courses, feminist publishing and feminist conferences rest upon the labour of less well-paid female secretaries, office cleaners and catering staff. The economic privileges of many middle-class feminists inevitably also involves the economic exploitation of many working-class men.

Although most middle-class white feminists today consider themselves to be anti-racist and opposed to class privilege, many have failed to confront such problems or to concede that the women's movement or their own behaviour could be seen as racist. As Deborah King has said 'Many white feminist activists have often assumed that their antisexism stance abolished all racial prejudice or discriminatory behaviours... At best, this presumption is naive and reflects a serious ignorance of the pervasiveness of racism in this society' (King, 1993, p. 229).

Today, some middle-class white feminists continue to treat their own experiences as central. Nevertheless, recognition of the differences among women is more widespread than in the past, and some *white* feminists today argue that the perspectives of black women are of central theoretical and practical importance. The willingness to play at least lip service to the diversity of women's experiences is in part a response to the impact of post-modernist theory and its suspicion of generalising, totalising theories. More importantly, however, it is also the product of black feminist political activity and analysis.

Who is the most oppressed?: from hierarchical to interdependent oppressions

Much feminist ink has in the past been spilt on the question of whether or not oppression based on gender is more important than that based on class or race. Debates have often seemed to confuse questions of causation with those of intensity or longevity of oppression. They have also tended to forget that people are members of more than one social group, and have therefore contrasted the experiences of women with those of workers or ethnic minorities as if women have no class or ethnic identity, workers are all white men and minority ethnic groups are undivided by gender or class.

The radical feminist approach saw patriarchy as the oldest and most significant form of oppression for women. Kate Millett argued that women's relation to the class system is 'tangential, vicarious, and temporary', while 'sexism may be more endemic in our own society than racism' (Millett, 1985, pp. 38 and 39); Robin Morgan has even claimed that class and race were invented by patriarchy to divide and conquer women (Morgan, 1970, p. xxxix).

In contrast, Engels' application of Marx's ideas to 'the Woman Question', which was for many years the orthodox Marxist position, argued that women's oppression began with the first private property and class society, for it was only then that men's desire to pass their property to known heirs motivated them to control and possess women. As such, it would be ended in future communist society, and he claimed that it was already disappearing within the working classes, as proletarian marriage was no longer based on property and economic dependency (for fuller discussion, see Bryson, 1992, Chapter 3).

Although few writers today would accept such crude reductionism, some do insist on the primacy of class analysis. Anna Pollert criticises the idea that patriarchy exists as an autonomous or semi-autonomous system, arguing that in contrast to capitalism, which is driven by the pursuit of profit, 'There is no necessary internal connection between men and women as gendered subjects which defines a self-perpetuating material dynamic or economic/social system'. She also argues that 'There are no gendered relations without a class dimension at some level, and the same operates for "race"' (Pollert, 1996, p. 643 and 646). Ellen Meiksins Wood has written of the 'determinative primacy' of class struggle. She says that this 'is not because class is the only form of oppression or even the most frequent, consistent, or violence source of social conflict, but rather because its terrain is the social organization of production which creates the material conditions of existence itself' (Wood, 1995, p. 108). She does not, however, argue that gender and race inequalities are caused by capitalism. On the contrary, she says that 'there is a positive tendency in capitalism to *undermine* such differences, and even to dilute identities like gender or race, as capital strives to absorb people into the labour market and to reduce them to interchangeable units of labour abstracted from any specific identity' (Wood, 1995, p. 276). This means, she says, that race inequality is not inherent in capitalism, and that capitalism could also survive the eradication of all oppressions specific to women as women; the existence of capitalism is, however, inseparable from class exploitation.

Although it might technically be possible to eliminate racism and sexism within a pure capitalist system, this is highly unlikely. Wood herself accepts that gender and race oppressions are useful to capitalism because they conceal its nature and divide the working class, and that gender oppression also serves as a way of organising social reproduction in what is thought to be the least expensive way. Other writers have used similar analysis to argue that because race and gender oppressions play a material role in increasing capitalist profit (by providing readily identifiable groups which can be 'super-exploited' at the point of production), they are 'a function of class society as well as being a product of it (Davis, 1995, p. 105). The importance of such oppressions for capitalism is strengthened by the production of gender as well as race oppressions through nationalistic conflicts, which may themselves be the product of international capitalist competition (although the ideological role of nationalism is changing in an era of multinational organisations operating within an international capitalist system). It also seems likely that while the economic relationships between men and women are hidden within the family and personal life, workers are protected from the full commodification of life. If, however, capitalism's potential to reduce men and women to 'interchangeable units of labour' were to be realised, such protection would no longer exist; this final triumph of alienation could have explosive effects.

None of these arguments need mean that gender and race oppressions are caused rather than utilised, modified and reinforced by capitalism; they also leave open-ended the question of whether they were originally the product of earlier class society, as Engels suggested, or whether they could have an independent, non-economic origin. Even within a Marxist framework such as Wood's, the concept of social reproduction, could suggest that because gender relations are as much a part of the 'material relations of production' as class, then they also have as much 'determinative primacy'. Although race oppression has no physical basis that is equivalent to biological sex and that has provided the basis for the kind of division of labour that exists in social reproduction, it in turn plays a critical role in the construction of gender and has become entangled with class in complex ways.

The interconnecting and interactive nature of different systems of oppression is also becoming apparent in relation to their relative intensity or violence. At a popular level, feminist concerns are often portrayed as trivial compared with such 'serious' problems as racial violence and unemployment. Radical feminists have however highlighted the horrendous violence to which women in all parts of the world and all social groups have been subjected because of their sex, and the ways in which women's labour has been exploited. In reality, women can both share class and race oppressions with men and experience them differently; similarly, they can be united by common experiences of sexism at the same time that these are filtered by their class position and racial identity. For example, it is clear at one level that a woman who has been raped or one who is bleeding to death from an illegal abortion is suffering as a woman. The first woman may, however, have been raped as a black woman by a man who would not dream of touching a 'respectable' white woman; the second may be dying in a society in which women with money or contacts have no problem in terminating an unwanted pregnancy. If the rapist in the first case is white, the woman may be unlikely to be believed if she reports him to the authorities; if he is black, she may be unwilling to 'betray' her community by involving the police. If the second woman is also black, she may have feared that if she were to go into hospital she would be sterilised without her consent. The complicating factors seem endless, and they show the futility of trying to talk of gender, class or race oppressions in isolation from one another.

Today, many feminist writers agree with bell hooks that 'suggesting a hierarchy of oppression, with sexism in first place, evokes a sense of competing concern which is unnecessary' (hooks, 1984, p. 35). Such writers agree that society is systematically structured by gender, race and class. Many also agree that 'Race, class and gender oppression are inseparable; they construct, reinforce, and support one another. The form which class first took was genderic and racist. The form racism first took was genderic and classist. The form the state first took was patriarchal' (Lerner, 1993, p. 245). From this new perspective, the buzz words are 'interactive', 'simultaneous', 'cumulative', 'dynamic' and 'multiple'; and research is aimed at exploring the interrelationships between the systems in historically specific situations, rather than in discovering which is the more fundamental. Patricia Hill Collins has summarised this approach:

> At this historical moment we have something very momentous happening – the linking of three historically distinct areas of inquiry with a renewed commitment to theorize connections on multiple levels of social structure. To accomplish this goal, all must support a working hypothesis of equivalence between oppressions that allows us to explore the interconnections among the systems and extracts us from the internecine battles of whose oppression is the more fundamental. (Collins, 1995, p. 492)

Beyond gender, race and class: disability and sexual orientation

Although most feminists have not done so, this interactive approach can be extended to other forms of oppression, particularly those around disability and sexual orientation (for a critique of feminism's neglect of disability issues, see Morris, 1991). It enables us to see that disability is not fixed and given, but fluid and open-ended, and that it is frequently socially produced and experienced differently by people in different social groups. For example, many people in western societies are disabled because they cannot afford a decent wheelchair or because buildings do not provide access to wheelchair users; at the same time, many who would otherwise be disabled by poor eyesight can function normally because corrective spectacles or contact lenses are readily available.

The ability to buy wheelchairs or spectacles can clearly be affected by both class and the nature of welfare provision; the meaning of being a wheelchair user or spectacle wearer can also be experienced differently by men and women. Although disabled men and women are both often treated as asexual and genderless (most obviously when public lavatories require people to classify themselves as male, female or disabled), a woman in a wheelchair can conform to some notions of femininity, as she is seen as dependent, passive and in need of protection. A male wheelchair user, in contrast, is seen as lacking in key attributes of masculinity such as strength and independence; if he is educated and white, he may, however, be able to compensate for through his earning power and intellectual authority. Meanwhile, a disabled woman is likely to be seen as an unsuitable or incompetent mother.

Similar arguments about the complex nature of social experience apply to sexual orientation, for being labelled as heterosexual or gay clearly has different meanings for men and women. The significance of sexual orientation also varies across class and ethnic lines and interacts both with economic realities and social attitudes in highly complex ways. Tackling the discrimination and disadvantage experienced by many people who are disabled and/or gay therefore involves understanding that disability and homosexuality are not simply individual experiences but socially created categories, and that their meaning is a variable product of other systems of power and inequality which they can at times both sustain and subvert.

Where do we go from here?

All of the approaches discussed in this chapter agree that gender, race and class constitute systems of oppression that cannot be reduced to individual acts, experiences or attitudes. Now that formal legal equality has largely been won, this understanding is an important prerequisite for collective political action to achieve further change. The idea that oppressions are interconnected but that none can be assumed to have causal primacy, also means that each system must be tackled directly and in its own right, rather than assuming that it will disappear as a by-product of change elsewhere. Because they are so inextricably linked, however, changes in one system will inevitably have effects on other areas.

For feminists, an important starting-point must be a recognition of the diversity of women's experiences and the specificity of the oppressions that particular women face. This is essential if marginalised groups are to become visible and develop their own perspectives, rather than being added to existing frameworks. As discussed above, this principle can be extended to include women's experiences around disability and sexual orientation, which again are both important in their own right and interactive with other social formations. A whole range of other experiences such as motherhood, infertility, physical appearance, bereavement, unemployment, incest or prostitution can also give rise to a sense of difference and to particular interests and political priorities. The danger here is that the process of recognising identities can become totally open-ended and fragmentary. This can be avoided if it is understood that the most politically significant differences are those that are related to structured inequalities of power rather than simply to personal experience. It is also important that recognition of differences is not treated as an end in itself, but as a basis for dialogue and the building of alliances.

The recognition of difference involves an understanding of the importance of race and class in the lives of women who appear to be advantaged within these systems, as well as those who are directly oppressed. It includes naming the racism of white feminists and the ways in which some women exploit others economically. For white feminists, acknowledging and confronting their own personal racism is however only a first step; if this self-knowledge is to be politically effective, it requires more practical changes to existing priorities and assumptions. For black women, the process of naming their identity may itself be empowering (see Hull, Scott *et al.*, 1982), and may help provide the basis for organisations which are more self-consciously political than earlier informal self-help or community groups. In Britain, for example, the Organisation of Women of Asian and Afro-Caribbean Descent (OWAAD) attempted to organise around the shared experiences of women on the receiving end of both racism and sexism. Other groups, of which the Southall Black Sisters is the best known, have campaigned against domestic violence within the black and Asian community (Wilson, 1991; Siddiqui, 1996).

Such groups seem to share values with white feminists. They are however confronted with a set of complex issues around priorities, allegiances and alliances, for if women seek to defend their own interests they may be seen as betraying their community or class. These problems are particularly acute for black and Asian women who seek to oppose male violence within their own community without reinforcing racial stereotypes or relying on a racist police force for protection. They were also vividly revealed when accusations of sexual harassment against an African-American man, Clarence Thomas, were made by an African-American woman, Anita Hill, during the 1991 Senate hearings to approve the appointment of the former to the Supreme Court of the United States. White feminists and black men were in general clear where their loyalties lay. Black women, however, seemed once again to be faced with a choice between their gender and their race in which their own identity as black women had no place. As women, they might recognise the force of Hill's case and want to celebrate the strength of a women's movement that could successfully insist that powerful men be called to account for their misbehaviour (for accounts from a white feminist perspective, see Wolf, 1993 and Farganis, 1994). As black people, however, they could not join in what Thompson succeeded in portraying as 'a high-tech lynching' (quoted in Farganio, 1994, p. 131). Nevertheless, some such women agreed with the African-American writer Toni Morrisson that 'The time for undiscriminating racial unity is past' (Morrison, 1993, p. iii); since then increasing numbers have recognised the sexual harassment of black women as a serious political issue, and have begun organising collectively against it (Bray, 1995. See also Crenshaw, 1993; Giddings, 1994).

If, as has been argued, oppressions are interconnected, some forms of collective action across class, race and gender lines will be necessary. Here bell hooks' idea of *solidarity*, introduced in the previous chapter can help steer a course between undiscriminating inclusiveness and separatism. A politics based on solidarity allows women to support each other rather than insisting on unity based on an identity of interests and experience. It also allows them to build upon interests which they may share with oppressed men, to treat men as comrades in struggle against race and class oppressions rather than simply as oppressors, and even to recognise the possibility that 'Men are not exploited or oppressed by sexism, but there are ways in which they suffer as a result of it' (hooks, 1984, p. 72).

Solidarity among oppressed groups cannot, however, be assumed. It is clear that those who are disadvantaged in one system do not automatically empathise with or support other oppressed groups. Just as white working-class men are capable of the most virulent racism and sexism, and black men can abuse and exploit women, so middle-class white feminists can actively damage the interests of other women. This means that 'sisterhood becomes a goal rather than a precondition of political agency: instead of anticipating solidarity among women, solidarity has to be achieved through dialogue' (Lutz et al., 1995, p. 15).

In terms of practical politics, women will sometimes need to organise collectively simply as women. They may, for example, campaign against restrictions against abortion rights or for action against sexual harassment. Even in such campaigns, however, they will need to be aware that these issues do not affect all women in the same way; they may, therefore, choose to work in alliances or coalitions, rather than as a single group. Women organising on the basis of shared gender interests may also be prepared to accept help from men. They should, however, be aware that men may be likely to dictate the terms on which this help is given. In 1979, for example, the British Trade Union Congress organised a huge demonstration in London against a restrictive abortion bill; the insistence by male union leaders that they should lead the march was seen by some women as a patriarchal take-over (Coote and Campbell, 1987, p. 158).

In some situations, the needs which women seem to share with each other will be less immediate than interests which unite them with some men, and the focus of their activity will lie with trade unions, anti-racist organisations or community groups. Here, however, feminist perspectives can help ensure that women's gender-specific needs are not lost in collective struggle. It will, for example, be important to recognise the needs of women workers, challenge sexism wherever it is found and insist that male leaders are not treated as the exclusive voice of minority communities.

Women may also want to support men who are fighting for their jobs. The best known recent example of this in Britain is the Women Against Pit Closures, formed during the 1984–5 coal dispute. Women here appeared to be defending men in a highly patriarchal community. Nevertheless, their activities went well beyond the traditional soup kitchens and fund-raising to include picketing and public speaking. These changes showed the impact of the women's movement on women who would never have described themselves as feminist. As mining women made links with other supporting groups, including black activists, lesbians and gay men and the women peace campaigners at Greenham Common, there was 'an extraordinary cross-fertilization of left politics... connecting the issues of the miners' strike with other issues of the left' (Coote and

Campbell, 1987, p. 179). The influence of this experience was clear more than a decade later, when the 'Women of the Waterfront' in Liverpool were active in support of dockers in the 1995–8 lock-out (Lavalette and Kennedy, 1996); in both communities, the long-term effects of women's new political activism are still being felt.

Even as they defended their men's jobs, women in the mining community faced opposition and hostility from some men who resented their new independence. Even greater problems can arise for women of colour who want to support oppressed men, but not the patriarchal values which they hold. This tension is clear in the mixed reaction of African-American women to the Million Man March organised in 1995 by Louis Farrakhan, the leader of the separatist Nation of Islam. This called upon African-American men to take responsibility for their own situation and to re-shape their lives in communities rife with crime, violence and drug abuse, and in a society where 46 per cent of African-American families are headed by a woman. Farrakhan also insists that although his followers should respect black women, they should reassert their patriarchal control over them; he calls for a return to the traditional gender roles of male provider and female home-maker. Some prominent black women, such as the veteran civil rights campaigners Rosa Parks and Coretta Scott King and the writer Maya Angelou have supported Farrakhan. However, other writers such as bell hooks have denounced his sexism, and Angela Davis insists that 'Justice cannot be served by countering a distorted, racist view of black manhood with a narrowly sexist vision of men standing "a degree above women"' (quoted in Freedland, 1995. See also Forna, 1996).

Similar disagreements arise among women of colour seeking to oppose repressive practices such as arranged marriage or infibulation without appearing to betray their culture. Such women may resent the attempts of white feminists to interfere, or the strident nature of their intervention (see Amos and Parmar, 1984). This does not necessarily mean that white feminists should remain silent on such issues, or that they should not offer support to women of colour. What they should not do, however, is to isolate arranged marriage or infibulation from wider issues of female subordination, or to assume that white cultural practices are necessarily superior. To put it mildly, the current state of marriage and sexual relationships has not brought unmitigated happiness and security to the majority of white women, while a culture in which an estimated 150,000

American women die each year from anorexia can hardly isolate infibulation as a danger to women's health (Wolf, 1990, p. 182. For a fictional exploration of the significance of infibulation for black women, see Walker, 1993; on the wider issues see Ramazanoglu, 1989; Lees, 1986). It is also important not to equate Islam with repressive practices, for this is, like Christianity, a religion with both conservative and feminist strands. Here the activities of Women Against Fundamentalism, established in 1989, suggests a way forward, as this group opposes religious intolerance and fundamentalism in all religions, and can therefore unite women from a wide range of cultures.

A politics of solidarity does not preclude separatist activity by particular groups of women. As long as society is structured by race and class, such separatism will at times be necessary, for these structures encourage the processes through which the interests and priorities of privileged women assert themselves, not least by the unthinking acceptance of these as the norm. This chapter has identified gender, race and class as three key structures which are built into the social and economic fabric of society. Other issues, such as sexual orientation or disability, will however also be experienced as important by some women. Organisation on the basis of these interests will be necessary if existing agendas are to be challenged. This may produce acute tensions, and Joni Lovenduski and Vicky Randall's study of contemporary feminist politics in Britain found that 'The difficulty of responding to the imperatives of lesbian politics and of the diverse and differentiated black and women's movements is more likely to lead to political exhaustion than to a confident politics' (Lovenduski and Randall, 1993, p. 84).

There are no easy answers to such problems, and there are many difficulties in the way of a politics of solidarity. Facing up to these is, however, essential if feminism is to continue as an active political force into the 21st century. This means that the issues discussed in this chapter are not self-contained, but are running themes throughout other feminist debates.

4

Feminism and the law

The demand that women should have the same legal rights as men has long been central to feminism, and many feminists today continue to believe that the law can be used to achieve their goals. Others, however, argue that it is inherently biased against women: they claim that not only is the legal profession strongly male dominated, but that the law fails to recognise women's needs or articulate their experiences, that it expresses a limited, male conception of justice and that it is both a source and reflection of men's patriarchal power. As such, it cannot provide a ready-made tool for feminists; some however claim that it can become a 'site of struggle' in which feminists can contest the current meaning of being a woman.

This chapter assesses these arguments, and concludes that feminist engagements with the law can be productive in both the short and the long term, provided that its existing biases are recognised and contested. In addition to some practical recommendations, it suggests demanding an end to legal classification by sex as a feminist strategy for change.

A male-dominated profession

Until the end of the 19th century, women's exclusion from any active role in the legal process was absolute. Without a vote, they had no role in choosing their country's legislators and they were denied both entry into the legal profession and the education that would have qualified them for this. If a woman married, her very legal existence was suspended: she could have no independent right to her own property or earnings or to the custody of her own children, and she was in effect the property of her husband. As the famous British philosopher John Stuart Mill said in *The Subjection of Women* in 1869, 'There remain no legal slaves, except the mistress of every house' (1983 edition, p. 147).

Although there have been major national differences in time-scale, women in western democracies have gradually gained access to the legal 'rights of man', including the right to enter the legal profession. This does not mean, however, that they play an equal role with men today, and there are still few women in top judicial positions. The situation is particularly acute in the federal courts in United States, where in 1994 only 14 per cent of judges were women. This low figure was, however, an all-time high, and represented an increase in absolute numbers to 120 from only five in 1976, when affirmative action programmes were introduced. Appointment methods for state judges vary widely; although women are still under-represented, it has been estimated that between 1980 and 1994 the number of female state judges has almost tripled (Martin, 1996). In Britain, where appointment procedures have been highly secretive and reliant on informal networking, 80 per cent of judges in the mid-1990s were white men who had been both to public school and to Oxford or Cambridge University, and the number who had been privately educated was actually rising (Travis, 1996, 1998). At the highest levels of the British judiciary, male domination is even more marked: in 1995, only one of the 32 Appeal Court judges and six of the 94 High Court judges were women (*Guardian*, 25 April 1995).

Although discrimination against women lawyers can be seen as a feminist issue in its own right, the under-representation of women in the judiciary does not necessarily mean that the courts are biased in favour of men. There is however some evidence from the United States that female judges tend to be more supportive of women's rights than male judges (Martin, 1996). More generally, the composition of the judiciary means that the courts appear alien to most women, as well as to black and working-class men. The narrow experience and background of judges can also make it particularly difficult for them to understand the needs and reactions of people who are economically and socially disadvantaged, or who have been abused. As Helena Kennedy has commented 'If any single category of human being is unaccustomed to being treated as inferior or subordinate, it is a white, male, British judge' (Kennedy, 1992, p. 30). It is therefore unsurprising that, as the following sections show, problems arise when women try to pursue equality within legal systems in which such men have written the rules.

Equality with men: employment law

In the United States, feminist demand for full legal equality seemed to have reached its logical conclusion in 1971, when an Amendment to the Constitution guaranteeing equal legal rights to women was passed by both Houses of Congress with huge majorities. Support for the Equal Rights Amendment (ERA) then waned however; it was never ratified by the necessary number of states, and the Amendment finally fell in 1982.

By this time, even some feminists were expressing doubts. Some feared that the ERA would absolve husbands from the responsibility of maintaining their wives and children, that it would involve the drafting of women into active military service and that it would rob working-class women of protection against bad conditions of employment. It also became difficult to see how the demand for maternity leave or for any kind of affirmative action to redress women's disadvantages could be reconciled with the principle of absolute gender equality.

The fear that 'equal treatment' can in practice disadvantage women seems to some to have been confirmed by the Canadian experience. Here, feminist pressure ensured that the 1982 Charter of Rights and Freedoms contained a section which gave full legal equality to all citizens. Subsequent court decisions have used this to justify treating divorcing spouses as independent and equal for purposes of financial support and to withdraw benefits aimed at lone mothers. Because women continue to earn significantly less than men and to be far more likely than men to be single parents, the result of these 'gender-blind' decisions has been an increase in female poverty (see Kingdom, 1991; Sedley, 1991 and Mossman, 1995).

In the United States, the requirement that women should be treated exactly the same as men has produced particular difficulties for pregnant women workers, because it suggests that to provide maternity leave constitutes 'special treatment' and is therefore discrimination against *men* (see Bacchi, 1990; Minnow, 1990; Kay, 1995). Laws against sex discrimination were therefore for a time interpreted to make it illegal for insurance policies or employment contracts to cover such leave. Although a series of legal battles during the 1970s succeeded in changing this interpretation, maternity leave can only be provided or insured against on the same basis as 'temporary disabilities' that may be experienced by men. In 1998, the United States remains the only advanced industrial society with no statutory maternity leave.

In Britain, the equality argument has not been pushed so far, and by the late 1990s all female employees were entitled to some maternity leave. However, discrimination against pregnant women workers only counts as sex discrimination if it can be shown that a woman has been treated less favourably than a sick man. As Carol Smart has said, 'The tortuousness of this logic defies belief, but it reveals the extraordinary lengths to which a legal system which has staked its policy on the equality approach, will go to prove that difference is sameness' (Smart, 1989, p. 83).

A commitment to complete legal equality between men and women has also caused problems for affirmative action programmes designed to improve women's situation in the workplace or to increase their political representation. Carol Bacchi's study of such programmes in six western nations found that affirmative action is seen either as a form of charity for the underprivileged or a form of unjustifiable discrimination against men (Bacchi, 1996. See also Eisenstein, 1994). In Britain in 1996, such thinking led to the finding that the Labour party's policy of all-women shortlists in some safe or winnable constituencies was unlawful (for further discussion, see Chapter 5). In the United States, it has produced a series of Supreme Court decisions disallowing consideration of race or gender in selection procedures.

Equality on women's terms

According to some recent feminist writers, these problems are the product of a model of gender equality which unquestioningly accepts male needs and experiences as a universal norm and fails to see the extent to which men are already privileged by existing practices and assumptions. Catherine MacKinnon has, however, demanded to know 'Why should anyone have to be like white men to get what they have, given that white men do not have to be like anyone except each other to have it?' (MacKinnon, 1993b, p. 370).

The dominant model, it is said, assumes that rights are exercised by self-sufficient individuals who scarcely have to look after their own physical needs, let alone anyone else's. The fact that few women can operate like this becomes a problem, and their family responsibilities are seen as a mark of 'difference', requiring special consideration or treatment, such as maternity leave, flexible working hours or the provision of a crèche. In contrast, equality on women's terms would recognise that women's biological role in reproduction and their socially produced domestic responsibilities are essential to the survival and well-being of society. Their sex-specific needs therefore represent the importance of women's contributions rather than a sign of inferiority or individual peculiarity. As Carol Bacchi says, 'Women are not "different". Quite simply, their sex-specific characteristics have been disadvantaged because society has been organised in such a way that pregnancy and childrearing are ignored' (Bacchi, 1990, p. 176).

From this new perspective, a key employment goal is not special treatment for women, but to give women and men the same opportunities to combine work and family obligations. Here the passing of the Family and Medical Leave Act in the United States in 1993 shows the possibility of moving away from the traditional male paradigm in order to improve women's situation. The Act, which had previously been vetoed by President Bush, entitles employees (male and female) to 'take up to 12 weeks unpaid leave per year for the care of a new-born, newly adopted, or newly placed foster child, or for the care of a seriously ill child, parent or spouse' (quoted in Thompson, 1996, p. 297). Leave entitlement is hedged round with restrictions, only 45 per cent of workers are covered and far fewer can afford to take advantage of it. Nevertheless, framing the proposals in terms of family needs rather than women's rights was a successful political strategy that widened the basis of support for the measure; it also meant that women were not singled out as a group with special needs that would be potentially expensive to employ.

As we shall see in Chapter 6, this kind of approach has gone much further in the Scandinavian nations, where employment legislation is also largely based upon a gender-neutral approach, but where labour market and welfare legislation has acknowledged that both men and women can become parents, and that workers cannot be treated as disembodied units of production. All the Scandinavian nations therefore provide far more generous parental leave than is available in

Britain or the United States, all allow for flexibility in working hours and all except Norway have good childcare provision. Similarly, relatively safe working conditions and a narrowing of the pay gap between men and women have been achieved through trade union activities designed to protect all workers and reduce inequality, rather than by special measures in favour of women.

An approach to equality that treats women as a central starting-point also raises questions about the nature of 'merit', and the extent to which this reflects male priorities and perceptions rather than objective criteria. Here Catherine MacKinnon has argued that 'virtually every quality that distinguishes men from women is already affirmatively compensated in this society' (quoted in Jaggar, 1994b, p. 56). From this perspective, deliberate action to improve the employment situation of women does not represent discrimination, but recognition of women's abilities and the ways in which women are systematically excluded by current practices.

Similar arguments have been used to argue for a re-valuation of the work done by women and men. Here the European Community Directive of 1975 that the principle of equal pay should be extended beyond the minority of women doing the same or similar work to men, and that it should include work of equal *value* has very radical implications. In practice, few British women have successfully pursued equal value claims, and the criteria through which value is measured have not been radically challenged: there has been, for example, no suggestion that nursery nurses should be paid the same as professors, that the work of cleaners is as important as that of solicitors, or that many organisations could survive the departure of their managers more easily than their secretaries. Nevertheless, significant numbers of women have benefited from revaluation of their jobs, and the principle can be seen as an important legal victory for women.

The above discussion suggests that if we expose the gendered nature of existing legal assumptions and insist that these incorporate women's perspectives, we can move beyond the debate over whether the law should treat women and men the same or recognise gender-specific needs. This does not mean that all women have the same interests and that these cannot be changed. On the contrary, as the example of parental leave shows, a 'dynamic' approach to sexual difference can recognise that although gender-specific responsibilities and needs exist, many of these can in principle become gender neutral. It is also important to remember that gender differences can vary from one social group to another, and that they are likely to be mediated by divisions of class and race.

Equality with men: the criminal law

Some feminists have argued that the criminal justice system as well as employment law has been distorted by an uncritical acceptance of male assumptions disguised as gender neutrality. This they say makes it particularly difficult to understand the behaviour of women where issues of domestic violence and/or sexual assault are involved. They argue that this has adversely affected the way that the courts treat women, particularly in cases where they are accused of killing their partner or where they have been the victims of rape. The following discussion draws largely on British research; its general principles are, however, applicable to other western societies.

According to British law, a successful plea of 'provocation' can reduce a charge of murder to the lesser one of manslaughter. For this defence to be allowed, a jury must believe that 'a reasonable man' might have experienced a sudden and temporary loss of control. Although in principle the term 'reasonable man' now includes 'reasonable woman', feminists have argued that the thinking behind it is based on typically male responses and fails to understand the reality of the circumstances in which women most commonly kill their partners (despite the publicity given to some cases, this is in fact an extremely rare crime). In practice, women who kill men who have been abusing them seldom use the plea of provocation with success, for although their action may represent a desperate response to years of cumulative abuse, it is likely to involve an element of planning and premeditation rather than an apparently spontaneous and short-lived outburst.

Women killers of men they know are more likely to have their sentences reduced on grounds of diminished responsibility than provocation; even so, in 1994 40 per cent of the 13 British women who killed men known to them were convicted of murder rather than manslaughter, compared with only 29 per cent of the 101 men who killed women they knew (Roberts, 1995). Some feminists have claimed that using a plea of diminished responsibility pathologises what might be seen as reasonable behaviour if men had not set the standards, and Jill Radford and Liz Kelly have therefore argued that in certain circumstances the killing of a violent partner should be understood as a rational form of self-defence (Radford and Kelly, 1995). Such arguments have had some success in the United States. In the United Kingdom, too, well-publicised campaigns on behalf of individual women have raised awareness of the issues among both the judiciary and the public at large, and Helena Kennedy has identified an increased understanding of issues around domestic violence in recent years (Kennedy, 1992, p. 213).

The inability of a man-made and male-dominated legal system to express women's experiences is particularly clear in the case of rape trials. Sue Lees' recent British study of women's own experiences found that their voices were systematically silenced by a criminal justice system in which traditional male assumptions and myths are institutionalised and which is, she claims, 'systematically allowing rapists to go free' (Lees, 1996, p. 455. See also Smart, 1989, 1995). Helena Kennedy has argued that in court women witnesses, defendants, lawyers and police officers, are all generally accorded less credibility and respect than men (Kennedy, 1992). In rape cases, the difficulty of a female complainant in making her voice heard is particularly great: if she appears upset and distressed her evidence is dismissed as hysterical, emotional and untrustworthy; but if she is calm and composed it is thought that she cannot possibly be the victim of anything so traumatic as rape. Beliefs about 'acceptable' and 'appropriate' female behaviour also frequently mean that she is required to explain behaviour that would be unremarked in a man: it is therefore the victim rather than the accused who is called to account for going out on her own at night, accepting a lift or drinking with strangers; the man who is accused is not similarly required to justify his presence or behaviour in public spaces. Although since 1976 a woman can only be questioned about her sexual history in British courts with the permission of the judge, such permission is still frequently given, and the sexual reputation of the victim rather than the accused is frequently put under scrutiny.

Lees found that women were often denied the opportunity to describe their experience in their own words. Dominant attitudes in the courtroom seemed to Lees to reflect the viewpoint of men who might be accused, rather than women who might be raped. This bias is built into courtroom procedures, such as the requirement that the judge inform the jury that they must be wary of convicting on the evidence of the woman alone; similar warnings are not given for any other type of offence, although conviction for a crime such as burglary may similarly rest upon uncorroborated evidence. According to Lees, lawyers and judges are 'woefully ignorant and prejudiced' about rape and sexual assault (Lees, 1996, p. 248). In particular, they tend to accept false stereotypes which see rapists as evil and identifiably abnormal strangers, or as unfortunate victims of female provocation who have been overcome by lust. Lees' research, however, confirms earlier findings that rapists are usually known to their victims and that, apart from the attack itself, their appearance and behaviour are perfectly normal; she also found that their rapes are frequently premeditated and planned, and that rapists tend to rape more than once. Lawyers and judges also seem to believe that women are likely to make false accusations of rape and that many men are being wrongly convicted. In reality, all the available evidence suggests that rape is massively under-reported and that the conviction rate is very low: although Home Office figures show that between 1985 and 1993 the numbers of rapes reported to the police nearly doubled, the conviction rate during the same period fell from 24 per cent to 10 per cent; this meant that of the 4,589 rapes that were reported in England and Wales, only 455 resulted in a conviction (Lees, 1996).

Helena Kennedy has also argued that in rape cases where the alleged attacker is known to his victim and where he is white, men throughout the legal system tend to identify with the accused. She and Lees both note, however, that such solidarity is not extended to black or stranger rapists; their treatment by the legal system rather than the actual behaviour of black men, may therefore explain their relatively high presence among convicted rapists. As Kennedy says 'the majority of men in court are stereotypically viewed as powerful, credible and independent. The men who do not involve stereotypical assumptions – homosexual, black, Irish, Arab, vagrant, gypsy, unemployed – can suffer as women do' (Kennedy, 1992, p. 263). For women who fall into these categories, the loss of credibility is even greater, as prejudices around race and class interact with those of gender.

Gender and justice: women's 'different voice'

Ignorance of the reality of rape is not confined to men: female judges do not automatically take the side of women in the courts, and the kind of women who succeed in the legal profession are perhaps less likely than average to display stereotypically female qualities such as care and compassion. Nevertheless, the underrepresentation of women in the judiciary seems likely to confirm the marginalisation of women's experiences. For some feminists writers, the problem goes even deeper, because they argue that our very processes of moral reasoning and thinking about right and wrong are gendered, and that once again the law has been based on a male model, in which female ways of thinking have no place.

Here the work of Carol Gilligan has been particularly influential. In *In A Different Voice*, first published in 1982, she said that her own research shows that there are empirically observable differences between men and women in the ways in which they think and moralise about the world. She claims that women's moral thinking recognises the importance of emotions, intimacy and relationships, and that this gives rise to what she calls an 'ethic of responsibility' which is very different from the dominant male 'ethic of rights', which is based upon much more individualistic assumptions. The female conception of justice has traditionally been held to be inferior and a sign of women's immaturity; Gilligan, however, asserts that a genuinely mature ethic of justice would incorporate both male and female perspectives. The resulting 'ethic of care' would, she says, combine ideas of responsibility with those of rights, recognising both human interdependence and an individual's sense of self. As such, she says it would be superior to both the selfish, individualistic male ethic and the self-sacrificing female ethic. Gilligan has sometimes been portrayed as an essentialist who valorises women's way of thinking above that of men. In fact, however, she is at pains to stress that it is women's typical experiences rather than innate biological differences that are responsible for observable differences in moral reasoning, that although men and women tend to focus on one system of ethics most people do use both systems, and that a mature theory and ethical standpoint must incorporate both.

Law in a patriarchal society

Many legal feminists argue that the early pursuit of formal legal equality with men did not simply fail to question male norms, but failed to understand the nature of the power relations involved. Here a key and influential writer is the American lawyer Catherine MacKinnon, who argues that women's voice is not simply *different* as judged by male standards, it is also *subordinate*. For MacKinnon, any analysis of law must be based on the understanding that we live in a patriarchal society in which control over women's bodies is central. This understanding, she says, has arisen from the grass-roots resistance of women in rape crisis and battered women's shelters which has created new forms of political practice and a new form of theory which

> Is deeply of the world: raw with women's blood, ragged with women's pain, shrill with women's screams. It does not elaborate yet more arcane abstractions of ideas building on ideas. It participates in reality: the reality of a fist in the face, not the concept of a fist in the face. It does not exist to mediate women's reality for male consumption. It exists to bear witness, to create consciousness, to make change. (MacKinnon, 1993b, p. 369)

MacKinnon argues that the law has served men's interests in opposition to women's and that it cannot be used as it stands to gain genuine equality; rather, it has to be radically re-shaped to addresses women's concerns. She argues that the concept of equality should be expanded to include the areas where women are in reality most disadvantaged – that is, as victims of sexual assault and as people forced to bear children because of a lack of legal or funded abortion. From this radical feminist perspective, sexual assault, pornography and restrictions on women's reproductive freedom should be seen as central issues of sex inequality, critical to the maintenance of patriarchal domination. MacKinnon therefore sees the extension of rape laws to include rape within marriage as an important feminist victory and has campaigned vigorously for anti-pornography legislation (see Chapter 8).

The British writer Carol Smart accepts that MacKinnon's work is important and agrees that the law is grounded in a patriarchal society. However, she disagrees with MacKinnon on a number of issues, including the importance of sexuality as the basis of women's oppression, MacKinnon's tendency to treat both men and women as unitary groups, and her belief in the omnipotence of male power; MacKinnon's approach, according to Smart has produced a contradictory analysis which both sees the law as patriarchal, and puts too much faith in its power to change things. In contrast, Smart argues that feminists should 'beware the siren call of the law' and become 'far more aware of the "malevolence" of law and the depth of its resistance to women's concerns' (Smart, 1989, pp. 160, 2).

Although Smart warns against seeing the law as a ready-made weapon that can be easily enlisted or hijacked to promote feminist aims, she also rejects the idea that it is a monolithic instrument of patriarchal oppression which men deliberately and consistently use to further their own interests, and that all feminist attempts to use it are therefore doomed to failure. Rather, she argues that the law should be understood as an important site of feminist struggle, within which gender identities and hierarchies are constructed. She and the American writer Mary Jo Frug have used post-modern ideas (see above) to argue that the law is a particularly powerful form of discourse which helps create the meaning of what it is to be a man or a woman (Smart, 1989, 1995; Frug, 1992). These meanings can both reflect and help maintain gender inequalities and arrangements.

Susan Millns has applied such arguments to an analysis of the ways in which legislation in Britain during the 1990s on reproductive technologies, child support and pregnancy rights in employment helped construct and reinforce dominant ideas of parenting. She found that the laws assert both children's need for a father and men's financial responsibility for their children; they do not, however, recognise men's responsibility for practical childcare and the consequences for employment that this would imply (Millns, 1996. See also Smart, 1984 on family law). If we accept that gender identities and roles are not fixed, such constructions can be identified and challenged, as can the dominant legal conceptualisations of domestic violence and sexuality discussed earlier. It is also possible to see and challenge the ways in which legal constructions of womanhood reflect white middle-class experiences and assumptions; for example, child support legislation assumes both a particular version of the nuclear family and the availability of reasonably paid work for a male breadwinner.

Such analysis suggests that 'legal discourse should be recognized as a site of political struggle over sex differences' (Frug, 1992, p. 126), and that feminist theorists and practitioners can use the law to assert a version of the world very different from the male perspective perpetuated by the legal establishment. Feminism can therefore '(re)define harmless flirtation into sexual harassment, misplaced paternal affection into child sexual abuse, enthusiastic seduction into rape, foetal rights into enforced reproduction, and so on' (Smart, 1989, p. 165). Similarly, despite the shortcomings of equality legislation, this 'has had a profound effect on the content and language of political rights in Britain. It has altered consciousness' (O'Donovan and Szyszczak 1988, p. 87). From this perspective, the importance of legal changes extends well beyond their immediate practical effects, for such changes also play a powerful ideological role. Feminists can therefore use demands for legal independence, protection and equality as part of a complex strategy for change, rather than simply as goals in themselves.

Strategies for change

Although it is certainly not a uniform body of thought, recent developments in feminist legal theory have enabled us to understand that the law operates within the framework of a patriarchal society in which women's voices have been silenced, and that it is not enough simply to extend to women the rights it has given to men. Rather, the gendered nature of its assumptions and principles must be systematically questioned, and women's experiences and values asserted as a valid starting-point. This can give rise to a new perspective, in which women are no longer seen as 'special' or 'different', for they are no longer measured against male norms. Such analysis need not imply that all women or all men speak with a common voice; it should recognise that the law is not only rooted in patriarchy, but in racism and class society, and that it therefore does not have any one meaning or defining principle.

In terms of employment law, a woman-centred understanding of equality can become the basis for strategies that go far beyond the outlawing of discrimination against women. A consultation document produced by the British Equal Opportunities Commission in 1998 shows something of what such an approach might look like in practice. Declaring that 'A law is an unequivocal declaration of public policy' and that 'A new, clear, effective Statute will encourage the next step change in the attitudes and actions of individual men and women', it recommended a consolidation of existing legislation into a single statute based on the principle of 'a fundamental right to equal treatment between men and women'. Its practical recommendations included proposals for shifting the burden of proof in sex discrimination cases from the complainant to the employer and for enabling industrial tribunals to make general findings rather than ruling only on individual cases, as at present. It also argued that equal treatment must include support for women's childbearing role, without which 'equality of opportunity will remain no more than an aspiration'. In addition to maternity leave, this support would include good quality, affordable childcare and 'family-friendly working arrangements'; it therefore advocated paternity and parental leave as well as maternity leave. It also recognised that gender differences in employment prospects and pay frequently reflect gender stereotyping and the undervaluing of skills associated with women rather than direct and deliberate discrimination; it therefore recommended that employers be legally required to take a much more proactive approach to equality by monitoring their workforce and pay structures and taking action to remedy any disparities in their treatment of men and women that emerged (Equal Opportunities Commission, 1998, pp. iv, iii and 9).

The implementation of such policies would have a major impact upon the legal profession, where, as Helena Kennedy has said, an improvement in women's career prospects 'will only be achieved by removing blinkers about what constitutes merit and experience'. She argues that 'Most women lawyers, who can manage a home and a reasonably successful career can manage a court', and that patience, open-mindedness and courtesy should be considered as relevant skills (Kennedy, 1992, p. 268). This would mean that affirmative action programmes aimed at increasing the number of women judges would not constitute 'positive discrimination', but a revaluation of selection criteria to recognise qualities associated with women as well as those associated with men. At the very least, the resulting increase in the number of female barristers and judges would help make the environment of the courtroom more 'woman friendly' and expand the width of personal experience available to the judiciary. If, as some argue, the law is more deeply gendered, such change is a necessary precondition for a more balanced system of justice.

One result of a more balanced system would be a greater awareness of the need to protect women from violence and sexual assault, including that which is experienced within the home, and for more sensitive court proceedings when such cases come to trial. Such a system would challenge popular and judicial ignorance about the effects and prevalence of domestic and sexual violence, at the same time as insisting both that this be recognised as a crime that crosses racial and class boundaries, and that legislation designed to protect women should not be used to attack black and/or working-class men.

Although the above proposals are far-reaching, they are essentially practical. Some of the issues discussed by legal feminists seem however to be much more esoteric and remote from the lives of 'ordinary' women. Nevertheless, the purpose of legal feminism is not to elaborate theories for their own sake, but in order to improve feminist practice. For example, as Carol Smart says of her own application of post-modernist theory: 'the idea of investigating the legal construction of... the raped woman, is of little value unless we are also talking to women who have been raped' (Smart, 1995, p. 231); her work therefore includes research among such women as a basis for challenging the way they are silenced within the legal system. As discussed in the following section, post-modernist ideas can also be used to question our legal classification as 'women' and 'men'.

Sex as a legal fiction

Post-modernism suggests that the law can be seen as both a particularly powerful form of discourse and a form of social practice which can sanction, control or punish particular forms of behaviour; as such, it can play an important role in enforcing as well as creating particular conceptions of what it is to be a man or a woman. Such conceptions have varied over time. In 19th-century Britain, the legal category of 'woman' meant, among other things, someone who was in need of male protection, someone who was unfit for higher education, someone who was barred from many occupations and someone who was not entitled to vote. Until very recently, it meant someone who could retire with a state pension at 60 and who, if married, had to reveal her earnings on her husband's tax form; in most nations of the world today it means someone who can marry a man but cannot marry a woman, and someone who is particularly likely to win custody of her children in a contested divorce settlement.

Although the content of the legal category 'woman' has varied, the classification of the population into male and female persons has remained constant. As discussed in Chapter 3, however, the biological basis for dividing the human race into two mutually exclusive categories simply does not exist. At the very least, there are a minority of people whose genital or chromosomal characteristics are ambiguous or contradictory; other attributes such as strength, aggressiveness or sexual orientation show a degree of overlap rather than binary opposition; and the inability to give birth is not confined to men, but is shared by all females at some stage in their life. In the face of such fluidity and overlapping characteristics, the claim that we can all be neatly labelled as male or female can only be a legal fiction. This fiction is, however, extremely powerful. At a practical level, it prevents lesbians or gay men from marrying, and therefore excludes them from the legal benefits of marriage, such as pension rights, or the right to be joined by a non-British spouse; it also restricts the lives of trans-sexuals, who are unable to change the sex classification that appeared on their birth certificate. At an ideological level, it perpetuates the perception that differences between all men and all women are fundamental and unchangeable. Any progress towards equality or to the acceptance of a multiplicity of genders therefore comes up against thinking constructed around binary division and essential difference.

In Britain legislation against racial discrimination is in place. There are also limited affirmative action programmes to promote racial equality, and ethnic monitoring aimed at ensuring equality of opportunity both within institutions and in society as a whole. Babies are not, however, classified at birth according to their racial origin, and most of us would be horrified at such a suggestion; in contrast, it is accepted without question that babies should be classified by sex. The above analysis suggests that this classification is no more justified than classification by race, and that genuine equality will only be possible if it is ended (for a similar argument, see O'Donovan, 1985b).

Such a change would have some immediate practical consequences. It would make the question of whether trans-sexuals should be allowed to change the sex on their birth certificate redundant. It would cut through the debate over whether gay and lesbian couples should be allowed to marry; any two consenting adults would therefore be able to share the social, financial and legal advantages of matrimony. It would enable rights and benefits to be given to people who need them, rather than to abstract individuals who turn out to be male, or to pre-determined categories, such as 'mothers' or 'fathers'. It could, for example, state that the presumption in contested child custody cases should be that this would normally be awarded to the primary carer. It would also enable the specific needs and interests of different groups of women to be addressed, rather than losing sight of these in universalistic claims or in an insistence that gender divisions are more important than those of class, race or other structured inequalities.

The idea that we should announce 'It's a baby!' when a woman gives birth seems ludicrous. It also seems obvious that there are practical reasons for needing to know a person's sex: for example, women offenders would be at risk of rape in a mixed prison, and girls may benefit from being educated apart from boys. If however we focus on human rather than sex-specific needs and recognise the existence of more than one structure of disadvantage, the problems seem less deep-seated. Thus, men in prison today are also at risk of being raped by other men, and many boys suffer from the low expectations of their teachers. What is needed is prison conditions which ensure the safety of all inmates, and educational programmes that meet the needs of under-achieving groups (such as Afro-Caribbean boys) without essentialising membership of such a group through law. Such thinking underlay the recommendation of the British Equal Opportunities Commission in 1998 that the provision of women-only transport services is unlawful sex discrimination, but that transport organisations should treat public safety as a priority for both men and women (Equal Opportunities Commission, 1998, p. 24).

The abolition of sex as a legal category would not mean that we would stop thinking of ourselves as women and men, or that sexual inequalities would be magicked away. It would not, therefore, prevent us from analysing shared oppression or campaigning collectively as women. At a basic level, however, it would disempower the law as a way of constructing our identity as male or female. It would therefore open up the possibility of a much more fluid and open society, in which the complex interplay of bodily appearance, behaviour, sexual orientation and role-playing could allow for a much greater degree of choice and self-determination. Such a change is unlikely to be conceded in the foreseeable future. The very articulation of such demands can, however, provide an important role in creating awareness and challenging 'common sense' assumptions about what it means to be a man or a woman. As such, it is not a self-contained goal, but part of a wider strategy, which includes more practical and immediately achievable demands.

Conclusions

Although the uncritical pursuit of legal equality can be counter-productive, it seems clear that the legal system cannot be written off as a uniformly patriarchal institution that can never further the interests of women. On the contrary, feminist engagement with the law can produce important practical results. Even when these results appear disappointing, or where attempts to achieve legal changes fail, such engagement can still be important at an ideological level, affecting not only our behaviour but also our consciousness: as Carol Smart has said, 'While it is the case that law does not hold the key to unlock patriarchy, it provides the forum for articulating alternative visions and accounts' (Smart, 1989, p. 88).

This implies that feminist approaches to the law can be both more fruitful and more complex than some critics have suggested. Feminist legal strategies cannot however be successfully pursued in isolation from other forms of political activity, both conventional and unconventional. It is to these that we now turn.

5
Politics and the state

Feminist disagreements about the meaning and nature of politics are at the heart of theoretical debate; they are also of critical practical importance. This chapter begins with an analysis of theoretical debates and developments. It links these with recent practical experiences to argue both that feminists can achieve real change by working through formal political institutions and that informal political activity is also vital. A final section focuses on women's representation in legislative assemblies; it argues that their under-representation is a cause for concern and that quotas may be necessary if this is to be changed.

Feminist theory and political concepts

For feminists coming from a liberal perspective, politics tends to be understood in a 'common sense' way as public activity to do with political parties, pressure groups and parliaments. Feminist politics therefore involves using the political rights for which earlier generations fought, and working to increase the numbers of women in positions of public power. Other feminists have, however, attacked this as a naive approach which fails to understand the nature of state power and rests upon a gendered and untenable division between the public and the private. As such, it cannot see the need for new forms of political organisation or that political resistance to patriarchy extends to the family and personal relationships. Critics also claim that conventional approaches have failed to see the importance of women's informal political activity within local communities and have therefore unfairly depicted women as less committed citizens than men. These claims are examined in the following sections.

The public/private dichotomy

The idea that human society can be divided into public and private spheres, and that in a free society politics should be kept out of the latter, is central to liberal democratic thought. This also sees the public sphere as one in which the particularities and personal differences of private life can be transcended, and in which all adults are treated as equal citizens under the law, irrespective of their sex, skin colour, physical strength or economic resources.

Some recent feminist writers have argued, however, that the supposedly universal, objective, rational and dispassionate values of the public sphere are, in fact, based upon qualities traditionally associated with men. Liberal thought contrasts these values and qualities with those found in the private, female world of personal relationships, emotion and subjectivity; it also treats the former as inherently superior. This means that the public/private dichotomy is both gendered and unequal and that, despite modern liberalism's claim to include women on the same terms as men, the individual citizen does not relate to the two spheres as an abstract individual, but as a man or a woman. As a result, a man can be himself in the public sphere, for his sex is treated as an unproblematic norm, but women can only be admitted if they abandon their female identity. In other words, if women want to gain a public voice, they are expected to speak 'like men', rather than as women, for 'womanly' concerns or forms of expression have been deemed inferior and inadmissible in the public sphere. At a practical level, the result has been that qualities and experiences associated with men, such as a combative debating style and trade union, business or military experience, are seen as political assets; those associated with women, such as conciliatory skills and setting up a playgroup or running a home, are not.

As we saw in Chapter 2, radical feminists have further argued that the public/private distinction ignores the ways in which men's collective power over women is exercised in private life. As such, it can be seen as a mystifying patriarchal device, designed to conceal oppression and the ways in which the gender division of labour in the home affects both practical opportunities for political participation and the values and priorities of politicians.

In terms of feminist politics, a rejection of the conventional public/private distinction suggests that resistance to patriarchy can or should involve a range of activities far removed from conventional party politics. This has sometimes been interpreted to mean that any male/female interaction is political, because it involves members of a dominant and oppressed group, and that any woman who asserts her interests against a man is engaged in feminist politics. Such an interpretation, however, ignores the shared nature of oppression on which both the theory of patriarchy and the claim that 'the personal is political' were originally based, and the consequent need for collective as well as individual forms of resistance. Critics such as Anne Phillips have therefore warned against a retreat into individualistic solutions and total abandonment of the notion of public and private spheres. Phillips agrees that what goes on in the home is important and that feminist activity need not be confined to conventional or formal politics; she does, however, insist that 'There remains a distinction between the general and the particular, and it is important not to blur this divide' (Phillips, 1991, pp. 118–19).

Whether or not such public/private, general/particular and personal/political distinctions can or should be made in principle, and, if so, where the line should be drawn, continue to be matters for feminist debate. There is, however, more general feminist agreement that the *traditional* distinctions are both invalid and detrimental to women, and that the relationship between different spheres of life is not fixed and absolute, but fluid and interactive.

Informal political activity

Conventional approaches to politics suggest that women are on average significantly less interested and active than men. If, however, we look beyond the formal political system to less institutionalised forms of collective activity, a very different picture emerges.

Although the overall involvement of women in community groups, voluntary organisations, protest groups and wider social movements may not actually be greater than men's, it is certainly significant, and at the level of local community action women frequently play a leading role. This kind of activity represents an important form of political participation for those whose situation, resources, preferences, temperament or organisational style rules out more conventional political forms; it also frequently arises out of women's domestic and family responsibilities.

Many women have always been involved in voluntary and charitable work and in the organisation of fund-raising and social events. Traditional organisations such as the Women's Institute (WI) in Britain can provide an important source of political skills and self-confidence. Although the WI is usually seen as non-political, it has campaigned both locally and nationally on such issues as school closures, family allowances and environmental issues, and Vicky Randall has claimed that it may be an important source of recruitment for Conservative women councillors (Randall, 1987). Like other large voluntary women's organisations its membership is now in decline (Social Trends, 1992), but as an organisation which at the end of the 1980s had over 340,000 members, it still represents an important link between individual concerns and wider political issues, especially for women in rural areas.

Women in all social groups are particularly likely to become involved in local campaigns around housing and the education and welfare of children. For some working-class and/or black women, political activity may be at the most basic levels of community survival, involving action against racism and a struggle to retain self-respect and self-definition in a society that denies their worth and the legitimacy of their culture. Such activity is important in its own right; it can also extend outwards from the home and the immediate community and into the churches, the educational system and local government, so that the centrality of women in family and neighbourhood can make their informal networks a basis for more formal political action. Although women's involvement tends to decline if a movement expands and becomes successful, women's activities in tenants' rights and welfare movements can also have a long-lasting effect on participants, involving a general radicalisation and sense of empowerment.

Women's involvement in neighbourhood and community politics is not usually overtly feminist; it can, however, lead to an increased consciousness of the collective interests of women and to links with the wider women's movement. This may arise from shared goals, as when apparently spontaneous campaigns for improved childcare provision, for better street lighting or against the closure of child health clinics link up with national networks. Such networks sometimes have the potential to cross class and ethnic boundaries. Consciousness of shared interests may be further increased if apparently reasonable and important demands are dismissed by those in authority, or by men in mixed campaigning groups, as unworthy of serious political attention.

All of this lends support to Yasmin Ali's claim that although many women are uninterested in politics as defined by men, many are involved in a system of 'parallel politics'. For most women, she says, watching politics on television is like watching 'one of the more arcane Olympic sports', with incomprehensible rules and customs; many women are, however, active in a parallel system of informal networks and community activities, and many gain political information and values, not from 'serious' newspapers and broadcasts, but from women's magazines and daytime television, through which the voices of 'ordinary' women can frequently be heard unmediated (and unnoticed) by political 'experts' (Ali, 1996). If feminists are to develop a form of politics that is relevant and responsive to the needs of all groups of women, not just of an elite minority, it is important that they recognise the potential of this parallel system and continue to understand that there is much more to politics than conventional approaches are able to see.

Citizenship

An insistence on the importance of women's activities is also central to much recent feminist work on citizenship. This concept, which has enjoyed something of a revival in recent years, implies a set of entitlements and obligations linking the individual, the community and the state, and promises equal respect and treatment for all full members of a society. It has, however, been criticised by feminists who argue that once again the promise of equal treatment requires women to conform to standards laid down by men, and that discussion of citizenship has failed to recognise either women's needs or the socially important duties which they perform.

Nevertheless, some feminists argue that, if women are fully included in the human standard, citizenship can provide both an inspiring ideal of a genuinely equal and inclusive society and 'an invaluable strategic theoretical concept for the analysis of women's subordination and a potentially powerful political weapon in the struggle against it' (Lister, 1997, p. 195). Such a version of citizenship would see that caring for children or others unable to look after themselves is as much a civic responsibility as paid employment. It would insist that, as economic independence and bodily integrity have long been seen as preconditions of male citizenship, they are serious political requirements for women too. This enables us to challenge the current division of rewards and labour which produces economic dependency for many hard-working women and enables many men to pursue careers and political interests by opting out of 'private' responsibilities. It can also legitimise demands for reproductive rights and freedom from sexual harassment or fear of violence, transforming these from private concerns to issues of civic entitlement.

The rejection of hierarchy and the call for separatism

For some feminists, informal or uninstitutionalised activity is not only an important form of politics, it is one which can enable women to develop new and better ways of working together to achieve their aims. In particular, an important strand of recent feminism has rejected hierarchical organisational forms, and has attempted to develop more fluid, open, participatory and democratic forms of grass-roots activity. Criticism of the elitist and quasi-participatory nature of conventional politics has been extended to Marxist and other left-wing organisations, and some socialist feminists have argued that feminist critiques of all forms of power must be central to socialism both as a movement for change and as the future form of society (see in particular, Rowbotham *et al.*, 1979). For some writers, these ideas are linked to important differences between women's and men's attitudes to power, and it has been claimed that while men are interested in power over others, women have a liberatory understanding of power as something which is enabling and empowering but which does not have to involve the subordination of other groups (see Harstock, 1985. For criticism, see Deutchman, 1996).

Attempts to create new forms of activity have at times met with significant success. Many women have been empowered by participation in small-scale groups, where for the first time their voices were listened to and they could feel a sense of worth. On a larger scale, the women-only peace camp established in Britain at the Greenham Common nuclear weapons base in 1981 provides an extraordinary example of the scale of activity that could be generated through informal networks and word of mouth, without any formal structure or organisation. For example, in December 1982, over 30,000 women from all over Britain arrived at the base to express their opposition to the projected arrival of American nuclear cruise missiles; rather than listening to speeches, they encircled the nine-mile long perimeter fence and tied to it items of personal significance, such as photographs, diaries or children's toys. For many participants, such activity seemed to represent not only an effective form of publicity, but a new and womanly form of politics, in which the values of nurturing were opposed to those of destruction and the values of participatory democracy could become a reality.

The initial decision to make the peace camp women only was based less on feminist principles than on tactical considerations (it was thought more likely to produce media interest and publicity and less likely to provoke a violent reaction from the authorities than a mixed group), and many of the campers always welcomed male support. Nevertheless, the camp seemed to many, supporters and opponents alike, to symbolise a strand of radical separatism within the women's movement. As such, it was celebrated as a safe space for women where they could celebrate their strength and their independence from men; it was also hated and feared as a destructive form of extremist, man-hating, lesbian separatism.

Some feminists, particularly those coming from a liberal perspective, have always disliked any kind of women-only groups, seeing these as discriminatory, divisive, and less effective than mixed political organisations. Others see them as tactically useful, a short-term political necessity. From this perspective, women-only groups may be an important initial step in raising feminist consciousness by enabling women to share their experiences and establish their own priorities in a safe atmosphere. Such groups can also provide the opportunity for women to develop self-confidence and political experience, to acquire leadership skills and to establish alternative networks. As such, women-only groups may be a temporary measure, or provide a secure basis for more permanent feminist activity; either way, they do not preclude working with men in other mixed campaigning groups or political parties.

For a minority of feminists, however, the difficulties and dangers of working politically with men outweigh any potential gains, and some see separatism as a goal in itself. Here it is argued that, if feminists are to escape violent oppression by men, they must withdraw as far as possible from political, economic, social, sexual or cultural contact with them and rely on each other for protection and support. This perspective rejects conventional politics on the grounds that 'the master's tools will never dismantle the master's house' (Adrienne Rich, quoted critically in Wolf, 1993, p. i); and it argues that feminists have more important and productive things to do than to play political games in a system that men have designed and for which they have written the rules.

Feminist theories of the state

As with definitions of politics, feminists coming from a liberal democratic perspective have not challenged conventional approaches to the state. For such feminists, the state is a potentially neutral institution from which women have historically been excluded, but which they can and should now use to assert their rights and realise their collective power. Although liberal theory tends to be suspicious of state power, the liberal feminist approach does not see any particular problems in using the state to advance women's interests and meet their needs. Liberal campaign groups such as the National Organisation for Women in the United States have therefore demanded not only equal access to welfare benefits, but also childcare provision and maternity leave.

Critics of the liberal approach point out the painfully slow rate of progress towards equal political representation and caution against increasing women's dependency upon the male-run, capitalist state. They accuse liberal feminists of failing to understand the depth of an oppression which goes far beyond personal disadvantage or individual acts of discrimination and the ways in which this is both reflected in and maintained by the state, which is profoundly, and possibly essentially, hostile to both the articulation and the realisation of feminist goals.

This kind of analysis has been made particularly forcefully by the American feminist Catherine MacKinnon, who insists that feminists must develop a woman-centred theory of the state and understand it

98 *Feminist Debates*

in their own terms, unmodified by male perspectives and theoretical interpretations. The starting-point for a feminist theory of the state must, she says, be the understanding that 'the state is male in the feminist sense. The law sees and treats women the way men see and treat women' (MacKinnon, 1983, p. 644). Although some feminists use this kind of analysis to argue for radical separatism (Anderson, 1994), MacKinnon does not think that women should simply abandon the state; rather, she argues that they must struggle to speak within it on their own terms *as women*, challenging the state's spurious claims to gender neutrality, and insisting on the validity of female voices.

Other writers have used Marxist analyses to attempt to understand the ways in which the state furthers the interests of the capitalist economy and the oppression of women within this. Such analysis has influenced feminist thinking on the welfare state. From a Marxist feminist perspective, the apparently benign use of the state to provide welfare for its citizens may in fact simply represent the most cost-effective way of reproducing labour power; it also assumes and reinforces women's domestic responsibilities and their economic dependency on a male breadwinner within the patriarchal family. As discussed in Chapter 2, there has been fierce debate about the nature of the relationship between capitalism and patriarchy; but many feminists who disagree as to which has primacy have agreed that, far from freeing women, welfare provision has helped to maintain oppressive gender roles, and that it has also involved increased surveillance of sexual and reproductive behaviour and of child-rearing practices.

The experience of welfare provision as a form of control is particularly acute for working-class and/or minority ethnic women, who are likely to find that if they attempt to claim benefits they are treated as undeserving scroungers. In Britain, Afro-Caribbean women are disproportionately likely to have their children taken into care, and welfare institutions are sometimes used to police immigration controls.

Recent theoretical developments

Most of the above analyses seem to suggest that feminists should be very cautious in their engagements with the state, or even that feminists should direct their energies outside the formal structures of state power and political parties if they are to achieve genuine change. Although some feminists have never had any problem with conventional political activity, such thinking had a strong effect on feminist politics from the late 1960s. It meant that direct involvement with the agents or structures of the state seemed like a reformist 'sell-out' to patriarchal and/or capitalist values; if feminists were to retain their integrity, and avoid being co-opted into an oppressive system, they must therefore work outside the state and develop their own separate organisational forms.

Today, although there are still many activists who reject 'collaboration' with the state, there seems to have been a widespread shift in feminist thinking about the state and a perception that conventional political activity cannot simply be rejected out of hand. Cynics might see this change as simply the result of an age-related conservatism on the part of a generation of feminists who were radical in the 1960s. It is, however, also the product of more general theoretical changes and of practical political experience; these have combined to produce a more open-ended and less consistently hostile attitude to the state and to conventional political activity.

Post-modernism and the nature of power

Changes in feminist thinking on the state are, to some extent, linked to changes within western Marxism from the 1960s, and can be seen as part of a more general movement away from ideas of determinism and towards more open-ended understandings of state/society relationships. Recently, post-structuralist and post-modernist thinking has taken such ideas much further; as we shall see, however, the implications of this for feminist politics are ambiguous. Although it has had less impact on feminist theory, the increasingly fashionable notion of 'governance' also questions conventional state/society and public/private boundaries, suggesting a more inclusive and potentially more woman-friendly approach to the study of government than in the past (see Kooiman, 1993).

At first sight, these new approaches seem to support the radical feminist rejection of conventional politics and its stress on grassroots activity and direct action. Like radical feminists, the post-structuralist Michel Foucault has argued that power is exercised and experienced at the 'micro-levels' of society, and that it is here, rather than at the level of the central state, that power may be resisted by marginalised and subjugated groups (see Foucault, 1980, especially Chapter 8). This approach seems to support a very broad definition of politics and a rejection of any rigid distinction between the public and the private; it also suggests that because there is no central source of power, then attempts to use or undermine state power are meaningless. From this perspective, feminist attempts to develop a theory of 'the state' are themselves misguided, and Judith Allen has therefore argued that:

> 'The state' is a category of abstraction that is too aggregative, too unitary and too unspecific to be of much use in addressing the disaggregated, diverse and specific (or local) sites that must be of more passing concern to feminists. (Allen, 1990, p. 22)

By the same token, however, attempts to deny meaning or specificity to 'the state' could also be interpreted as encouraging feminists engaged in conventional political activity, for if the state is not to be distinguished from other social institutions, then there is no particular reason to avoid political structures. Indeed, the idea that power is dispersed rather than concentrated in a unitary state also opens up the possibility of subversive activity within its fragmented structures: rather than tackling an oppressive and centralised monolith, feminists may be able to infiltrate or influence, for example, local government, state education, state broadcasting or the law. This means that although there might not be a state in the sense of one central body serving patriarchal and/or capitalist interests, the state can be more loosely conceptualised as an arena of conflict, or a set of arenas, within which feminist gains can be won and resistance expressed. Michelle Barrett, for example, argues that:

> The state is not a pre-given instrument of oppression, but is a site of struggle and to some extent at least responsive to concerted pressure. To reject this struggle altogether is to lapse into the romance of anarchism. (Barrett, 1986, p. 246; see also Cooper, 1995)

From a post-modern perspective, state agencies and institutions are also particularly important because of the ways in which they help construct and enforce the meaning of what it is to be a man or a woman in our society. For example, welfare services have assumed and encouraged a view of women as economic dependants of breadwinning husbands, and the aggressive style of parliamentary politics seems to confirm that this is a tough man's world in which the qualities traditionally associated with women have no place. Such meanings can, however, be contested as well as constructed, and an understanding of this gives a double significance to many political campaigns. Thus the call for independent welfare benefits and efforts to elect more female members of parliament involve a challenge to traditional understandings of what it is to be a woman; as such, they have important ideological effects, in addition to any immediate and practical changes which they might achieve.

Practical changes are also important, of course, and the state is not only a site of discourse. Even if feminists are not predisposed to be interested in the state, they cannot escape the impact of its policies: even the most militant separatists can be affected by government decisions on a whole range of issues from artificial insemination for lesbians to tax, welfare or transport policies. Moreover, while the state may be diffuse and fragmented, and its boundaries may shift and blur, it is not simply one institution, or set of institutions among many; rather, it is unique both in its claim to power and in its reach. As John Hoffman has recently argued, the classic Weberian definition of the state as the institution which claims a monopoly of legitimate force for a particular territory does not mean that its authority is unchallenged or that force is not exercised elsewhere (for example within families). It does mean, however, that the state 'has (at least potentially) a hand in everything' (Hoffman, 1995, p. 478), that it can sanction or outlaw violence inside and outside the home, and that it can impose penalties on those who break its rules. From this perspective, it is not only legitimate for feminists to engage with the state, it is vitally important and almost inevitable that they do.

Recent political experience in Britain, the United States and Scandinavia

The shift in feminist thinking on the state is not simply the product of developments at a theoretical level, but also represents a response to feminist experiences of organising both outside state structures and within them.

Separatist and non-hierarchical groups

Many feminists continue to believe in ideals of democratic participation and 'womanly values', and prefer direct action to conventional political participation. Such ideas are particularly influential within green and environmental movements. The Greenham Common peace camp has also inspired women throughout the world to develop new ways of protesting against militarism, such as the silent vigils of the Women in Black in Israel (see Pope, 1992; Chazan, 1993; Cockburn, 1995; Bryson, 1996a).

Nevertheless, the experience of Greenham and other movements suggests that unstructured forms of protest have problems in continuing on a large scale over time, and it has led some writers to a less optimistic view of separatist and/or non-hierarchical forms of organisation. The emergence of bitter personal and ideological disputes at Greenham and in radical groups elsewhere showed that women-only movements are certainly not immune from conflict. Many have also found not only that it is extremely difficult to eliminate hierarchies, but that attempts to do so can create new problems. A group which attempts to give everyone an equal say is likely to be inefficient in terms of using the talent and time of its members, and in terms of relating to other groups which it might want to influence. It is also unlikely to prevent the emergence of leaders; indeed their role may actually be greater than in more structured groups, because it cannot formally be checked. Today, therefore, although many feminists remain highly suspicious of any kind of structured organisation and many more insist that existing structures need to be democratised, many have come to see the values of some formal structures, and would agree with Anne Phillips that 'when the ideals of democratic equality are set impossibly high, they can produce contradictory effects' (Phillips, 1991, p. 145).

At the same time, a more optimistic view of formal politics is emerging as a result of recent feminist engagements with the state. Such engagements have taken a number of forms. Here I will focus upon 'municipal feminism' in Britain, attempts to exploit the potential power of women voters in the United States and Britain, and the more far-reaching attempts to create a 'woman-friendly state' in the Scandinavian nations; it should also be noted that attempts to develop a 'bureaucratic feminism' have been particularly important in Australia (see Eisenstein, 1991, and the essays in Watson, 1990).

'Municipal feminism' in Britain

The distinction between formal and informal politics is often particularly blurred at the level of local government. Community or neighbourhood initiatives and campaigns around issues such as transport, childcare, housing or health frequently involve demands on local authorities either for policy initiatives or for the funding and provision of services. In a number of local authorities, self-consciously feminist groups have both produced such demands and helped secure the establishment of women's committees within the authorities. In some cases these committees have in turn sought links not only with feminist groups and networks, but also with marginalised and unorganised women, whose voices they have attempted to incorporate into the policy-making processes of local government.

The first, largest and in many ways the most influential of these women's committees was set up in 1982 by the Greater London Council. The motives behind this, which went far beyond liberal feminist ideas of equal career opportunities, arose from a form of socialist feminism that was concerned with breaking down hierarchies and with reducing inequalities among women, as well as between women and men. As such, it was both in line with and a radicalising force behind the new left-wing Labour administration, whose stated aim was to channel 'power, resources and opportunities to the deprived, marginalised and disadvantaged sectors of London's population' (quoted in Coote and Campbell, 1987, p. 105).

In addition to attempting to improve the employment situation and prospects of women in London, the committee acted as an internal pressure group within the council and supported voluntary groups in the community. Elaborate consultative mechanisms were introduced, including open meetings, which were on occasion attended by 500 women, and the co-option of women to ensure that the committee represented the views of working-class, ethnic minority, lesbian and disabled women. By 1986, the women's committee had a budget of £90 million and a staff of 96, and it had given out nearly 1,000 separate grants, worth a total of £30 million, to a whole range of voluntary groups, including women's refuges, lesbian centres, health centres and childcare providers. Joni Lovenduski and Vicky Randall have described its initiatives as 'an unprecedented experiment in local democracy' which mobilised many women who had never been politically active before (Lovenduski and Randall, 1993, p. 194), while Anna Coote and Beatrix Campbell claim that:

> For a short time, women had a taste of what power might be like, and what could be achieved if women could command extensive resources in women's interests, over a longer period. (Coote and Campbell, 1987, p. 107).

The GLC experiment did not survive, for in 1986 the council itself was abolished. Although by the late 1980s there were nearly 60 other local government women's committees throughout the country, the power of these to implement radical policies has been restricted both by financial constraints and a lack of genuine political backing or understanding of feminist issues; by 1994 their numbers had fallen to about 43. Even in those authorities where there is a genuine commitment to open, inclusive and democratic processes, it has proved difficult to combine these with the formal procedures of local government, or to include women who are not already politically active or organised. There are also problems in co-opting individual women onto the committees to represent groups, such as disabled women or lesbians, which may themselves be divided or fragmented; tensions have also arisen around class and ethnic differences, with committee members being accused of failing to understand the significance of ethnic identity, and of favouring middle-class white women over black and working-class white men.

There is, nevertheless, still room for optimism. Today, women's committees continue to play an important role in some Labour authorities, both in terms of influencing policy and as a link between the authority and the voluntary sector. Some women's committees have done particularly important work in relation to domestic violence. Posts have been established to co-ordinate local approaches to the problem, local funding has been provided for refuges, and the problem has increasingly been articulated in feminist terms, as 'an issue of power and the result of the unequal status of women and men in society' (Mackay, 1996, p. 210). Most significantly, the Zero Tolerance Campaign, which seeks to raise public awareness and challenge dominant myths about domestic violence against women and children, originated in 1992 in the Edinburgh District Council's women's committee, and has since been copied by many other authorities. Fiona Mackay's study of the Edinburgh campaign found that feminist activists were able to work with and through the women's committee without the issues being modified or re-defined; she therefore argues that feminists 'may be gaining some leverage from their intervention in the state through women's committees and women's units to control and define certain issues' (Mackay, 1996, p. 209). Despite their problems, the history of women's committees does therefore suggest the possibility of a productive engagement with local state power, and a way of linking formal and informal political activity.

The United States and the politics of the 'gender gap'

In 1920, a Constitutional Amendment gave all women in the United States the vote on the same basis as men. However, the hopes of some suffrage campaigners that women would use their electoral strength to pursue feminist ends were unrealised. Most women, like most men, voted according to their class, religion and family traditions, and for many years the most commonly observed differences between women and men voters were that women were both less likely than men to use their vote and more likely to vote Republican. The apparent ineffectiveness of the vote as a way of achieving improvements in the lives of women meant that elections were not a natural focus of the new feminist movements from the 1960s. In recent years, however, greater knowledge of voting patterns and a reversal of earlier trends have combined with an increasingly effective feminist lobby to mean that some feminists are once again seeing the vote as a key political weapon.

Since at least the early 1980s, women in all ethnic groups have been significantly more likely than men to vote for Democratic candidates. This trend reached an all-time high in the 1996 Presidential election, when 54 per cent of women voters chose Clinton and only 38 per cent preferred Dole; men in contrast gave 44 per cent of their votes to each of the two main candidates. Although Clinton's lead among white women was relatively low at 7 per cent, white men gave an 11 per cent lead to Dole (*Guardian*, 7 November 1996). There was also a gender gap of around 10 per cent for Congressional candidates.

The political causes of this gap are complex, and it is clear that women are not a cohesive voting block. Nevertheless, its identification in the early 1980s inspired a registration drive by feminist organisations determined to exploit its potential:

> In the gender gap the women's movement saw an opportunity. If women really were voting in ways different from those of men, and if women voting did help elect progressive candidates, then unleashing the untapped source of 30 million unregistered women voters might turn the tide of the 1984 election. (Mendelson, 1988, p. 63)

Feminist efforts helped produce a rise of 1.75 million women voters in the 1984 election (with an especially marked increase among black women); because there are more women than men in the population, a continuation of this trend meant that by the 1992 Presidential election 54 per cent of votes were cast by women (McKay, 1993, p. 108). Although in 1984 women's differential voting had not been enough to defeat Ronald Reagan, the popular Republican incumbent, in 1996 the Democratic lead among women was so great that their votes won the election for Clinton, despite a drop of 7 million in the white female vote (*Guardian*, 17 February 1997).

Awareness of the importance of the women's vote has had clear effects on the political parties. In the early 1980s the Republican party deliberately set out to close the gender gap by appointing some women to highly visible positions, supporting more female candidates and enacting some minor legislative reforms aimed at women. Most feminist campaigns have, however, been aimed more directly at the Democratic party, where the gender gap was exploited successfully to ensure the selection of Geraldene Ferraro as vice-presidential candidate in 1988, and where women's perceived electoral clout has been used to demand protection of abortion rights and to insist that issues such as childcare, equal opportunities or sexual harassment are placed on the mainstream political agenda. The willingness of politicians to listen to such demands means that some sections of the women's movement must now be seen as a significant force in mainstream politics at the national level. By 1988, the National Organisation for Women 'was being taken seriously as part of the Democratic party's decision-making process' (Frankovic, 1988, p. 123); other well-established groups such as the League of Women Voters have been joined by newer groups in their attempt to encourage women to become politically active, and there is now a whole range of lobbying, education and fund-raising groups aimed both at increasing women's political representation and at achieving particular policy goals. The impact of such efforts was clear in the 1992 Congressional elections, held amid the political fall-out of the Clarence Thomas hearings (see Chapter 3). Women were not united in opposing Thomas, and black women in particular were subject to divided loyalties. Nevertheless, the sight of an all-white, all-male Senate Committee deciding to recommend the appointment of a man to the Supreme Court of the United States, despite allegations that he had sexually harassed a female colleague, and reporting their conclusions to a full Senate of 98 men and only two women, forced the political under-representation of women into dramatic focus. As women across the nation protested that 'Men just don't get it', the apparent failure of men to understand or address the issues that concern women motivated some individual women to stand for political office and others to vote for them. Campaigning women's groups were able to exploit this new tide of opinion and to use their political knowledge and financial resources to support female candidates. The result was a record number of women elected to both Houses in what has become known as 'The Year of the Woman'. In the same year, Clinton's Presidential campaign promised to prioritise women's issues and to create an administration that 'looks like America' in terms of its gender and ethnic balance. Once elected, Clinton rewarded his feminist supporters by appointing a significant number of women to key Cabinet positions; almost as soon as he had taken office, he also both issued executive orders lifting restrictions on abortion rights and signed the Family and Medical Leave Bill, which had previously been vetoed by Bush (see Chapter 4).

In the 1996 elections, women voters were treated by political campaigners as critical to the outcome. The lack of any cohesive 'women's vote' was, however, also clear, and groups supporting anti-abortion women candidates succeeded in winning four House seats with the help of female votes (Kalb, 1996). Despite such complicating factors, the vote now seems to many American feminists to be an effective means of bringing about change. Far from seeing it as a mere formality, they would therefore agree with Carol Meuller that:

> From the combined effects of women voters, modern polling, organized feminism, the media, and the major parties arises the potential for

women's collective influence. It is a substantially greater potential than that which accompanied the passage of the suffrage amendment 60 years before. (Meuller, 1988, p. 18)

The gender gap in Britain

In Britain, the gender gap in voting behaviour is much less dramatic than in the United States, and feminist attempts to exploit the potential of women's votes has been less extensive. Nevertheless, by the 1990s, feminist academics and campaigners were publicising the political importance of women's votes by showing not only that more votes are now cast by women but that women are more likely to be floating voters rather than party loyalists; as such, their votes may be potentially winnable by either party, and could determine the results of an election.

Women's voting behaviour is a matter of particular concern for the Labour party as, although the gap is reversed for young people, women as a whole have been more likely than men to vote Conservative. Encouraged by feminists within the party, efforts have been made to understand the party's lack of appeal to women and to present a more women-friendly image. In the early 1990s, a quota system was introduced for officers and delegates at all levels throughout the party, and for a short while included the selection of parliamentary candidates. In the run-up to the 1997 election, political advisers drew on the experience of the 1993 Australian election, when for the first time more women than men voted for Labour. Candidates were encouraged to focus on issues such as childcare and health, and advised both on how to dress and how to talk in order to improve their communication with women voters (*Independent on Sunday*, 17 November 1996). It is easy to dismiss some of these changes as merely cosmetic, and the result of opportunism rather than any serious commitment to improving the lives of women. Nevertheless, the organisational changes within the Labour party are likely to have real and long-term effects on the party's culture and priorities; they will also provide increasing numbers of women with the political experience that will help them achieve elected office. At a more immediate level, the Labour party did manage to attract more female voters; according to an internal party report the votes of women switching from the Conservatives were in themselves sufficient to win Labour the election (*Independent on Sunday*, 25 May 1997). Greater awareness of the importance of women as voters is both cause and result of increasing political activity on the part of groups such as the Fawcett Society (whose roots go back to the earliest suffrage campaigns) and the National Association of Women's Organisations (an umbrella group for a whole range of groups from the Women's Institute to small feminist organisations), which are now working with feminist academics and politicians to publicise the political concerns of 'ordinary' women and the need to address these if votes are to be won. As in the United States, there seems to be an increased sense that the vote is not an empty formality, but something which feminists can use as part of an overall strategy for real change.

The Scandinavian experience

Although there are important differences among the Scandinavian nations, there are two general features of Nordic politics which immediately strike anyone interested in gender relations: the high numbers of women elected into national parliaments and the positive use of the welfare state to promote gender equality. These features are clearly interconnected, and for many feminist writers, the 'Scandinavian model' represents a new form of 'woman-friendly' state. Others have been more critical, arguing that women have been excluded from the powerful corporate structures of the Scandinavian states, through which many policies are made in close consultation with both business and organised labour. They point out the clear social and economic differences between women and men that remain, and some have even claimed that women have moved from dependency on individual men to dependency on the patriarchal state. Today a lively debate continues as to the nature and significance of women's achievements; most recent writings by Scandinavian feminists are, however, both highly positive about the gains that have been made and optimistic about the possibility of further progress, even in a political climate in which welfare provisions are, as in other nations, increasingly under threat.

Women's entry into the structures of the Scandinavian states is most immediately visible in national parliaments and governments.

By the early 1990s, more than 30 per cent of members of parliament and cabinet ministers were women in all the Scandinavian nations except for Iceland; in the 1993 Norwegian elections, all three main political parties were led by women; and after the 1994 elections in Sweden, women's representation reached an international all-time high of 41 per cent in parliament and 50 per cent in the cabinet. These figures compare with just under 10 per cent female representation in the British House of Commons and the American House of Representatives at the same period, and are without precedent anywhere else in the world. Although women's representation has been high relative to other nations throughout the century, the real breakthrough in numbers has occurred since the 1970s. There has been a parallel, although less dramatic, gain in local government, where around one third of elected members were female in the early 1990s; women have also made steady inroads into government bureaucracies, where 'femocrats' (feminist bureaucrats) have consciously used their position to promote women's interests.

Until recently, women's political representation has not been matched by their presence in corporate structures. Over the past decade, however, they have made significant inroads here as well. This is partly a reflection of women's entry into employment and hence into institutions which participate in government committees; it is also a result of feminist pressure and positive action by central governments in response to this. Such action has been most direct in Norway, where a legally established target of 40 per cent representation on government committees has almost been met (although with marked variations between departments); throughout Scandinavia as a whole, women's representation on corporate bodies has now reached about 30 per cent.

All of this suggests that, for feminists, the key questions now are not 'Could women ever gain access to political power?', but rather 'How have they managed to do so in Scandinavia?' and 'What have been the results?' Attempts to answer these questions suggest a complex interaction of causes and consequences. The dominant social democratic political culture provided an initially favourable environment that was friendly to ideas of group rather than individual representation and to the use of the state to achieve equality. Once women had gained a foothold in political structures, they were able to use these beliefs to promote further increases in women's representation, for example by pushing for gender quotas for parliamentary candidates and corporate appointments. Such policies are much less easy to implement in the United States or Britain, where they run counter to liberal ideas of individual competition, and where electoral systems make the use of quotas especially difficult. Women politicians in Scandinavia have used their position to push for women's rights in employment, and for welfare and employment policies which ease the burden of women's traditional caring responsibilities and enable them to be both shared with men and combined with paid work. This in turn means that women's lack of the key political resources of time, money and contacts is less acute than in other nations, and therefore facilitates their further political involvement. The entry of yet more women into the political arena provides role models and a woman-friendly environment for other women; it also ensures that gender equality and issues of particular concern to women remain high on the political agenda, and that women's own perceptions and experiences are heard.

Today, women politicians remain disproportionately involved in policy areas to do with welfare, health and the family rather than defence or the economy as a whole, and recent studies show that they still often bear the sole responsibility for placing 'women's issues', such as gender equality, pornography, sexual violence, prostitution and women's health, on the political agenda. For pessimists, such concentration on traditional areas might suggest that stereotypes of womanly interests and abilities remain unchallenged, and that women are still excluded from the most powerful and central policy decisions. Women are, however, not *confined* to particular areas, and the high level of welfare spending in the Nordic countries means that this is central to the economy and to social organisation, so that welfare issues are not marginal concerns. Women's concentration on certain issues can therefore be seen as an assertion of feminist priorities, rather than as exclusion from more important forums.

As I have argued elsewhere (Bryson and Lister, 1994; Bryson, 1996b), although problems remain, it seems that in Scandinavia the 'vicious circle' of women's political, economic and social disadvantages is being replaced by a 'virtuous circle', through which gains in one area interact with gains in another, to produce a general picture of cumulative progress. By the mid-1990s, Karvonen and Selle found that a central theme of their book on *Women in Nordic Politics* was that 'political institutions and politics do make a difference', and that 'government can be an important actor in promoting women's interests and the individual freedom of women in Scandinavia'(Karvonen and Selle, 1995, p. 9). Clearly, this offers encouragement to feminists in other nations, and suggests that engagement with formal politics and state institutions can produce practical improvements in the quality of women's lives.

Feminism and the political representation of women

The idea that meaningful change can be achieved by working through the formal political system raises major issues to do with the continuing under-representation of women in elected legislative assemblies. For a range of interconnected reasons, many feminists today see this as a central political issue.

For some, it is an obvious matter of justice that there should be an approximate gender balance, and it simply does not seem right that one sex should be able to dominate to the near-exclusion of the other. In contrast to the under-representation of the very young or the very old, which can be seen 'as part of a normal and natural lifecycle' (Phillips, 1993, p. 63), many feminists argue that this exclusion is politically significant because it both reflects and helps maintain discrimination and oppression. In the influential *Justice and the Politics of Difference* (1990), Iris Young has argued that justice requires that we give political recognition to the existence of gender difference (and also to other group differences such as those based on ethnicity and physical ability), and that denying their existence contributes to oppression rather than equality. She therefore argues for an elaborate system of representation in which all oppressed groups, including women, would have a guaranteed role in policy formation; such guarantees would not be necessary for the privileged, who already have access to decision-making positions.

Such arguments assume that women have shared interests as members of an oppressed group. For some radical feminists, these interests are directly opposed to men's; if women are to use the state to improve their situation they must be represented in it, for they can expect only opposition from their oppressors. Although others argue that men can benefit from or support feminist demands, experience suggests that they are unlikely to prioritise them. To the extent that women's claims for better pay and employment opportunities involve exposing and attacking men's privileged workplace situation and its basis in inequalities within the home, the interests of the sexes would appear to be in conflict, at least in the short term. As Joni Lovenduski has argued: 'The core of women's interests is comprised of their disadvantaged position in the division of labour within the family, and for as long as that division persists it is sufficient reason for insisting that women's interests may be represented only by women' (Lovenduski, 1986, p. 208).

Although liberal feminists are less likely to see the issue in terms of group oppression, they too can agree that women's biology and social situation can give rise to distinct concerns and priorities that they need to articulate themselves. Most feminists therefore believe that it is wrong that men can legislate on issues to do with reproduction or sexual violence without women's voices being adequately heard. Most also see that, as the primary carers of children, disabled adults and elderly people, and as the bulk of poorly paid, part-time workers, women also have particular concerns and interests in relation to welfare and employment policies, even when these appear to be gender neutral.

A further set of arguments stems from the claim that women can bring special qualities and/or experiences to politics. Such claims have a long history, and formed an important strand of earlier claims for the vote, when it was asserted that the 'womanly values' of temperance, purity and peace would lead to an improvement in the standard of public life. Today, the idea that women are more peaceful, compassionate and caring remains a powerful one, as does the claim, discussed in the previous chapter, that they have a distinctive way of thinking about justice. At a more practical level, many claim that women politicians would have no time for the infantile, 'yah-boo' trading of insults that today sometimes passes for political debate; the British politician Shirley Williams has also argued that women members of parliament are more able than men to provide the caring qualities needed for effective constituency work (Williams, 1997). Although some argue that such 'womanly' values are based in biology, many others see them as a product of women's experiences; from this perspective, it may be important to have decision-makers who have had experience of caring (see Okin, 1990; Ruddick, 1990).

None of the above claims is straightforward, and they have all been heavily criticised. For many critics, they seem to rest upon a freezing of gender identities, and an essentialism which labels individuals by one attribute and ignores both the differences between women and the interests which some women share with some men. As such, they run counter to post-modern accounts of the fluid and changing nature of gender, and, as so often in the past, they tend to equate the interests of women with those of the minority who are the most likely to win political office.

Such criticisms are not without foundation. Quite clearly, women are not all mothers or badly paid, part-time workers, nor do they all feel themselves to be sexually exploited or oppressed, and many are positively opposed to feminist goals. Moreover, the kinds of women most likely to be elected to parliament are those who have most access to political resources and whose lives most closely resemble those of successful men; unlike men, this means that they are disproportionately childless, as well as being white and middle class (in the early 1990s, 40 per cent of British women MPs did not have children, and only one was black. See Bawdon, 1995). Such women may be no more likely than many men to understand the needs and priorities of women intimidated by racism, or struggling to survive on state benefits; they may also have even less experience of childcare than male legislators, most of whom are or have been part-time fathers.

This does not mean that the under-representation of women is not important, but that it cannot be isolated from other forms of inequality. As discussed in Chapter 3, the meaning of what it is to be a woman varies with class and ethnicity, and women may at times feel that their primary allegiance is to the men of their class or ethnic group rather than to other women. Feminists interested in improving the situation of all groups of women, rather than that of an elite minority, must therefore retain an awareness of the complex nature of a 'politics of solidarity'. They must also remember that it is not simply the number of women in political office that is important, but what women do when they get there, and Anne Phillips cautions that 'However plausible it is to say that male-dominated assemblies will not adequately address the needs and interests of women, it cannot be claimed with equal confidence that a more balanced legislature will fill this gap' (Phillips, 1995, p. 71).

As we have seen, however, the behaviour of female politicians in Scandinavia provides grounds for optimism, as they have acted to prioritise needs and interests which male politicians have overlooked. The more limited experience of women representatives in the United States and Britain also suggests that they have had an impact on political agendas and they are generally more supportive of feminist issues than men, regardless of their party affiliation. Although there are many examples of female politicians who have done nothing for their sex, the general pattern does seem to confirm intuitive expectations; it therefore reinforces the claim that increasing the numbers of women in parliament is an important feminist goal.

Causes of under-representation

With the exception of Scandinavia, the under-representation of women is an international phenomenon. It is, however, particularly acute in the United States, where in 1996 the overall figure in Congress was about 10 per cent (with 8 women senators and 51 house representatives). After the British 1997 general election, about 18 per cent of members of the House of Commons were women, the second lowest figure in Europe. Although these figures are low, they are dramatically higher than in the recent past: in the United States before the 1992 'Year of the Woman', only 2 per cent of senators and fewer than 5 per cent of house representatives were women, and women did not break the 5 per cent barrier in the British House of Commons until 1987.

General reasons for women's under-representation are not hard to find. At a practical level, as we shall see in the next chapter, women's continuing responsibility for caring and domestic work and their generally disadvantaged employment situation mean that they have less access than men to money, influential contacts and time; each of these is a critical political resource. Discrimination against women can also still be a problem. Although conscious and deliberate refusal to endorse female candidates is much less common than in the past, unconscious discrimination is much harder to eradicate, and 'If selectors base their assumptions about suitable applicants on the image of established MPs, this may produce a systematic bias in favour of maintaining the status quo' (Norris and Lovenduski, 1995, p. 127). At a deeper level, the whole process of socialisation into gender roles, and the underlying ways in which perceptions of masculinity and femininity are constructed, contribute to a perception that politics is the preserve of men. This is exacerbated by the confrontational and adversarial style of party politics, and means that while a man who succeeds as a politician is also confirming his masculinity, a female politician has either to set her femininity to one side or to employ it as a deliberate political weapon; because of her minority status in a masculine world, neither she nor others can treat her gender as 'normal' and unremarkable.

These factors combine to mean both that fewer women than men enter the race for political office, and that women who do enter are less likely than men to succeed. Pippa Norris and Joni Lovenduski's study of legislative recruitment in Britain in the early 1990s found that both the supply of female applicants and the demand by party selectors for particular kinds of candidates contributed towards the low number of women chosen by the parties to stand for parliament. Contrary to popular assumptions, they also found that women face more problems from party selectors in the Labour party than in the Conservative party, where the problem seemed to be less the reluctance of selection boards to choose women than a shortage of women coming forward (Norris and Lovenduski, 1995).

Recent changes and proposals for reform

These factors have been common to political systems everywhere. As family structures alter, increasing numbers of women achieve economic independence and traditional gender stereotypes are challenged they may, however, be declining in significance, and recent increases in the representation of women already mean that both that legislative assemblies are a less hostile environment for new women members and that there are more female political role models.

Recent gains are also the result of activity by increasingly effective, experienced and well-resourced feminist networking, fundraising and campaigning groups. Such groups have been particularly important in the United States, where financial backing is critically important at all stages of the complex selection process, and where feminist groups played a key role in increasing the number of women elected to Congress in 1992. One of the largest and most effective of the new groups was EMILY's List (the acronym stands for Early Money is Like Yeast – it makes the dough [money] rise). This attracted both big sums of money from wealthy individuals and large numbers of small donations which combined to provide over

$6 million to support female candidates within the Democratic party. In Britain, this success inspired the formation of EMILY's List UK, a group which has helped aspiring female candidates in the Labour party with the costs of childcare, transport, accommodation and campaigning. The longer established 300 Group also provides support, training and advice for women in all political parties, and campaigns for reforms to facilitate the election of more women. The ability of women to act collectively in these ways is itself a product of gains that have already been made, and reflects the increased political experience and financial independence of many women and the outstanding success of a few high fliers; a generation earlier, the resources for such large-scale organisation by women were simply not in place.

All of this suggests to some observers that it is only a matter of time before more balanced representation is achieved; the most that political parties need do, therefore, is to streamline selection processes to ensure that any residual discrimination against women is eliminated. In practice, however, progress does not seem to be so automatic as this scenario suggests. In the United States, the great leap forward of 1992 was not matched in 1994 or 1996, when only a few more women were elected to Congress. In Britain, there were fewer Conservative women members or candidates in 1997 than in 1992; although there was a dramatic increase in Labour women members from 39 to 101, this was almost entirely due to the controversial 'all women shortlist' policy discussed below. For many feminists, therefore, more deliberate action is needed, and a number of key demands for political or constitutional change have emerged.

In Britain, the most straightforward demand is for the establishment of a crèche in the Houses of Parliament. This would be of clear symbolic value, affirming Parliament's commitment to good employment practices for all its workers (85 per cent of whom are women). It has, however, been refused on grounds of lack of space; moves to have the Commons' shooting range converted to a crèche have been rejected (Bawdon, 1995). Attempts to change the hours of work of the House of Commons have also not yet succeeded, although the new Labour administration is in principle sympathetic. The situation whereby Parliament does not sit in the morning but sometimes has sessions that last all night is obviously difficult for those with family responsibilities. The argument that these hours enable members to engage in outside work which keeps them in touch with the 'real

118 *Feminist Debates*

world' is rejected by those who think that being a MP should be a full-time job, and by those who query the middle-class male assumption that the world of lawyers and businessmen constitutes 'reality', whereas participation in family responsibilities does not. In the United States, where the party system is much weaker than in Britain, progress has been blocked by a high rate of incumbency return (that is, sitting members are very likely to be re-elected). Time limitations on the term of office would do much to open up the system to women; Congressional approval for this, however, seems as likely as turkeys voting for Thanksgiving or Christmas.

For many campaigners, electoral reform holds out the promise of a more woman-friendly system. Cross-national studies suggest a strong correlation between proportional representation and levels of female representation, with the kind of first-past-the-post system that exists in both the United States and Britain being a major obstacle to progress. Even when a party is genuinely committed to increasing the number of female members, single member constituencies make it difficult to achieve this, as individual men have to be rejected if more women are chosen. Most forms of proportional representation, however, make the overall gender balance more visible and make it easier to take into account group as well as individual characteristics. For example, in a system of large multi-member constituencies, the British Labour party would find it difficult to justify nominating five men and no women in one area; with a 'party list' system (whereby seats are allocated to parties at national level according to how many votes they receive) it would be similarly unlikely to produce a list in which nearly 90 of the first 100 names were male. Until the 1997 election, however, its failure to select women for many winnable seats had the same overall effect as these more obvious forms of bias.

Although electoral systems are clearly important, proportional representation on its own does not provide a magic wand. In the first place, not all forms have the same effect, and although the Labour party has shown signs of support for electoral reform, the measures preferred by its leading figures have not been those most favourable to women. Second, electoral systems do not operate in isolation, but interact with other political factors. This is shown clearly by the example of Israel. Here there is both a near-perfect form of proportional representation (the party list system operates within a single national constituency) and an active feminist movement; religious and military pressures mean, however, that female representation is still under 10 per cent (Bryson, 1996a). Third, and most important, the opportunities for increased representation which proportional representation can provide can only be realised if the political will is there, and the principle of the group representation of women is conceded. Where this principle leads to an acceptance of the need for gender quotas, proportional representation means that these can be implemented without requiring individual men to stand down; the desirability of such quotas is itself, of course, fiercely debated.

The debate over quotas

Feminist supporters of gender quotas for elected positions have invoked arguments about both individual equality of opportunity for candidates and fairness to the female half of the electorate (see Squires, 1996). Opponents, however, have focused on the former alone; the result has been a lop-sided debate in which the second set of arguments have frequently become lost.

Concentrating on the first strand of the debate, opponents of quota systems see these as a form of unjust discrimination against men, as aspiring male candidates are unfairly expected to compensate women for past discrimination for which they were not responsible. Quotas are also seen as condescending to women, and as likely to produce a decline in the quality of candidates, as well-qualified men are forced to stand aside in favour of less-qualified women. Diana Maddock, the Liberal Democrat spokesperson on women's issues has denounced quotas on these grounds, saying 'We want equal treatment for women, not special treatment. Our aim is equality of opportunity, not equality of outcome' (quoted in Squires, 1996, p. 75), and the Conservative MP Angela Rumbold has similarly declared 'We want neither tokenism, nor the kind of favouritism that turns our concept of fairness on its head. Women, I believe, want real opportunity; they want to be able to "make it" on the basis of merit' (Rumbold, 1991, p. 6).

In direct reply to this, advocates of quotas argue that discrimination is not a thing of the past, even if it is less overt than formerly, and that our understanding of 'merit' is biased in favour of men. They also point to the collective disadvantages faced by women, which mean that many able women are unable to compete equally with men, despite formal equality of opportunity. As Anne Phillips has said, 'Either society treats men and women as genuine equals, in which case they will turn up in equal numbers... or it treats them unfairly, in which case we need special arrangements to guarantee an equal presence' (Phillips, 1991, p. 156). This argument moves away from an individualistic approach to one which recognises the importance of structural inequalities and group disadvantage. As such it is likely to find favour in the kind of social democratic political culture which is dominant in Scandinavia, or in political parties, such as the British Labour party, which have a tradition of recognising collective problems and the need for collective action to overcome them. The political culture of the United States and the British Conservative party, with their stress on self-help and individual merit are, however, unfavourable; as the British feminist Beatrix Campbell says, 'Many Conservative women believe in women's equality without having a theory of inequality, which often leaves them without a political strategy to deal with inequality' (Campbell, 1987, p. 200).

Although advocates of quotas have frequently found themselves arguing on the limited question of fairness to individual candidates, the right of female voters to be represented by women can also provide an important strand of their argument. From this perspective, it is unfair to women voters if politicians are overwhelmingly drawn from a group whose members tend to have different perceptions, needs and priorities, and whose group interests may at times even conflict with those of women.

Such ideas about group representation are again alien to the individualistic assumptions of the British Conservative party. They are, however, in line with the traditional assumptions of the Labour party, which was built upon the recognition of class interests, and which has long had a small number of 'reserved seats' for both trade unionists and women on decision-making bodies. By the late 1980s, arguments about both fairness to women candidates and the need to represent women voters had combined with the political argument that giving women a greater and more visible role within the party would be a vote-winning strategy. The result was a series of conference decisions requiring the introduction of gender quotas of at least 40 per cent women at all levels of party organisation; from 1993, this included the requirement that Labour candidates in half the winnable seats and half the safe seats where sitting members were retiring should be selected from all-women shortlists.

Politics and the state 121

Quotas were instinctively and bitterly opposed by many women and men within the party, as well as by its political opponents. The strength and vociferousness of this opposition reflects the extent to which the assumptions of liberal individualism dominate the terms of political debate even in a party with an egalitarian and collectivist tradition, as attention focused on the unjust treatment of individual men rather than on the collective experiences and interests of either women candidates or the female electorate. Such liberal thinking was reflected in the decision of an industrial tribunal in 1996 that the policy constituted unlawful sex discrimination, because it excluded men from the possibility of employment as an MP. The Labour leader, Tony Blair, did not share the enthusiasm of his predecessor, John Smith, for the policy, and the decision was not contested.

Although short-lived and divisive, the policy was successful, as it was largely responsible for the more than threefold increase in Labour women members at the 1997 election; in 'unlikely but possible' constituencies where it did not apply, only 11 of the 66 new Labour seats were won by women. This has created problems for the Conservative and Liberal Democratic parties, whose lack of women members is now more visible in contrast to the Labour party, and who are now reluctantly considering related proposals. At the end of 1997, a Conservative green paper proposed that 25 per cent of candidates interviewed for selection should be women (*Independent on Sunday*, 2 November 1997); at the time of writing, the Liberal Democrats are proposing to alternate male and female candidates in the new party list system for the European elections, and there is strong pressure in the main Scottish parties for formal mechanisms to ensure adequate female representation in the new Scottish Assembly. The issue is therefore not dead, and those who oppose quotas have yet to produce any effective alternative.

Conclusions: feminist political strategies today

Feminists are, increasingly, not only outside the formal political system, but are becoming influential insiders. As such, many are in a position to make or influence decisions affecting the lives of other women; experience indicates that this can produce meaningful changes, which may in turn facilitate further political gains. This suggests that we should not see the state as monolithically patriarchal and that state welfare can be provided in forms that empower women and enable them to live as independent citizens, rather than as economic dependants.

Feminists will, however, be more politically effective if they understand that the state is not gender neutral. Such understanding can help them expose the patriarchal assumptions behind the dominant perception that 'women's issues' are of marginal political importance and that a politician who attempts to speak as a woman is obsessive, parochial and biased. It is also important that feminist politicians remain in touch with grass-roots movements and 'ordinary women', for there is a danger both that an elite minority of powerful women could become assimilated into existing power structures and that such women will represent the interests of middle-class, mainly white, career women, and have no more understanding than many men of the needs of less privileged groups.

This means that feminists do not need to choose between formal and informal politics, or between mainstream activity and autonomous women's movements, for both are necessary. Grass-roots groups are important in their own right; they can also help keep feminist politicians informed and in touch with the needs of a wide range of women. For example, when the British Labour politician Clare Short was Shadow Minister for Women, she worked with women who had first-hand involvement in rape crisis and women's refuge centres in order to produce a powerful consultative document on domestic and sexual violence against women (Short, 1995b). As Joni Lovenduski and Vicky Randall say in their study of British feminism at the beginning of the 1990s, 'In the long run, feminists inside a system are more likely to be effective and motivated if there is a strong autonomous feminist movement outside the system' (Lovenduski and Randall, 1993, p. 12).

Although the autonomous women's movement is widely depicted as being in decline, in some areas it is clearly thriving. To some extent, its apparent decline reflects its increased diversity, and the 'normalisation' of many of its activities into social, academic and economic as well as political life. The result is that today there exists a very wide range of feminist activities and networks, both formal and informal. These networks are not simply the tool of ambitious career women, but have the potential to link and inform feminists whose interests are diverse in the extreme; they also have the potential to mobilise large groups of women on particular issues.

6

The family and paid employment

This chapter outlines recent changes in family life and paid employment, and the ways in which feminists have reacted to them. It shows that, contrary to popular mythology, most feminists today are neither dedicated career women, who believe that someone who is 'just a housewife' is wasting her life, nor man-hating earth mothers, living off the state and bringing up children in women-only households. It finds that although there are still major disagreements, there is an increasingly widespread feminist understanding that women's family and employment situations cannot be analysed or changed in isolation from each other. This means that a genuine expansion of choice and opportunity must involve both a recognition of their interdependence and a reassessment of the values attached to each.

The family

The family today

Family life has always taken diverse forms, and its structure has varied between and within nations and over time. Nevertheless, there are clearly identifiable trends in western societies since the 1960s. Increases in divorce and births outside marriage have produced a striking rise in the numbers of lone parent families. Combined with a general movement of women, including married women with young children, into the paid workforce, this means that the 'cornflake family' of wage-earning husband and dependent wife and children is an increasingly small minority of all households. These international trends in family composition have been particularly marked in the United States, where by the early 1990s nearly 30 per cent of families with children were headed by a lone parent, and in Britain, which, at just over 20 per cent, had the highest rate of lone parenthood in the European Community (Bradshaw *et al.*, 1996). Within the United States and Britain, African-American and Afro-Caribbean families are particularly likely to be female headed. Further changes in family structure have resulted from an increase in life expectancy which has in most western nations combined with a falling birth rate to produce an ageing population.

The vast majority of lone parent households are headed by a woman, and such families in all nations are disproportionately likely to live in poverty. There are, however, huge national differences in the size of this effect: in 1996, a comparative study of 20 industrialised nations found that in Britain 56 per cent of lone parent households were in poverty, compared to only 3 per cent in Sweden (Bradshaw *et al.*, 1996).

A different kind of poverty can also be experienced by women who are married to prosperous men, but who have no independent source of income. There is widespread evidence that, although many men are generous towards their partners, financial resources are not usually shared equally within the family. As a result, non-earning or low-earning women can experience a personal poverty that is hidden within the family, and which prevents them participating independently in society. This means that although divorce appears to produce an increase in poverty among women, many 'poor' women report that they feel financially better off on their own, as they have an independent income and are in control of their own finances.

Despite recent changes, the majority of women still marry or cohabit with men, and most children still grow up in a two-parent family. Although there has undoubtedly been some shift in attitudes and expectations, particularly among younger people, and some increase in men's contribution to housework and childcare, studies in every country consistently find that 'new man' is more of a myth than a reality, and that the traditional domestic division of labour remains remarkably unchanged, even when women are in paid employment. Women also remain primarily responsible for caring for disabled or elderly family members. This means that a 'good son' is one who ensures that his elderly mother is looked after, while a 'good daughter' is expected to do the caring herself (Dalley, 1988). Spouse care provides an exception to this general pattern; in Britain, as many men care for elderly wives as women care for elderly husbands (see Parker, 1990).

Despite the ups and downs inherent in almost any long-term relationship, many women are happily married and do not feel exploited or envy their husband's breadwinning responsibilities, while many enjoy staying at home and looking after their children. Many however are less content, and in a study carried out for Reading University in 1996, Lynne Murray found that nearly half of her sample of mothers who were at home full-time suffered from depression severe enough to inhibit the long-term development of their children (*Guardian*, 4 November 1996). A significant minority of women are not only treated as unpaid servants but also experience violence from their husbands. There is nothing new about this, and, as official reports to the 1995 Beijing World Conference on Women made clear, domestic violence is a problem in all social groups and in every nation of the world (United Nations, 1995). In Britain, although only a tiny fraction of attacks are reported, domestic violence accounts for about a quarter of all reported violent assault; analysis of the 1992 British Crime Survey suggests that there are a minimum of half a million domestic violence incidents per year (87 per cent of them against women).

Both the changes and the continuities in family life have deep-seated and complex causes, and none is simply the product of feminism which, as the following section shows, has itself developed in response to women's varied and changing experiences.

The family in feminist thought

As discussed in Chapter 2, liberal feminists have long demanded that women should be liberated from domesticity and enabled to work outside the home. However, although few women now devote their whole lives to keeping house and caring for their family, many women today do not feel liberated, but exhausted and exploited as they are expected to go out to work as well as retaining their traditional family responsibilities. Many who choose to stay at home with their children also resent the implication that bringing up a family is not 'real' work, and in the mid-1990s the writer and journalist Maureen Freely claimed that feminism had failed mothers by devaluing motherhood and treating children simply as an obstacle to fulfilment (Freely, 1996).

Although Freely condemned the whole of feminism, many feminist writers would argue that the problems she identified are a product of liberal feminist thought, rather than feminism *per se*. For such critics, liberalism has never developed an adequate theory of the family, but has simply assumed both that it is a necessary basis for a civilised society and that it is an area of personal life which should be free from political interference. As a result, it has failed to see the extent and social importance of the work done by women within the home, or to consider the consequences if women are no longer available to do it. Because it draws a sharp line between personal relationships in the home and the public world of politics, it sees domestic roles and financial arrangements as a matter for individual choice and negotiation, and it treats domestic violence as a personal tragedy rather than a political issue of male power (for further discussion of the public/private distinction, see Chapters 2 and 5).

Conventional socialist and Marxist approaches have also often ignored the family and the division of labour within it, seeing these as either 'natural' or as a by-product of conditions of economic production. This approach seems to suggest that there is no need to address inequalities within the family directly, and that feminist energies are more appropriately directed towards workplace organisations and campaigns for socialist change. There is, however, a long strand within socialist thought that is highly critical of conventional family forms and that favours more collective and communal ways of life. Such values found more recent expression in Michelle Barrett and Mary McIntosh's 1982 book *The Anti-Social Family*, in which they argued that the family plays an important ideological role both in socialising children to accept oppressive gender roles and in encouraging selfish, individualistic values that are hostile to ideas of socialist collectivism. As discussed in Chapters 2 and 3, recent developments within Marxist theory have also attempted to understand the economic importance of women's domestic and caring labour and the interconnected but at times conflicting ways in which both capitalism and men may benefit from it. Such analyses suggest that the family is part of the material basis of society, and that changes or challenges to the way household work is organised are as important as conditions of work outside the home.

In contrast to other approaches, the family is the starting-point of much radical feminist analysis. This insists that personal relationships within the home are not simply matters of individual choice, but both reflect and maintain men's patriarchal power. From this perspective, most men's continuing failure to accept their fair share of domestic responsibilities is not accidental, but a refusal to give up a position of privilege which, by restricting their employment prospects, helps maintain women's financial dependency. Domestic violence is also seen as a product of unequal power relationships, rather than aberrant behaviour by a few individual men.

The influence of this analysis now extends well beyond those who would call themselves radical feminists, and the 'black box' of the family has increasingly been opened up to feminist political scrutiny. Men's failure to make a greater contribution to domestic and caring work is a recurrent theme in much recent feminist writing on public policy; at a more theoretical level, Janet Radcliffe Richards and Susan Moller Okin have used the ideas of the liberal theorist John Rawls to argue that a just society is impossible until there is justice within the family, and that this requires a radical restructuring of domestic and caring responsibilities (Richards, 1982; Okin, 1990). There is growing understanding that the personal economic dependency and poverty experienced by many women within marriage is incompatible with either equal citizenship or domestic partnership, and that women need access to their own financial resources if they are to escape or resist domestic abuse.

Some radical feminist critiques of the family go further than this, however, arguing that women's oppression cannot be ended while the institution itself remains, and that even the best marriage represents a form of domination disguised by love (see, in particular, Firestone, 1979). For some radical feminists, rejection of the family is also tied in with a rejection of heterosexuality as an oppressive institution, and the belief that heterosexual mothers will inevitably teach their daughters patriarchal values within the family (see Copper, 1994).

Such views are rejected by those women who have found joy, contentment, security or fulfilment through their role as wives and mothers, and probably never represented majority opinion even within radical feminism. Many have agreed with Adrienne Rich that, rather than rejecting motherhood and the family outright, feminists should attack the ways that they are 'defined and restricted under patriarchy' and seek ways of transforming them into sources of creativity and power (Rich, 1977, p. 14). Rich's arguments provided a basis for pro-family feminist arguments which developed during the 1980s and formed part of a feminist re-evaluation of motherhood and the 'womanly values' of nurturing, co-operation, peace and harmony, which led some writers to develop 'eco-feminist' ideas, and which Lynne Segal disparagingly refers to as 'maternal revivalism' (Segal, 1987, p. 145).

Renewed stress on the values of nurturing and the possibility of reforming the family is also to be found in some influential feminist psychoanalytic theory, particularly that linked with Nancy Chodorow and Dorothy Dinnerstein. These writers have argued that the present female monopoly of childcare damages both girls and boys, producing emotionally inadequate men, and women who over-invest in caring; Dinnerstein further argues that it means that adult men and women are unable to cope with women in positions of authority, for such women re-activate the sense of childish rage and frustration that they felt as infants. Their solution, however, is not the abolition of the family but an increased involvement of men in parenting (Chodorow, 1978; Dinnerstein, 1987). Shared parenting is also advocated by Sara Ruddick, who argues that the practice of mothering generates a set of values, particularly those associated with the peaceful resolution of conflict, which it is important that men as well as women learn (Ruddick, 1990. See also the related 'ethic of care' debate, discussed in Chapter 4).

Although some lesbian feminists argue that the heterosexual nuclear family is inherently oppressive, a lesbian perspective can also see marriage and the family as privileged forms of social organisation from which same-sex couples are unjustly excluded. Lesbians do not have the right to make a public declaration of love and commitment through the marriage ceremony, or to the status, legal rights and financial privileges (such as immigration rights or tax allowances) that marriage can bring. Lesbians have also been denied the right to become mothers, by being refused access to artificial insemination or *in vitro* fertilisation programmes, and they have been discriminated against as adoptive mothers and in custody disputes.

Similar discrimination has been experienced by some disabled and/or minority ethnic women (some of whom are also lesbian). Feminism has had much to say about the needs of women care givers; until recently, it has ignored the needs of care receivers, who are frequently denied the right to the kind of family life that other people take for granted. This life may include responsibilities for others, for women and disabled people are not mutually exclusive categories, and many disabled women want to marry and have children, and to be enabled to carry out maternal and household duties rather than being treated as dependent objects of other people's care. From this perspective, childcare and housework are not simply oppressive, as feminist analysis sometimes suggests, but important activities from which disabled women have been excluded (Morris, 1996). Similar arguments apply to elderly people, who frequently support each other rather than simply being on the receiving end of care, but who may require support if they are to remain in their own home (Arber and Ginn, 1990).

The experience of many black women has also been ignored by white feminist critiques of 'the family', which have had little to say about the brutal destruction of traditional kinship patterns under slavery and the ways in which immigration laws today can deny minority ethnic groups the right to family life. The demand by white feminists that women should resist motherhood and domesticity also has little meaning for minority ethnic women who today raise their children in a society which sees them as an unwanted drain on resources (see Roberts, 1995) or who live in communities in which women have always gone out to work because men have never been able to earn enough to support their families. In such communities, staying at home to look after a house and family can seem like a luxurious dream rather than a form of oppression, and the family can be experienced as a sanctuary from the racism of the wider society. Nevertheless, minority ethnic women are as likely as white women to experience exploitation and abuse within the home. Such women are likely to face particular problems, as it is politically very difficult for women in minority groups to report domestic violence to white authorities, or to gain access to a suitable women's refuge; women who have entered the country in order to marry may also risk deportation if they leave their husbands (Corrin, 1996, p. 81).

Policy implications and ongoing debates on the family

Whether it is seen as a burden, a source of fulfilment, or a complex combination of the two, increasing numbers of feminists today recognise the social and economic importance of the work traditionally done by women within the home. Most also agree that the rise in divorce and lone parenthood is unlikely to go into reverse, but reject the claim of right-wing politicians and social commentators that fatherless families are both symptom and cause of the growth of an alienated, crime-ridden, drug-abusing and welfare-dependent 'underclass'. Here most feminists argue both that the link between lone parent families and anti-social behaviour has been exaggerated and that it is a product of poverty and acrimonious split-ups rather than the absence of a male authority figure. In this context, the task is to ensure that lone parents have the resources and support they need to bring up their children.

Although most feminists today do not want to exclude men from family life, a majority probably believe that lone parent and lesbian families can be at least as good as most traditional families, and that the heterosexual nuclear family should therefore not be legally, financially and socially privileged over other forms. For some, this means that lesbians should be entitled to get married, for others it means that marriage as a legal contract should itself be abolished. If, as suggested in Chapter 4, sex ceased to be a legal category, the same legal regulations would apply to same-sex as to heterosexual relationships.

A majority of families are likely to contain men for the foreseeable future. Most feminists can agree that in such families women's caring responsibilities should not force them into personal dependency, that these responsibilities should be shared more equitably with men and that both men and women should be enabled to combine family responsibilities with paid employment. They will also agree that women and children need the full protection of the law from violence within the home and that they should not be trapped in abusive relationships through lack of financial independence.

Disagreement remains, however, on how women's traditional work in the family is to be financially recognised without reinforcing their responsibility for it. Marxist analysis of the economic importance of domestic labour has led some socialist feminists to demand 'wages for housework'. Many critics argue, however, that this will inevitably be interpreted as 'wages for housewives', and that, because any achievable wage rates would be unattractive to men, the campaign reinforces the idea that domestic work is women's responsibility (see the discussion in Tong, 1989, pp. 54–61). Although she says that men should be encouraged to apply for it, similar problems could arise from Melissa Benn's call for a 'carer's income' (Benn, 1998), and from the more widely accepted claim that caring responsibilities should be recognised as a basis for pension entitlements. The idea that a basic 'citizen's income' should be paid to all adults appears a gender-neutral way of ensuring a degree of economic independence for all; however, this fails to distinguish between those who are contributing to society by their caring work and those who are idle, and it could actually weaken women's link with the labour market (see Lister, 1997, pp. 189–90).

Related disagreements stem from the question of whether lone parents (who are usually women) can expect to be provided for financially by their child's absent parent or by the state, or whether they should be required to enter paid employment. Although many feminists support the principle that absent fathers should contribute financially to the upbringing of their own children, others see this as a way of returning women to dependency upon men and reasserting the values of private patriarchy. In Britain, the Child Support Agency, which was set up with the apparently simple aim of making men financially responsible for their own children, soon ran into a host of practical problems, and feminist critics argued that its aim was not to reduce child poverty, but to cut government spending.

International comparisons suggest that a high rate of paid employment is linked to relatively low rates of poverty in lone parent families (Bradshaw *et al.*, 1996), and most feminists would agree that parents who want to work outside the home should be enabled to do so, and that they should not be deterred by the lack of childcare provision or the workings of the benefit system. However, many lone mothers, like many women with husbands, believe that it is in their children's best interests that they do not go out to work. When in 1997 the newly elected Labour government in Britain highlighted paid employment as the key to giving lone parents a stake in society, critics were quick to point out that parenting itself represents both hard work and a commitment to the future of society, and that sending lone mothers out to work was likely to create rather than solve social problems:

> Labour says the family is the most important thing, but it is about to send the head of the most fragile families out to market and its kids to homework clubs and after-school supervision. (Benn, 1997)

132 Feminist Debates

If lone parents are expected to work outside the home rather than be maintained by the state, this has to be conditional upon the availability of good-quality, affordable childcare and reasonably paid employment that is compatible with family responsibilities. If, and it is a big if, these conditions are met, it might seem reasonable to agree with Ruth Lister that lone parents should be required to register for at least part-time work when their youngest child reaches school age (Lister, 1997). Although politicians have not generally made the connection, it might also seem reasonable to say that similarly situated married women also be encouraged to work outside the home, rather than being dependent upon the earnings of their husband.

Such arguments suggest that the provision of care has to be seen as a matter of public as well as private concern and responsibility. Many feminists argue more generally in favour of collectivist policies, based on the belief that society as a whole has in interest in the welfare of all its citizens, including both the providers and receivers of care, and in the upbringing of future generations:

> Women need their independence to be effective as carers. Children need carers who are not second class citizens... childcare has to become an area of public concern, all the time, not just in the last resort'. (New and David, 1995, p. 15)

> Public policy should recognise that the essence of successful family life is neither enforced dependency, not isolated individualism, but interdependence. (Coote *et al.*, 1990, p. 7. For related arguments, see Bubeck, 1995)

Such policies would involve state provision or funding of childcare and the allocation of resources to enable elderly and disabled people both to choose the kind of assistance they want and to provide adequate payment to those who supply it. It would also require legislation to require or enable conditions of employment to be more flexible and more readily combined with caring responsibilities.

This kind of thinking has gone furthest in the Scandinavian nations. Although it is less in tune with the more individualistic assumptions of American and British politics, it is increasingly accepted by a number of liberal activists, including the veteran feminist campaigner Betty Friedan, who now argues that a 'new vision' of family and community must take precedence over short-term profit and individual gain (Friedan, 1997). From 1997, the promise of the British Labour government to develop a national childcare strategy also represented an important recognition that this is not simply a private responsibility. Socialist critics, however, argue that good, affordable childcare for all who need it is unlikely to be provided in an economy based on the profit motive and in which governments are unwilling to use the tax system to produce a meaningful redistribution of resources.

For some feminists, collective responsibility for caring can also be met through informal community and friendship networks, and through the development of more fluid and open family forms which do not see children as the property or exclusive responsibility of their parents. Such ideas can be traced back to 19th-century socialist feminist thought. Today, they are in part a response to the complex new forms of extended family produced in societies where marriage for life is no longer the norm, and where a child can have several sets of grandparents as well as a host of step-brothers and sisters. They have also been developed in recent black feminist writing. A number of African-American and Afro-Caribbean feminists argue that their communities can provide a model for an open and non-patriarchal family form, in which women are central both as nurturers and providers, and 'mothering' is shared by wider family and friendship groups, rather than being the exclusive responsibility of the blood mother. Far from seeing black lone mothers as aberrant, this perspective can see it as a sign of female strength, so that 'It may be in the lives of those most outcast by patriarchy that we will catch a glimpse of liberated motherhood' (Roberts, 1995, p. 562).

Despite such celebration of female strength, there is today an increasingly widespread feminist consensus that society's caring needs should not simply be shifted from individual women to the state or the extended family group, but that they should be redistributed between women and men. Such ideas are now influencing public policy. Educational and employment policies in Scandinavia have for many years been committed to increasing men's domestic role, and in 1992 a European Community Recommendation on childcare included more equal parenting as an aim. Opinion polls also suggest that most men as well as most women now believe that childcare and household tasks should be more or less equally shared. As we have seen, however, changes in actual behaviour are more apparent than real, and although men's 'help' may have increased, the primary responsibility for the family remains, in general, firmly with women. To some extent, this is a product of employment conditions which, as we shall see in the following sections, can make it difficult for men to increase their contribution within the home. The Scandinavian experience suggests however that working arrangements cannot entirely account for men's continued reluctance to share day-to-day caring responsibilities, for they have been much slower than women workers to take advantage of family leave entitlements and flexible working arrangements and still do less than their fair share of domestic and caring work.

According to the British sociologist Catherine Hakim, men's failure to contribute more in the home reflects a continuing acceptance of the traditional gender division of labour by most women as well as by most men (Hakim, 1996). Others point to the fragile nature of gender identity, arguing that this has to be constantly reasserted through appropriate action, so that people are in effect making statements about their gender at the same time as performing other tasks: 'Her doing the laundry and his fixing the light switch not only produces clean clothes and a lit room, they also produce a reaffirmation of gender roles' (Blumberg, 1991, p. 20. See also West and Zimmerman, 1991). From this perspective, men's gender identity is under threat if they take on household or caring roles: 'Caring as an activity, disposition, and attitude forms a central part of probably all cultural conceptions of femininity and is virtually absent from or even incompatible with, conceptions of masculinity' (Bubeck, 1995, p. 160). Other writers argue that the problem has been compounded by some feminists' devaluation of women's work: given that they have stressed the tedium and frustration rather than the joy and fulfilment that can be part of their traditional role, it is unsurprising that men have been unwilling to participate more in the home (see Burgess, 1997).

This does not mean that changes in gender roles are impossible, or that men are genetically programmed to be unable to see dust or operate washing machines. It does, however, seem likely that changes in men's behaviour are likely to be slower and more difficult than many earlier feminists thought, and that although changes in employment practices are a necessary precondition for men's increased domestic role, they are not sufficient. In this context, feminist demands for greater state support for women's family responsibilities is not letting men off the hook but, like family-friendly employment practices, an essential starting-point if their own labour market participation is to be on reasonable terms.

Paid employment

Recent changes

In the last few decades, women have entered the paid labour market in unprecedented numbers, and in most western nations they are now well over 40 per cent of the workforce. Although some women have always worked outside the home, they have only gradually won the right to do so on the same terms as men. Earlier restrictions on women's right to education and entry into the professions were dropped from the late 19th century onwards and were followed by the abolition of the marriage bar, which had formerly excluded married women from many occupations. Today, women in most western nations have a right to employment which is backed up by laws against sex discrimination and by the provision of maternity leave. They are increasingly well educated in comparison with men, few give up employment when they marry, and in recent years it has become increasingly normal for women to remain active in the workforce when their children are small.

Increasingly, politicians and policy-makers are working on the assumption that the employment of women is both good for the economy and desirable in itself, and few serious politicians would now publicly state that a woman's place is in the home. This reflects a clear shift in public opinion on the employment of women. In 1989, the British journal *Social Trends* described this as a rare case of a radical change in attitudes, reporting that the numbers of people thinking that mothers of children under five should stay at home had fallen from nearly 80 per cent in 1965 to less than 50 per cent in 1987, and that support for other groups of working women was even greater.

Such changes are not simply a result of feminist pressure, but also reflect structural changes in the economies of western nations, which have seen a shift from manufacturing to service industries which has involved a loss of traditional male jobs and an increase in those traditionally done by women. It is also clear that, as in the past, many women work outside the home through economic necessity rather than because they want to.

The gendered labour market

Although women are now a major and permanent part of the workforce, their situation differs in many ways from that of men. First, their employment is much more likely to be part-time. In the United States, about a fifth of women workers but only seven out of every 100 men are in part-time employment; in many European countries, including Britain and Sweden, the rate of part-time employment rises to around 40 per cent of women workers, while remaining at 10 per cent or less for men. Although part-time workers in most nations have gradually won most of the legal rights and protections now held by full-time workers, their conditions of employment are generally inferior and often precarious, with lower wage rates and poor promotion and training opportunities.

Full-time women employees also work on average fewer hours than men. British men work the longest hours in Europe: by the mid-1990s, a quarter of British male employees worked for over 48 hours a week (an average increase of an hour since the mid-1980s). In the United States, the working week is even longer; as in Britain, but contrary to trends in most western nations, this has increased in recent years. In Sweden, in contrast, working fewer than 35 hours a week is becoming increasingly normal for both men and women.

The right of workers to take time out of employment for family reasons also varies widely. At one extreme, the United States has no statutory provision for maternity leave and a very restricted right to 12 weeks' unpaid parental leave on the arrival of a new baby, which is taken up by less than 4 per cent of workers (see Chapter 4). At the other extreme, in addition to maternity and paternity leave, all Swedish parents are entitled to 18 months' parental leave, of which the first 360 days is paid at 90 per cent of earnings. Part of this is non-transferable between parents, and there is a take-up rate of 78 and 90 per cent by male and female workers respectively. All families are also entitled to 120 days' leave a year for each child under 12, to be used if either the child or the child's normal carer is ill. British entitlements compare unfavourably with most other European Union countries. After its election in 1997, the Labour government accepted European measures to restrict compulsory working hours and to enable men to take unpaid paternity leave; it did not, however, propose the more radical changes in conditions of employment that some senior Labour women had earlier demanded (see, in particular, Harriet Harman's *The Century Gap*, 1993).

Despite equal opportunities policies in education and employment, all labour markets are highly segregated on gender lines. Horizontal division into male and female employment sectors (with women concentrated in caring, service and clerical work and in the public sector, and men in manufacturing and industry and in the private sector) has historically been combined with vertical segregation, whereby senior positions have been almost exclusively held by men and female employees have been concentrated in low-status, poorly paid jobs.

In recent years, there have been some changes. The male monopoly of trades and professions such as plumbing and engineering is no longer absolute, and some men are entering female areas of employment, such as nursing and secretarial work. There has also been a steady movement of women into management and administration, and a few women have had high-profile success at the highest level. However, the high publicity attracted to some individual cases disguises the extent to which earlier patterns continue. Many areas of employment remain almost exclusively single sex, and women are still massively over-represented in low-paid, low-status jobs and under-represented in higher posts. Even in the United States, where the movement of women into high-status occupations has been particularly marked, it is very difficult for women to reach the most senior positions. Many now identify the 'glass ceiling' effect – that is, the invisible but effective barrier which prevents women from moving beyond a certain point on the promotion ladder: in March 1995, the Glass Ceiling Commission set up by the Senate leader Robert Dole reported that white males continued to hold 95 per cent of senior management jobs, although they were less than 30 per cent of the workforce (*Guardian*, 17 March 1995). The general pattern is found even in areas traditionally dominated by women; for example in Britain, although there are over four times more female than male teachers in primary schools, slightly more men than women are *head*teachers (Equal Opportunities Commission, 1996). For minority ethnic group managers, the barriers are even greater, and a recent study argued that they face a *concrete* rather than a glass ceiling (Davidson, 1997).

Although the gap has generally narrowed over the past 30 years, women workers continue to earn significantly less than men. The gender gap in pay is particularly high in the United States, where full-time women workers earn only about 70 per cent of the pay of full-time men. In Britain the gap for full-time workers had fallen to 20 per cent by the mid-1990s, but the hourly rate for part-time women workers was only 62 per cent of that of full-time men; the lowest rates of all are found among homeworkers. In most other European countries, however, earnings are generally more equal: the gender gap is lowest in Sweden, where the hourly wage differences between female and male workers is about 10 per cent (Dulk *et al.*, 1996).

Frustration with workplace culture and a lack of career prospects has led some ambitious women to self-employment. Others see this as an escape route from poverty, or as a way of reconciling work with domestic commitments. However, self-employed women continue to face discrimination, particularly from financial institutions, and they are further disadvantaged by lack of training and access to advice and support systems; the barriers are most acute for those attempting to set up all-women co-operatives. In contrast to self-employed men who can frequently call upon the unpaid labour of family members, self-employed women workers are unlikely to have such support, and frequently have to juggle their work with their domestic responsibilities. Despite an increase in their numbers, they remain a minority of the self-employed: in Britain, for example, by 1996 they were only 24 per cent of all self-employed workers (Sly *et al.*, 1997).

Labour markets are structured not only by gender but also by class and frequently by race. The disproportionately high rate of employment among lone parents in most European nations suggests that poverty drives many such women into the labour market. In Britain, however, lone mothers in general are less likely to be in employment than their married counterparts; many commentators attribute this to the lack of childcare and the workings of the benefit system. In general, minority ethnic women have a disadvantaged workplace situation compared to majority group women. Disabled people also face a lack of understanding and discrimination in a labour market which sees them as expensive to employ and underestimates the contributions which they can make. As discussed in Chapters 2 and 3, these different structures of inequality can combine to produce complex interactive rather than simply cumulative effects. For example, although African-American and Afro-Caribbean women in the United States and Britain are disadvantaged in the employment market by both their gender and their race, they are particularly likely to be highly educated and in full-time rather than part-time employment, even when they are lone mothers.

It is clear that in general women and men have a different relationship to the labour market, and that in many ways women appear to be disadvantaged. It is also clear that differences are both interconnected to each other and related to women's family situation. Most feminists would agree that the causal relationships involved are not inevitable and that they should be challenged; these relationships are however highly complex.

Feminist perspectives on employment

As we have seen, liberal feminists have insisted that women should have the same employment rights and opportunities as men, and they have tended to see employment as a source of fulfilment and an escape route from the drudgery and confinement of family life. Today, they argue both that anti-discrimination legislation must be improved and more rigorously enforced and that it is up to individual women to make the most of their opportunities. This perspective is well summed up in a self-help book for women:

> This book is all about what you can do to help yourself. It is not about what your family should do for you, what the government, your partner, your manager, or your organisation should do for you. It's about you accepting the responsibility for yourself, realising that no-one hands you life on a plate... and looking the world in the eye, believing that 'I can do this'. (Willis and Daisley, 1990, p. 2)

Although it has tended to devalue women's family role, liberalism's individualistic approach also leads it to see women's concentration in part-time employment as a freely chosen solution to the problem of balancing work and family responsibilities. Writing in this tradition, Catherine Hakim has argued that, contrary to feminist 'mythology', women's failure to achieve equality in the workplace is not evidence of discrimination but of a lack of commitment to their employment by women who 'choose to spend a part of their life producing children and rearing them, and they prefer to be supported by someone else when they are doing it, either a husband or the state' (Hakim, 1996, p. 179).

Socialist, radical and black critics have accused liberal feminists of holding narrow and class-based assumptions which forget that in capitalist class society only a minority can be successful and that in reality many women are forced to choose between economic dependency within marriage and poverty outside it, or between a career and a family (while men can reasonably expect both). They argue that, rather than being a source of prestige and fulfilment, most employment involves mindless drudgery and exploitation, and that a preoccupation with women's right to a career reflects the interests of privileged white women only. Such criticisms meant that the kinds of career opportunities that by the late 1960s were opening up for educated young women seemed to many left-wing feminists to represent a sell-out to capitalist values; from this perspective, the pursuit of a successful career was equated with becoming an exploiter of other people's labour, and therefore rejected.

Although it has never advocated the individualistic pursuit of a career, the orthodox Marxist position has, however, held that the entry of working-class women into the paid labour force is progressive, as it represents a strengthening of the ranks of the working class in the forthcoming battle against capitalism. Later socialist feminist thinking has supported this, but argues that women's employment is also important in the struggle against patriarchy. Alison Jaggar, for example, says that 'When women workers achieve a living wage, they are not just workers winning a concession from capitalism, they are also women winning economic independence from men' (Jaggar, 1983, p. 328). This suggests that part-time employment may not be the way forward for women, for it is unlikely to provide such independence or to require a radical reassessment of traditional family roles, so that 'Being "able" to engage in a combination of exploitative part-time employment and unpaid homework is a dubious privilege' (Smith, 1987, p. 247).

Despite lip-service to women's need for economic independence, trade unions have a long history of neglecting women's employment interests in favour of defending the male 'family wage', through which a man could earn enough to maintain a wife and children. Some have been overtly hostile to the articulation of women's perspectives. Nevertheless, many feminists have argued that trade union activity can be the key to improving women's employment situation, both in terms of their specific needs and as part of a class movement to improve conditions for all workers; they have therefore worked to encourage women to become active members and to push for feminist demands within the movement.

Although the radical feminist analysis points to the importance of financial independence for women, it does not see employment as an easy route to liberation, for it argues that patriarchal power is exercised in the workplace as well as in the home, and that it is exercised not only by employers but also by the male-dominated trade union movement. From this perspective, women's concentration in low-waged, low-status jobs is not an accident, or the result of individual acts of discrimination, or of women's lack of qualifications or ability. Rather, it reflects the structured inequalities of a system in which men's values and priorities are systematically privileged over women's, and in which women's disadvantaged workplace situation helps maintain patriarchy in the home.

For some radical feminists, sexual harassment, defined as unwanted sexual behaviour and attention, provides the clearest and most direct manifestation of male power over women in the workplace. In its most overt form, sexual harassment can represent a collective attempt by men to intimidate women and secure their continued exclusion from areas of employment such as the armed forces, or to resist their promotion. It can take the form of initiation rituals, sexual comments or the display of nude pictures which help create a sexualised working environment. Although some women may see this as harmless fun, or even as enjoyable, others may feel uncomfortable, vulnerable and intimidated and resent being treated as sex objects rather than co-workers. Sexual harassment can also take a more individualised form, particularly when men in authority use their position to subject female subordinates to unwanted sexual attention or to coerce them into sexual activity. Surveys consistently find that such behaviour is experienced by at least one in three women, and some radical feminists argue that this demonstrates the centrality of sexual coercion to the oppression of women, and the political nature of apparently individual experiences. Other feminists, however, claim that the problem is exaggerated, and that women must stop seeing themselves as sexually passive victims (for further discussion, see Chapter 7).

The more general argument that men's values and priorities must be questioned, and that they are the basis for deep-seated discrimination against women now extends well beyond radical feminist circles. Although discrimination is still sometimes overt, conscious and deliberate it is today often much more subtle, and can arise even when equal opportunities policies and objective selection and promotion procedures appear to be in place.

Ann Phillips and Barbara Taylor have argued that rather than being objective and neutral, 'skill' is frequently an ideological category, arising from the struggle of men to maintain their dominance in the sexual hierarchy (Phillips and Taylor, 1986). This means that attributes traditionally associated with men, such as strength, mechanical knowledge or firm leadership are more positively valued and rewarded than the attributes traditionally associated with women such as dexterity, childrearing experience or a conciliatory and cooperative managerial style. Moreover, because the emotional, nurturing and caring work which women perform in the workplace is often very similar to their unpaid domestic activities, it has been undervalued and taken for granted as part of women's natural attributes, rather than recognised as a skilled and valuable workplace contribution. The traditional secretary–boss relationship provides perhaps the clearest example of this, with the former expected to smooth ruffled feathers, look decorative and make the tea as well as effectively running an office, briefing her boss, keeping track of his appointments and reminding him of his wife's birthday (see also the discussion in Chapter 4).

Subconscious discrimination can also arise from a desire to appoint or promote someone who will fit in with the existing working environment, an assumption that a successful candidate will closely resemble the previous office holder and an inability to see women as potential candidates for high office. Discrimination can also arise from the unnecessary use of age, an unbroken employment record and geographical mobility as selection criteria, and from the use of informal networks rather than open advertisements in selection processes. Women with family responsibilities are further disadvantaged by working practices which equate commitment with long hours and see career breaks or part-time working as barriers to promotion. Unsurprisingly, those women who do succeed in reaching top positions are much less likely than their male colleagues either to be married or to have children.

The radical feminist claim that women's workplace situation both reflects and maintains their subordination within the home is also increasingly widely accepted by other feminists. Because many women's earnings are not sufficient to provide them with economic independence they remain at least partially dependent on their male partner for economic survival, and most feminists agree that such personal dependency is not compatible with the status of an adult citizen. Such dependency clearly reduces women's 'negotiating power' within the family and their ability either to leave an abusive relationship or to insist that family responsibilities are more equally shared. This in turn means that they continue to enter the labour market on terms very different from those experienced by men. Challenging women's workplace situation is therefore integrally bound up with changes to the traditional division of labour within the home.

Policy implications and ongoing debates on paid employment

Although a few high-flying women insist that they want no concessions, today an increasing number of feminists agree that employment on the same terms as men is neither a viable nor a desirable goal for women, so long as those terms themselves remain unchanged. Many therefore argue that women should not be required to slot themselves into existing practices, but that a much more radical transformation of working patterns and values is required. Key aspects of this would clearly be the kind of parental and family leave provisions which already exist in Sweden and a general reduction in working hours.

Such changes, along with provision or financial support for childcare, can be seen as forms of positive action to improve the competitive situation of women in the workplace. More direct forms of positive action include training or education aimed at providing women with the kinds of marketable skills which they have traditionally lacked (for example, single-sex science lessons in schools, or courses for women returners), or advertising vacancies in places or publications where women are most likely to see them. They can also include a standardisation of selection and promotion procedures to allow both for a more formal assessment of 'merit' and a recognition of qualities, such as interpersonal skills, that have been typically associated with women.

Because existing bias is often so widespread as to be invisible, and because dominant liberal assumptions see discrimination in terms of individual behaviour rather than structural inequality, some critics see such measures as unfair discrimination against men. Even more opposition has been generated by attempts to introduce formal gender quotas in appointments procedures. Contrary to popular mythology, neither the establishment of rigid gender quotas nor the selection of female or minority group candidates who are less well qualified than white men is now legal in either the United States or Britain. Although feminist supporters of quotas have generally seen them as a way of questioning the nature of these qualifications, they have been widely opposed as unfair, preferential treatment. Today, many feminists feel that, even if quotas are justified, the high risk of backlash makes them politically counter-productive (see the discussion in Chapters 4 and 5).

Because so many are badly paid, more women than men benefit from measures to introduce or raise minimum wage rates. Without wider changes, however, paying all women a decent wage can cause problems for others whose earnings barely meet their childcare costs; it also causes problems if disabled people have to pay their carers more without any increase in their own resources. This does not mean that the current low pay of many women is either necessary or defensible. It does, however, show the complex implications of change, and the need for a reassessment of resources and responsibilities, so that individual women workers are not expected to bear the full cost of childcare without help from their partner or the state and the needs of disabled people are balanced against those of their paid and unpaid carers.

If feminist demands for better employment conditions are to have any chance of success, women will have to work through trade unions and political parties rather than negotiating on an individual basis. In recent years, feminist pressures and the need to attract new members have combined to make unions more open to feminist issues than in the past, and female membership of unions has generally increased. Unions themselves have, however, declined in economic and political importance, and feminist demands can appear both expensive and incompatible with the market-led thinking which has become increasingly dominant in western democracies. Nevertheless, the improved political representation of women and the recognition of their voting power discussed in Chapter 5 have helped ensure that their employment needs are at last beginning to be recognised; in Scandinavia, women's high political presence means that earlier gains can be built upon or defended even at times of economic retrenchment.

Conclusions: towards a better balance in the interests of all

In the past, 'family-friendly' employment practices have been seen as concessions for women workers with family responsibilities. The preceding discussion suggests, however, both that such women should be seen as 'normal' workers and that employment policies should challenge rather than accommodate traditional family roles by enabling and encouraging male workers to contribute more in the home. This would also make it easier for 'absent fathers' to maintain regular contact with their children after separation or divorce. The breakdown of the worker/carer distinction would help develop a wider and more realistic awareness of both the pleasures and the difficulties of everyday parenting. While recognising that family structures are likely to be more varied and fluid than in the past, it would also enable them to be freely chosen rather than entered into or endured through economic necessity.

It now seems that the chief obstacle to employment equality is not that women currently spend a significant part of their lives in activities outside the workplace, but that men do not. It is therefore men's 'domestic absenteeism' that has to be problematised, rather than women's inability to work the kind of hours that would give them financial independence. As Cynthia Cockburn has argued: 'A 45-hour week, a 48-week year and a 50-year working life cannot be sustained by both sexes. It should be worked by neither' (Cockburn, 1991, p. 104). Because it would enable women to compete in the labour market on reasonable terms and men to increase their family role, Catherine Marsh has suggested that reducing the hours worked by British men might be 'the single most effective means of promoting equality in the workplace' (Marsh, 1991a, p. x).

Neither good-quality childcare that all parents can afford nor family-friendly workplaces will be produced by market forces alone, but will require both legislation and government expenditure. As such, they require a shift from individualistic to collectivist approaches. However, it seems likely that the cost of family leave schemes and a reduction in the working week have been exaggerated in an environment in which 'presenteeism' (being seen to be at work) is frequently a cultural rather than a practical requirement. The intuitive belief that workers will be more efficient if their hours are shorter and they are less tired is supported by British experience during the 1983–4 coal dispute, when productivity did not go down despite industry being put on a three-day week. If the introduction of parental leave or a reduction in working hours is accompanied by an increase in numbers employed, the costs of unemployment benefits will also fall; a recent international comparison of parental leave schemes therefore concluded that the costs for government are 'surprisingly low' (Wilkinson, 1997, p. 17). If the social costs of unemployment are also considered, a more equal distribution of employment appears even more attractive.

Swedish experience suggests that women will initially take more advantage than men of family-friendly employment policies, and that many men will continue to behave as if married to a full-time housewife. However, some recent research suggests that this is at last beginning to change, and that a new model of a more democratic family may be evolving in Sweden (see Wilkinson, 1997). As discussed in Chapter 5, it seems that the old vicious circle, whereby women's domestic responsibilities prevented them from competing effectively with men in politics or employment, and their lack of political voice or economic independence prevented them from challenging conditions of family life, is at last beginning to be converted into a virtuous circle of cumulative and progressive change.

Meanwhile, it is becoming increasingly clear that the financial and long-term social costs of traditional working patterns in the United States and Britain are unacceptably high. Earlier class divisions among women are becoming more acute, as dual career couples can afford to buy domestic support while many lone mothers or those whose partner is unemployed or badly paid are bringing up children in poverty. While the majority of women attempt with various degrees of success to juggle their responsibilities, a significant minority of career-minded women are neither marrying nor have children, while those who spend their lives caring for others are often neither adequately paid nor properly valued. Overwork and inflexible hours contribute to ill-health, alcohol abuse, mental illness and family break-up (Walker, 1995); when they are combined with a lack of good quality, affordable childcare, they can also contribute to the neglect of children's welfare and educational needs and a rise in juvenile crime. They also make it increasingly difficult for people to engage in any kind of voluntary or community activity, and Arlie Hochschild has argued that in the United States the expectation that women and men work increasingly long hours 'is leading us toward not only the parent-free home, but also the participation-free civic society and the citizen-free democracy' (Hochschild, 1997, p. 243). From this perspective, changes in employment practices and family life are not feminist luxuries but central political demands.

During the mid-1980s, this chapter would probably not have appeared in a book on feminist debates. The campaign for abortion rights could then be described as 'almost the definitive issue of contemporary feminism' (Randall, 1987, p. 263), and the one thing that appeared to unite feminists was the belief that women have a right and a need to control their own fertility.

However, such feminist agreement had not always existed, and it was to prove more apparent than real. Many late 19th- and early 20th-century feminists had opposed birth control because they saw it as a male-led ploy to facilitate the sexual exploitation of women; others feared that it would be used coercively to restrict the size of the working class or other 'undesirable' social groups. By the 1980s similar fears were again being expressed. Earlier concerns about sexual exploitation were repeated by radical feminists. Black and/or disabled women and lesbians argued that they were denied the right to *have* children: they claimed that they were coerced into abortion, sterilisation and the use of long-term contraceptives with unpleasant side-effects, and that they were refused access to fertility treatment. For such women, feminism's focus on abortion rights reflected its preoccupation with the needs of heterosexual, able-bodied, white women and its lack of sensitivity to the interests of 'other' women.

These arguments did not, however, disrupt the basic claim that women themselves, rather than male politicians, lawyers, religious leaders and doctors should decide what they could or could not do with their own bodies. Many feminists in all groups therefore agreed both that abortion should be available to women who wanted it, and that all women were entitled to have children. They also agreed that women should be able to choose where and how to give birth, and that doctors should not intervene in the birth process without their informed consent. New perspectives could therefore be combined with earlier feminist demands by replacing the narrow call for 'abortion on demand' with the broader claim for 'reproductive rights' or 'a woman's right to choose'.

Recently, however, a number of more deep-seated disagreements and debates have emerged among feminists. Feminists are divided over whether developments in reproductive technology, infertility treatment and the use of 'surrogate mothers' are to be welcomed as an extension of choice or opposed as new forms of patriarchal control and exploitation. Many continue to insist that abortion must be seen as an absolute right, and that to concede otherwise is to risk losing the limited gains that have recently been won. Others, however, are expressing reservations about abortion, trying to find common ground with some of those who oppose it, or even arguing that it is possible to be a feminist without supporting abortion rights. These disagreements are linked to theoretical disputes about whether free choice is possible in a patriarchal, capitalist society and whether feminists demands should be expressed in terms of 'rights' at all.

This chapter begins with a brief outline of the current situation, focusing on the United States and mainland Britain. It then analyses the ways in which competing interpretations of 'rights' claims have affected feminist thinking on reproductive issues and links this to the above debates, particularly those on abortion. It argues that this analysis is not simply of academic interest, but has practical implications for the conduct of feminist campaigns.

The situation today

Contraception and abortion

In most western democracies during the 1960s and 70s, contraception became available to women who wanted it and abortion laws were liberalised. There was, however, no uniform pattern, and both the circumstances and the outcome of these changes varied widely.

In the United States, access to both contraception and abortion has been legally defended as part of a constitutional right to *privacy*. Thus in 1972 the Supreme Court defended the right of single people to buy contraceptives, because:

If the right of privacy means anything, it is the right of the individual, married or single, to be free of unwarranted governmental intrusion into matters so fundamentally affecting a person as the decision whether or not to beget a child. (quoted in Sapiro, 1990, p. 309)

A year later, the famous 1973 *Roe* v. *Wade* Supreme Court ruling said that in the first trimester abortion was a private matter between a woman and her doctor which should not be subject to state regulation; it did, however, restrict women's right to abortion during the later stages of pregnancy. Since then, abortion has become a major and explosive issue in mainstream political life. Large and powerful 'pro-choice' and 'pro-life' groups have become important players in electoral and legislative processes at local, state and federal levels, and some commentators claim that abortion was the decisive factor in the 1992 presidential election (see O'Connor, 1996, p. 148).

The resulting election of Bill Clinton, the pro-choice candidate, seemed to signal a major shift from the policies of the Reagan–Bush years. During the 1980s, anti-abortionists had won significant successes, as many states introduced a series of restrictive rulings, and access to state funds and to information was steadily restricted. The related 'fetal rights' movement attempted to regulate the behaviour of pregnant women, including their use of legal drugs, and to justify medical intervention against a woman's wishes. Intimidatory tactics by some 'pro-life' groups also forced the closure of some abortion clinics and deterred women from attending: between 1977 and 1995 the use of violence by anti-abortionists included 5 murders, 11 attempted murders, 40 bombings, 100 arson attacks and hundreds of acts of vandalism (O'Connor, 1996). Clinton's victory and subsequent legislative changes and judicial decisions have, however, helped protect the principle of free choice.

Despite the restrictions, the abortion rate has been consistently higher in the United States than in most western nations: Craig and O'Brien cite figures suggesting that around 20 per cent of American women of reproductive age have had an abortion, and Pollitt says that by the time they reach the menopause this figure will have risen to 46 per cent. As in Britain, fewer than 1 per cent of abortions are carried out after 20 weeks of pregnancy (Craig and O'Brien, 1993, p. 251; Pollitt, 1995, p. 13).

While some women in the United States have difficulty in obtaining contraceptive services and abortion, others have been 'encouraged' to be sterilised or injected with the long-term contraceptive Depo Provera. This reflects official concern about the growth of a welfare-dependent 'under-class', particularly among African-Americans, which has led some states to deny additional aid to mothers who become pregnant while on welfare. The courts have also ruled that a doctor can refuse to treat pregnant Medicaid patients unless they are sterilised, and sterilisation is the only publicly funded form of birth control that is readily available.

Although such demographic policies have not gone so far in Britain, there is evidence that coercive sterilisation and contraceptive practices have been imposed on some poor and/or minority ethnic women. Contraception is, however, generally more freely available in Britain than in the United States; although services have been affected by recent funding cuts, free contraceptive advice and information have since the mid-1970s been available on the National Health Service.

The basis of the present British law on abortion was established by the 1967 Abortion Act. This permitted women to have a legal termination if two doctors believed that continuing the pregnancy would involve greater risk to the woman's life, or to the physical or mental health of the woman or her existing children, than a termination, or that there was a substantial risk that the baby would be born with a serious disability. During the 1970s and 80s, a series of attempts were made to restrict the circumstances in which abortion could be legally performed. These produced huge counter-demonstrations by feminists, and none passed the House of Commons. Although the 1967 Act did not specify a time limit, it was generally understood to permit abortions up to 28 weeks; the 1990 Human Fertilisation and Embryology Act reduced this to 24 weeks, unless there was a risk of death or permanent injury to the woman, or of an abnormality which would lead to the birth of a seriously disabled child.

In practice, British law has generally been interpreted quite liberally to allow abortions to most women who want them. The availability of National Health Service abortions has, however, always varied from one part of the country to another, and funding cuts during the 1980s and 90s have produced delays and lack of information which effectively limit the options of women unable to afford private provision. In 1971, 12 per cent of pregnancies were legally terminated; by the late 1980s this had risen to around 20 per cent;

despite some short-term fluctuations (due partly to scares about the safety of the contraceptive pill) this pattern continued into the 1990s. Historical and international comparisons suggest that abortion legislation bears little relation to the numbers of abortions actually carried out, which may have more to do with contraceptive knowledge and availability, attitudes to single motherhood and the costs of having a baby and looking after a family. Thus in Britain in 1939, when a pregnancy could only be legally terminated to save the mother's life, the Birkett Committee estimated that 16–20 per cent of pregnancies ended in abortion, a rate similar to that found today (O'Donovan, 1985a). The Republic of Ireland has the most restrictive legislation in the western world and in the Netherlands abortion is readily available, but proportionately as many Irish women have abortions in England as Dutch women do in the Netherlands (Ketting and Praag, 1986). The illegality of abortion has not prevented Brazil from becoming the country where one tenth of the world's abortions take place (*Guardian*, 11 August 1992); a total ban on abortion in Romania in the late 1980s was accompanied by an abortion rate four times higher than birth rate (see Chapter 3). The damage done to the status and health of women who undergo illegal abortions under unsafe conditions is clearly enormous; indeed, the World Health Organisation has estimated that it produces the death of around 200,000 women a year (Jacobson, 1994, p. 298). The availability of legal abortion would prevent many of these deaths; it would not necessarily increase the number of abortions actually performed.

Reproductive technology, fertility treatment and surrogacy

Developments in scientific knowledge have transformed both our perception of pregnancy and the meaning of motherhood. Ultrasound images encourage us to see the fetus as an autonomous person, and the image of it as a kind of thumb-sucking astronaut, independent but vulnerable, floating in the space of its mother's womb is now deeply embedded in popular consciousness (Petchesky, 1990, p. xiv). Ante-natal tests also enable us to discover many of the characteristics of a fetus, including its sex and the likelihood of disability; as genetics and ante-natal screening continue to progress, the possibility of the 'designer baby' is moving from

Reproduction 153

science fiction into the real world (for a full discussion of the range of ante-natal test available, see Zaleweski, 1996).

Some of the ante-natal tests routinely offered to women in western nations involve danger to the health of the mother and/or her fetus. There is, however, evidence that women are not always fully informed of the risks and that pressure is sometimes put on women both to take the tests and to undergo abortion if the outcome is 'unfavourable' (Rowland, 1992; Zaleweski, 1996; *Guardian*, 8 February 1997). Concerns have also been raised by western feminists that knowledge gained through ante-natal tests could be used to abort female fetuses. There is no evidence that this has occurred on a significant scale in the United States or Europe, and the sex of a fetus is not considered to provide legal grounds for abortion in Britain, unless there is a risk of sex-linked disease. In India, however, selective abortion of female fetuses has been widespread and with dramatic results: according to a report by the United Nations Children's Fund in 1995, it has meant that 50 million girls and women are missing from India's population. Sex selection tests are now banned, but the practice seems to be continuing (Narasimham, 1993; *Guardian*, 20 November 1995, 11 January 1996).

Other reproductive technologies which a generation ago would have seemed like science fiction are now well established. Perhaps the most important of these is *in vitro* fertilisation (IVF), through which an extracted egg is fertilised with sperm before being placed in the womb. The first such 'test tube baby' was born in Britain in 1978. IVF is particularly useful for women who have blocked fallopian tubes, or whose partner has a low sperm count. It also enables women to become pregnant without having sex with men, as does artificial insemination with donor sperm (AID). Perhaps even more controversially, IVF opens up the possibility of new forms of surrogate motherhood. The possibility of one woman bearing a child and giving it to another has always existed; it is now possible for the child she bears to be the product of an embryo conceived outside the womb using both the sperm and the egg of the adoptive parents: in such a case the birth mother and the genetic mother are two separate women.

Possible future developments in reproductive technology include cloning, the growth to term of a fetus outside the womb, and techniques to enable men to bear children (for a critical discussion of these, see Rowland, 1992).

Policy-makers have responded to these developments in a number of ways. In general, however, control over reproductive decisions has not been given to women, whose access to fertility treatment is limited by its expense and screened by a range of statutory bodies and voluntary restrictions. These restrictions are usually based on the perceived interests of the child, as in Britain where the 1990 Human Fertilisation and Embryology Act stated that 'A woman shall not be provided with treatment services unless account has been taken of the welfare of any child who may be born as a result of the treatment, including the need of that child for a father' (quoted in Millns, 1996, p. 165). Although this does not categorically rule out the possibility of fertility treatment to single women or lesbians, it makes it less likely. Many nations also recommend age restrictions on treating potential mothers. Older British women have, however, travelled for treatment to Italy, where no such limits are in force, and in 1997 a woman in California and another in Britain gave birth at the ages of 63 and 61 respectively, after lying to fertility clinics about their age. Although direct comparisons are not available, it is here worth noting that in 1997 the journal of the National Childbirth Trust reported that one third of the men who father children in Britain each year are over 45 (*Independent on Sunday*, 25 May 1997).

Commercial surrogacy is permitted in some parts of the United States. The legal status of such agreements is, however, highly contested, and disputes have arisen over parental rights when a birth mother has changed her mind and refused to surrender the child. In Britain, commercial surrogacy is illegal, although birth mothers may be paid 'reasonable' expenses. It is also unlawful for a woman to sell her eggs, although women may be offered priority in fertility treatment as a form of payment in kind. Men are, however, paid for sperm donation. British law defines the parents of a child as the woman who gives birth to it and her partner; this means that egg and sperm donors (that is, the genetic parents) have no legal rights and obligations, even if a surrogacy agreement has been signed (Millns, 1996).

Feminists have reacted to all of these developments in a number of different and frequently competing ways. These differences are partly a product of the different theoretical approaches that were discussed in Chapter 2. The following sections outline the implications of these for reproductive rights before examining the claim that the public debate on abortion has been conducted on inappropriate terms, which have alienated potential supporters of feminist goals.

Competing perspectives on 'a woman's right to choose'

Liberal feminism

Liberal principles have been used to claim reproductive rights for women on the grounds that these are a necessary precondition for self-determination and autonomy: if women are to compete with men in the labour market and act as citizens, they must first be enabled to control their own fertility. This right is also defended as a straightforward extension of the basic liberal principle that individuals are entitled to do what they want with their own bodies and live their lives free from unnecessary state intervention. To refuse to allow a woman to make her own reproductive choices is, therefore, a violation of her right to privacy and freedom.

According to liberal theory, adult citizens have rights because they are intelligent beings capable of making rational decisions. This implies that because a fetus lacks such qualities it can have no 'right to life' which might qualify a woman's right to expel it from her womb. Thus Mary Ann Warren has used liberal principles to argue that 'in the relevant respects, a fetus, even a fully evolved one, is considerably less person-like than the average fish', and that a woman's right to terminate her pregnancy is therefore absolute (Warren, 1991, p. 114).

A liberal position would therefore seem to imply that terminating a pregnancy has no more moral significance than having a haircut, and that a pregnant woman has the same right to smoke, drink alcohol or use legal drugs as any other adult. From a liberal perspective, there also seems to be no reason why a woman should not choose to abort a fetus of the 'wrong' sex, although she should not be pressurised into making such a decision. This perspective also welcomes the choices provided by reproductive technology, and argues that a woman should be as free to contract out her womb or sell her eggs as to let her house or sell her labour.

Although liberal principles have been used to argue for women's right to make their own reproductive decisions, a strict liberal insistence on the right to freedom from government intervention does not seem compatible with a demand that abortion or fertility treatment should be provided or financed by the state. In the United States, the Supreme Court therefore ruled in 1989 that states could be allowed to prohibit the use of public funding for abortion.

Socialist, black and disabled feminist perspectives

In recent years, socialist feminists too have demanded reproductive rights, particularly the right to abortion. Black and/or disabled feminists have tended to focus on the coercive uses to which fertility control has been put; most, however, agree that women are entitled to make their own reproductive decisions.

In general, these feminists have placed much more emphasis than liberals on the context within which rights are exercised. For some, claiming reproductive rights as citizenship rights locates them as part of a wider network of social rights and responsibilities (Shaver, 1993; Lister, 1997). More generally, socialist feminists argue that legal rights are meaningless if economic and social circumstances prevent women from exercising them. Rosalind Petchesky has therefore argued that access to abortion is a necessity for women, which should be provided as a 'social good' along with education and healthcare (Petchesky, 1990). From this perspective, genuinely free choice for a pregnant woman would mean that neither abortion nor bearing and rearing a child would be ruled out by economic considerations. Today, however, an economically disadvantaged woman, or one who finds she is carrying an 'abnormal' fetus, is free to make reproductive choices only in the sense that workers are free to sell their labour under capitalism; such a woman is frequently faced not with a genuine choice, but with an agonising dilemma.

Disabled feminists have further argued that genuine reproductive choice for all women requires rejecting the assumptions that disabled women should not have children and that the life of a disabled person is not worth living. They claim that to treat disability as automatic grounds for abortion absolves society from the need to support disabled people and implies that they should never have been born. They therefore reject as 'outrageous' the fact that according to British law 'a foetus of more than 24 weeks gestation is treated as having rights as a human being but loses these rights once it is diagnosed as being disabled' (Morris, 1991, p. 75). The concept of social reproduction developed by some Marxist feminists (see Chapter 2) has enabled them to argue that the conditions in which people reproduce is an important part of the material basis of society. From this perspective, the feminist demand that women be enabled to control their own fertility is part of a wider human struggle to use technology to increase human freedom and overcome alienating conditions of labour. According to this analysis, developments in contraception and reproductive technology are potentially liberating for women. As with other technological developments, however, these advances have not been used to free women but to further the need of the capitalist economy to make a profit; they have also been used to ensure that the 'right' kind of people are being produced (that is, future workers, not those who may be surplus to requirements, whose social situation seems unlikely to make them into docile workers or those whose disability may limit their economic contribution). For Marxists, a genuine 'right to choose' will therefore only be won in the context of more widespread social and economic change.

Although socialist feminists agree that women today need to be able to decide whether or not to have an abortion, they are divided as to whether this right would continue to exist in a socialist society. Alison Jaggar has argued that because individual reproductive decisions have social implications, they can be a matter of legitimate public concern, and that if in a future socialist society childcaring responsibilities were shared by the whole community, then 'the community as a whole should now have a share in judging whether or not a particular abortion should be performed' (quoted in Petchesky, 1990, p. 13). Rosalind Petchesky, however, argues that this kind of analysis ignores the basic fact that in any kind of society it is still women's bodies that are immediately involved; she therefore rejects the idea that they should ever renounce control over their own bodies and reproductive lives.

Socialist, Marxist and black approaches are generally critical of the liberal line on surrogacy. They insist that women's alleged right to rent out their wombs cannot be abstracted from the inequalities of a racist capitalist society, in which the commodification of motherhood seems to represent a final form of exploitation and alienation. Angela Davis has pointed out that black women's reproductive capacities were exploited under slavery when they were used as both breeding machines to supply plantation labour and as wet-nurses for white women's babies; she says that this historical precedent opens up the possibility that poor women of colour might be 'transformed into a special case of hired pregnancy carriers (Davis, 1993, p. 359).

Patriarchy and the control of reproduction

Radical feminists also reject an individualistic conception of reproductive rights in favour of an analysis of the context within which rights are exercised. For them, this context is that of men's patriarchal control over women's bodies. This means that the demand for genuine reproductive choice is not a matter of private, individual choice; rather, it is a collective demand by women which represents a profound challenge to patriarchy, so that 'Far from being a matter of social indifference or a "private affair", procreative choice will alter the dynamics of social power considerably' (Harrison, 1983, p. 55).

Like socialist feminists, radical feminists argue that legal rights have little meaning on their own, and that genuinely free reproductive choices cannot be isolated from other social changes. For Catherine MacKinnon, the most important of these is freedom from coercive sexuality. Without this, she argues, the availability of contraception and abortion simply serves men's interests by increasing the sexual availability of women, for in a patriarchal society it is virtually impossible for sexual relationships between women and men to be based on consent. This means that the right to refuse sex is basic to the struggle for reproductive freedom (MacKinnon, 1989b. For further discussion of MacKinnon's views on the exploitative nature of sex under patriarchy, see Chapter 8).

Radical feminists also generally agree with socialists that abortion must be affordable as well as legal, that women have a right not to be coerced into sterilisation or abortion and that genuine choice requires that parents are supported in their role by society. Like socialist feminists, they argue that surrogacy contracts do not increase such choice; they also claim that the application of such a contract to pregnancy represents a failure to understand what this involves, and 'reinforce[s] notions of human separateness and insularity rather than recognizing that the development of individuality and autonomy takes place through sustained and intimate human relationship' (Shanley, 1995, p. 168).

Some early radical feminists argued that reproductive technology held the key to women's liberation. Most famously, Shulamith Firestone argued in 1970 that women's reproductive role as both bearers and nurturers of children was basic to their oppression, which would only be overcome when technology enabled babies to be incubated outside the womb. This negative view of motherhood has, however, been challenged by later writers.

Today, few radical feminists share Firestone's optimistic view of reproductive technology, and many reject the idea that a woman's 'right to choose' can be realised by the purchase of high-tech fertility treatment, the use of other women's reproductive capacities or attempts to produce 'designer babies' of the 'correct' sex and genetic make-up. These 'rights', they say, rest upon a narrow view of children as possessions or commodities; they are therefore inimical to feminist values. Many also believe that reproductive technology is being used to control rather than to liberate women. They argue that it often carries risks to women's health, they see the selective abortion of female fetuses as a horrific form of genocide, and they argue that developments in the treatment of infertility represent new forms of social control rather than an expansion of choice. This view of the new technologies as a new male weapon in the battle to maintain patriarchal power has led some to organise resistance through the Feminist International Network of Resistance to Reproductive and Genetic Engineering (FINRRAGE) (see Rowland, 1992).

Post-modernism and rights

Because post-modernist approaches reject in principle the possibility of objectivity and certainty in human knowledge, they also reject the idea that humans are possessed of absolute and unchanging rights. Although it may be useful to claim rights as a matter of political strategy, post-modernists say that these can only be contingent, temporary and relative; to pretend otherwise is to be guilty of 'false universalism' and an inability to understand the diversity and specificity of human experience. In terms of reproduction, this means that women have no general rights and no unified experience or needs on which feminist demands might be based; although expressing these as rights may help legitimise their claims, it also involves using a pre-existing male discourse which is unlikely to be genuinely empowering for women.

Post-modernist approaches therefore suggest that feminists should handle 'rights discourse' with care. The analysis of the power of language to structure our thinking also alerts us to the ways in which it has been used by campaigners to manipulate sympathies and polarise opinion. This is particularly clear in public debates over abortion, where the shifting terminology of fetus/unborn child, pro-abortion/pro-choice and anti-abortion/pro-life prompts a range of powerful and frequently emotional reactions.

Feminism and reproductive rights today

As we saw in Chapter 2, the assumptions behind liberal feminist claims for women's rights have been attacked not only by post-modernists but also by socialist and radical feminists. These have insisted on the collective, social and contextualised nature of rights, and many have argued that women should not be claiming 'rights of man' based on rationality, autonomy and competitiveness; rather, they should base their claims on the 'womanly values' of emotion, interdependence and care. The language of individual rights is, critics claim, particularly inappropriate for discussing reproductive issues.

Despite the development of such criticisms, the terms of public debate on the legality and morality of abortion continue to be largely set by 'common sense' liberal assumptions about individual rights. This means both that feminists can find themselves using a language which at a theoretical level they reject, and that any feminist demand for the 'right to choose' is likely to be popularly understood in individualistic terms. This language is especially powerful in the United States; although Britain has a stronger socialist tradition, the understanding of rights in privatised, individualistic terms has become increasingly dominant in recent years.

According to critics, the result has been a distorted debate, in which clear thinking is made unnecessarily difficult, and in which many feminists find themselves defending positions with which they feel unhappy. In particular, the language of individual rights seems to allow no space for the ethical and emotional ambivalence which many women feel about abortion. As such, it can make pro-choice feminists appear selfish and cold-blooded, stifle debate by denying the legitimacy of feminist doubts and, by refusing to acknowledge the emotional experiences of many women, deny a basic source of feminist knowledge. The language of rights is also said to be politically counter-productive, because it triggers counter-claims on the part of the fetus which have helped legitimise the powerful 'right to life' and 'fetal rights' movements. It also has the effect of polarising the debate, which is expressed as a clash between absolute and competing rights; dialogue and compromise therefore become unnecessarily difficult.

The following sections examine these claims, and link them to the practical questions of whether it is possible for someone who opposes abortion to call herself a feminist, and whether feminists can find common ground with some sections of the anti-abortion movement.

Beyond rights: abortion and feminist debates

Absolute rights v. women's doubts

Feminist claims that women have an absolute right to abortion have frequently seemed to rule out the possibility that the fetus is anything more than 'a clump of tissues', or that abortion is a morally complex issue. This implies that, if women express moral reservations on the issue, these can only be a form of false consciousness produced by a patriarchal society, and not the product of genuine ethical conviction or doubt. Petchesky, for example, argues that the association of fetus with 'baby' is 'a heavily ideological notion', and she says that, if a woman feels guilty about terminating her pregnancy, this is the result of 'right to life' propaganda and puritanical attitudes to sexual pleasure. From this perspective, the 'ambivalence' of many women towards their experience of abortion is not evidence of a genuine moral dilemma; rather it is:

> A smokescreen that obscures a dense web of losses and sorrows related to ageing and childbearing and the precariousness of sexual relationships, as well as the longings for family ties and emotional commitment that a 'baby' may symbolise. (Petchesky, 1990, pp. 390, 372).

The problem with this kind of argument is that, as Susan Himmelweit has argued, it is out of tune with the feelings of many women, to whom it appears 'hopelessly insensitive' (Himmelweit, 1988, p. 49). For many such women, it is not the arguments of 'pro-life' groups but their own experience of pregnancy and/or termination that makes them unhappy with claims for abortion that ignore the potential humanity of the fetus. Many women who agree that abortion should be legally and freely available, also see it as a difficult and moral decision involving the choice of a lesser evil rather than the unproblematic exercise of a life-style choice. Kathleen McDonnell argues that feminists must recognise such feelings, rather than dismissing them as 'false consciousness':

> Gradually I found myself coming back to a basic feminist truth: that our 'politics' cannot afford to be divorced from our authentic feelings, no matter how vague or contradictory they may seem. Our real task is to search out and find ways to reconcile the two. (McDonnell, 1984, p. 13)

For McDonnell, it was her own experience of having a child that led to a re-examination of her feelings about abortion. She found that she 'felt a bit like a feminist heretic, attending pro-choice rallies and marches while secretly harbouring thoughts and feelings that seem to clash with what I saw as the official "line" on abortion'(McDonnell, 1984, p. 13). Recently, however, a number of other feminists have also been 'coming out' and articulating their feelings of unease with the 'orthodox' feminist position (see Luker, 1984; Hursthouse, 1987; Colker, 1992). Thus Angela Neustatter writes of her own experience of having an abortion:

> Although I had always marched and campaigned for a woman's right to choose... when it came to deciding to end a pregnancy, I was shocked by the distress and confusion I felt. I did not like having to take personal responsibility for ending a life, even though I believe that women have to make this choice when the odds make a child seem intolerable. (Neustatter, 1986, pp. 1–2)

The American feminist Naomi Wolf has gone further than this. In *Fire with Fire* (1993) she said:

> I would never want my subjective views to cast a shadow on another woman; and I will defend with all my strength a woman's right to an

abortion... But... for the duration of the whole unavoidable struggle for reproductive choice I have felt that I had to stifle some of my deepest convictions. (Wolf, 1993, p. 141)

More recently, she has said although she still agrees that women must make their own reproductive decisions, her own experience of pregnancy has confirmed her sense of the moral seriousness of abortion, which she suggests may even be seen as a sin for which women should atone and grieve (Wolf, 1995a). Other feminists have accused Wolf of playing into the hands of the pro-life lobby, and some insist that for many women abortion does *not* involve a moral decision. Thus Decca Aitkenhead has written of her own termination of an unwanted pregnancy that 'it was no harder to "decide" to abort that it would have been to "decide" to have a limb amputated after a horrible car crash', and she says that 'the decision to have an abortion is indeed sometimes taken "lightly"' (Aitkenhead, 1997; see also Neustatter, 1995; Wolf, 1995b). Such views remind us of the dangers of assuming a unity of female experience. They do not, however, undermine the claim that for many women abortion remains a genuinely problematic moral issue.

Women's rights v. *fetal rights*

Although feminist claims that women have an absolute right to do what they want with their own body seem to deny any status to the fetus, the language of rights almost automatically generates counter-claims by the opponents of abortion, with women's 'right to choose' clashing both with the claims of potential fathers and with the 'right to life' of fetuses.

In the United States, the official platform of the Republican Party in 1992 promised a Constitutional amendment to defend the fetal right to life. The growing fetal rights movement has also made claims for the unborn which have led to attempts to ensure that pregnant women provide a healthy environment for their fetuses. In pursuit of this aim, the law has been used both to force unwilling women to undergo Caesarean sections and to control the life-style of pregnant women; there have also been attempts to regulate the working conditions of all fertile (and therefore potentially pregnant) women. From this fetal rights perspective, for which Petchesky has coined the term 'fetocentrism', women represent a potential threat to the health and safety of the unborn, producing 'an adversarial relationship between pregnant women and their fetuses' rather than one of care and nurturance (Petchesky, 1990, p. xiii).

As many critics have pointed out, the fetal rights movement has more to do with the social control of women than the welfare of children, who are guaranteed no such rights to a safe, secure and healthy environment *after* they have been born. It also ignores the health needs of women themselves, as was dramatically obvious in the case of a woman found guilty of supplying drugs to a minor via her umbilical cord who had earlier been refused a place on a drugs treatment programme (Pollitt, 1995). Pollitt claims that such thinking has been made possible by the pro-life movement which has:

> Polluted the way we think about pregnancy. It has promoted a model of pregnancy as a condition that by its very nature pits women and fetuses against each other, with the fetus invariably taking precedence. (Pollitt, 1995, p. 178)

According to some feminists, this kind of thinking has been facilitated by feminist use of equal rights language. Thus Colker argues that 'As pro-choice advocates, many of us have called for private individualism and we have, in return, received the selfishness that accompanies private individualism...' (Colker, 1992, p. 158).

All of this suggests to some writers that the language of individual rights has been counter-productive for feminists seeking to defend women's access to abortion. They argue that feminists must find ways of expressing their demands that acknowledge ethical and humanitarian concerns, and do not legitimise counter-claims by their opponents. In terms of practical politics, some see this as a way of capturing the uncommitted middle ground of public opinion; others hope to go further and, by identifying possible areas of agreement, to open the way to negotiation and compromise with some sections of the 'pro-life' movement.

Towards a feminist morality of abortion

Acknowledging the fetus

Some feminist philosophers have tried to construct a justification for abortion which is based in individual rights, but which also recognises its moral complexity. Christine Overall, for example, says that 'Like some other feminists, I believe that although women are entitled to access to legal abortion, we must not lose sight of the fact that abortion involves the termination of fetal life' – and she argues that although a fetus may not be a person, it is not nothing. She attempts to 'combine a concern for the well-being of the fetus/embryo and respect for women's autonomy' by arguing that although a woman does have the right to expel a fetus from her womb, she does not have the right to kill it. Terminations, she says, must therefore be undertaken with the aim of maximising the chances of fetal survival (although the woman need no longer be responsible for the fetus she has expelled); Overall argues that the development of reproductive technology will enable such survival to occur at increasingly early stages of gestation (Overall, 1987, pp. 46, 68).

Other writers have reached similar conclusions from different premises. Here Eileen McDonagh has built upon the earlier work of Judith Thompson to argue that, even if a fetus is a human person from the moment of conception, this can only give it a generalised right to life, and not the right to occupy a woman's body without her consent. She therefore argues for both the legality of abortion in all situations and for state funding, claiming that a woman is as entitled to legal protection against an invading fetus as against any other form of assault (Thompson, 1984; McDonagh, 1996). However, she also agrees with Overall that although a woman is entitled to remove a fetus from her womb at any stage of pregnancy, she is not entitled to kill it.

The 'sliding scale'

For other writers, a rights-based approach produces a 'sliding scale' position. This recognises that, as Wendy Savage (a feminist obstetrician) has said, 'doing an abortion is not the same as removing an appendix because you have got this other potential person there'. It sees fetal rights as developing as the pregnancy progresses: Savage argues that although these are initially outweighed by the rights of the mother, 'as the foetus becomes larger, its rights become greater, and there comes a point... where the foetus's right to live equals the right to get the pregnancy terminated' (quoted in Himmelweit, 1988, p. 50). Similar arguments are often expressed in popular political debate, and are reflected in the legal codes of many countries including Britain and America, where late abortions are much more heavily restricted than early ones. They also appear more in line with many women's experience and perception of pregnancy than one which insists that their rights are unaffected by the growth of a potential child within their womb, even when they can feel it move. However, they can still appear to involve a somewhat cold-blooded calculation of competing claims, in which the rights of the fetus are opposed to those of the pregnant woman. They are therefore rejected by those who say that care and interconnectedness should be at the heart of feminist ethical thought.

Abortion and an 'ethic of care'

Susan Himmelweit has argued that an antagonistic, rights approach should be replaced by one which recognises that a pregnant woman is the active nurturer of the fetus within her womb. From this perspective, she says, it is in the interests of neither the woman nor her potential child that she should be forced to continue nurturing it against her will: 'It is cruel to an unwanted fetus, just like an unwanted child, to enforce it upon an unwilling mother, and it is a singularly cruel punishment to impose upon the woman' (Himmelweit, 1988, p. 50). Although aborting a fetus which she has nurtured for 28 weeks will be a more serious decision than an early termination, Himmelweit says that women should be able to make this decision without the need for medical approval; she argues that socialist feminists should be demanding this on humanitarian grounds rather than as an issue of rights.

Other writers have drawn upon the ideas of Carol Gilligan, who has argued that although thinking in terms of rights can be empowering for women, a mature sense of justice must also recognise the importance of responsibilities and human inter-dependence (see Gilligan, 1982 and Chapter 4). Here writers have argued that women do not think about the world in terms of abstract rights or build theories of morality based on 'cool, distanced relations between more or less free and equal adult strangers' (Baier, 1986, p. 248); rather, they express themselves in terms of emotions, relationships, practicalities and caring responsibilities. For many writers such 'womanly thinking' is a direct result of the experience of human interconnectedness which pregnancy and childcare involve. They argue both that a woman-centred approach to ethical thinking can be used to develop an 'ethic of care', and that this can be used to defend abortion in terms of a woman's concern for her fetus and a sense of responsibility for the welfare of others, rather than as a selfish assertion of individual will.

It should, however, be noted that such conclusions are not inevitable. Just as 'rights' claims have been used to argue against abortion, so too some 'pro-life' women, especially those in the working class, express their opposition to abortion in terms of family obligations and responsibilities, and their own experiences of pregnancy, abortion or infertility. At a more academic level, Celia Wolf-Devine has argued that a feminist 'ethic of care' does *not* permit abortion, which she sees as a violent, masculine response to the problem of unwanted pregnancy:

> Abortion is a separation – a severing of a life-preserving connection between the woman and the fetus. It thus fails to respect the interconnectedness of all life... it shows a willingness to use violence in order to maintain control... abortion is a failure to care for one living being who exists in a particularly intimate relationship to oneself. (Wolf-Devine, 1989, pp. 86–7).

Such views are not normally articulated by feminists. Nevertheless, they show that the opponents of abortion are not all uncaring, anti-feminist defenders of patriarchy. Some, indeed, may be feminists who genuinely think that women should enjoy the same opportunities as men, but who also believe that abortion involves the taking of human life. From this perspective, a woman is entitled to demand that others share responsibility for caring for her child; she is however no more entitled to abort it than to kill her elderly parents because caring for them is interfering with her career. For many women, an ambivalent attitude to abortion may also reflect their desire to assert simultaneously their right to compete on equal terms with men *and* the value of the caring and nurturing which have traditionally been performed by women. From these twin perspectives, the demand for abortion rights can appear positively as a necessary precondition for full female citizenship; it can, however, look like a selfish rejection of caring responsibilities.

Acknowledging such complexities suggests that it may be possible to find common ground with some anti-abortionists, or with those who are undecided or favour a 'sliding scale'. By disentangling abortion politics from other issues, it may also be possible to avoid the vicious polarisation of abortion politics that has occurred in the United States, and which is in danger of spreading to Britain.

Dialogue without compromise: the politics of 'the middle ground'

Today, the debate over abortion has become bound up with a broader clash between conflicting value systems, through which support for abortion is part of a feminist package and opposition involves a whole set of conservative beliefs around the family, motherhood, chastity and self-reliance. This clash of opposing world views is confirmed by the use of competing claims of rights, through which any compromise can only appear as betrayal.

Empirical analyses of the attitudes of pro-choice and pro-life activists have found that these do indeed frequently reflect wider sets of conflicting social values. However, that is not the end of the story, for the picture is not a simple one of conservative housewives and patriarchal men versus career-minded feminists and their male supporters. As social movements, both 'sides' are broad churches which draw upon a wide range of people with diverse beliefs and motivations, and wider public opinion is even less easy to classify into 'pro-feminist and pro-choice' versus 'anti-feminist and pro-life'. Studies consistently suggest both that there has been a gradual movement towards an acceptance of abortion in some circumstances, and that most people do not fully identify with either a 'pro-life' or a 'pro-choice' position, but prefer a 'sliding scale' which reflects both the duration of pregnancy and the reasons for wanting a termination.

A recognition of the complexity of the debate enables us to separate opposition to abortion from opposition to other feminist goals. A number of writers have therefore built upon the ambiguities and uncertainties that lie behind the polarised nature of public debate to argue that dialogue between the two sides is both possible and desirable. Such dialogue involves a restatement of feminist goals in language that enables us to recognise that at least some feminist values may be shared with at least some opponents of abortion.

In the first place, it can be stressed that feminists are as concerned as many 'pro-lifers' with the welfare of babies. However, unlike some of their opponents, they do not limit this concern to unborn fetuses but extend it to children and adults, arguing that all members of society are entitled to decent working and living conditions. Feminists can also agree that society needs the love, care and nurturance that many women have traditionally provided for their families (although many will point out that in practice the nuclear family has often been a source of oppressive dependency, exploitation and violence rather than love and fulfilment). They will, however, argue that such care should not be the sole responsibility of women and that society must be reorganised so that caring does not come into conflict with employment or other forms of social participation.

This position provides the basis for a list of tangible demands which a number of writers believe could command support from both the pro-choice and pro-life camps. These include family-friendly employment policies, a change in attitudes towards disability, comprehensive healthcare, adequate sex education and safe and reliable contraception. Such demands have gained support from those whose opposition to abortion is based on humanitarian grounds, and who understand that they are in fact likely to result in a *reduction* of the abortion rate; in the United States, a number of 'pro-lifers' have therefore resisted Republican welfare cuts which would reduce the social support available for mothers (Dione, 1995). The United States-based Common Ground network is also attempting to create 'an environment for dialogue, mutual respect, and shared commitment to non-violence in the community', in the belief that the increasingly violent nature of abortion politics cannot be in the interests of either women or of the wider society. It stresses that 'no-one is ever asked to change his or her belief about the core issue of abortion'; it therefore aims at understanding rather than agreement, and seeks to build upon areas of common concern, such as those outlined above (Common Ground, 1995).

Conclusions: feminism and the politics of reproduction

Some disagreements among feminists on reproductive issues are likely to remain for the foreseeable future. Feminists should, however, also be able to agree that it is important to listen to the experiences and perceptions of all groups of women, and not just those who express 'approved' views. This applies not only to abortion, but also to infertility treatment and ante-natal screening. Here it is important to understand the consequences for disabled people of an assumption that 'imperfect' babies should automatically be aborted; it is, however, also necessary to understand that for parents who have seen a loved child die in pain, ante-natal screening is not simply a matter of eugenics or 'designer babies', and that better social support would not solve all their problems. Similarly, feminists should not write off the anguish of a woman unable to conceive as simply the result of social pressures which offer her no meaningful alternative to having children. Such analysis may contain elements of truth or conform to ideas of feminist orthodoxy; applied to real flesh and blood women it can however be both fatuous and deeply insulting.

In the real world of politics, compromises have to be made, and if feminists want to enable women to control their own fertility, they have to capture the middle ground of public opinion, and enter into the kind of dialogue that makes political negotiations possible. This involves understanding the power of language to control and construct social reality, but it need not represent the cynical abandonment of principles. Most feminists will continue to focus on the legality of abortion whenever this is under threat and to campaign for the funding and information that would make it accessible for all groups of women. An understanding of the way that the language of rights has constructed the debate suggests, however, that these claims should be made as a prerequisite for women's citizenship and in terms that stress context and relationships rather than as a narrow assertion of individual rights. It also suggests that the demand for 'rights' should be accompanied by an emphasis on the caring needs of babies, women, families and the wider society. The right to abortion will therefore not be seen as an end in itself, but as one of many preconditions for full reproductive choice. Similarly, those who demand that lesbians, black and/or disabled women have full access to infertility treatment will see this as part of a wider movement to equality.

A few feminists may believe that abortion is so evil that it should not be condoned in a civilised society or legitimised by law. Significant numbers are also likely find it morally problematic, particularly during the later stages of pregnancy. This need not rule out dialogue, for many who dislike abortion will nevertheless understand that abortions do not cease when they are made illegal. They can therefore agree that safe, legal abortions are preferable to a return to the days of back-street abortionists, pierced uteruses and bottles of gin; they may also be able to set aside their differences and work with anti-abortionists who agree with them on other issues.

All of this makes it clear that reproductive issues cannot be resolved in isolation from other aspects of life. This means that feminists working in this area are faced with a double agenda: to control their own bodies and to change the social conditions within which reproductive decisions are made. These conditions include the context in which sexual relationships are conducted; this is the subject of the next chapter.

8
Pornography

Although it is often assumed that all feminists are in favour of censoring pornography, they are perhaps more bitterly and more deeply divided on this issue than on any other. These divisions occur at a whole range of levels from tactical disagreements among feminists who advocate different ways of combating pornography, through debates over whether pornography is a cause or symptom of women's subordination, to outright conflict between those who see pornography as the root of all oppression and those who celebrate it as a form of sexual freedom. These divisions have found political expression in the formation of pro- and anti-pornography and pro- and anti-censorship groups. They reflect deep-seated theoretical disagreements about the ability of the law to promote feminist ends, about the meaning of freedom and oppression, about the nature of human sexuality and about the relationship between representation and reality. They also frequently involve competing definitions of pornography itself.

This chapter attempts to disentangle these layers of disagreement in order to promote a clearer debate in which protagonists are addressing the same issues, rather than simply talking past each other. After an initial overview of the current situation and the debate over censorship, it explores the practical implications of the problems of defining pornography. It analyses the evidence for the alleged harm that pornography does to women, linking this to wider debates around sexuality and around the causes, extent and significance of male sexual violence.

Background

During the 1960s, the publication of increasingly explicit sexual material was hailed by many as part of a new era of permissiveness and sexual freedom. Public debate on the issue was dominated by arguments between those who defended it as a form of free speech and a source of sexual liberation, and those who condemned it as un-Christian, anti-family and immoral. In this context, women who disliked or feared pornography lacked the language to articulate their feelings without aligning themselves with those who opposed sex outside marriage, such as Lord Longford and Mary Whitehouse in Britain, or the Moral Majority in the United States. Since then, however, feminist analyses have transformed the debate, which has increasingly focused on whether or not pornography is harmful to women, rather than on whether or not it is immoral.

The pornography industry

Sexually suggestive or explicit material has become ever more readily available, not only through specialist outlets and publications, but in the mainstream media of newspapers, magazines, television, videos, films and the Internet. Some of this, such as the advice and information pages in women's glossy magazines and, increasingly, those aimed at teenage girls, depicts women confidently in control of their own sexuality, encouraging them to explore their own needs as well as those of their partner. Much, however, treats women as passively available and submissive, and mainstream material includes depictions of rape and other forms of violent sexual abuse, presented in the guise of entertainment. Legally available 'top shelf' magazines leave no part of women's bodies to the imagination, and cater for a whole range of sexual preferences: publications available from ordinary high street newsagents include those specialising in bondage, in obese women, in old women and in women with their pubic hair shaved; many also show women enjoying and being sexually aroused by violence and abuse. The depiction of erect penises has, however, usually been deemed unlawful. Although child pornography is illegal in the United States and Britain, very young looking teenage models are routinely shown in sexually provocative poses in the mainstream media, and are increasingly used in more explicit publications. All this adds up to a vast and profitable industry. Catherine Itzin, a British anti-pornography writer, cites evidence suggesting that by the mid-1980s, the pornography industry in the United States was grossing eight billion dollars a year (more than the music and film industries combined), and that over two million 'top shelf' magazines are sold in Britain every month (Itzin, 1992).

Such publications are legal. There is, however, an illegal international trade in videos and printed material showing all kinds of sexual activity in graphic detail; this includes activity with very young children and extreme violence. So-called 'snuff' movies even claim to show the real-life torture and on-screen murder of women or children; in 1976 one such film was shown at a mainstream cinema in Times Square, New York, advertising itself in huge neon signs as 'Snuff' and 'Made in South America, where life is cheap'. Partly because the law enforcement agencies lack the resources to investigate it properly, it is difficult to assess the extent of this market. Some feminists claim that it has been exaggerated, and that in most hard-core pornography women are not treated either violently or as passive objects. It should be noted that neither the 1979 Williams Committee *Report on Obscenity and Film Censorship* in the UK nor the 1986 report of the Meese Pornography Commission in the United States found evidence of the existence of 'snuff' material; the New York authorities refused to take action against the film *Snuff* on the grounds that the alleged murder was faked, and that even if it were not, it had taken place outside United States jurisdiction (Dworkin, 1988).

The legal situation

In the United States, freedom of speech is guaranteed by the First Amendment to the Constitution. The courts have ruled, however, that free speech does not include obscene material, and the 1980s saw an attempted crack-down, inspired by traditional pro-family and Christian groups. They also saw the development of a radical feminist analysis of pornography, particularly associated with Andrea Dworkin and Catherine MacKinnon, which led to the passing of the 'MacKinnon–Dworkin Ordinances' in the cities of Minneapolis and Indianapolis in 1983 and 1984. The Ordinances would have enabled any woman who thought she had been harmed by pornography to take action against its producers, distributors and retailers. Although the first ordinance was vetoed by the mayor and the second was ruled unconstitutional by the federal courts, they have been widely seen as a model by feminists elsewhere. Laws based on the ordinances have been considered in a number of American states; more successfully, the arguments that were used to support them contributed to a reinterpretation of obscenity law in Canada.

In Britain, there is a general consensus that the obscenity laws which restrict the publication of sexually explicit material are unworkable and unenforceable. Despite a continuing drift to ever more open and explicit depictions of sexual activities, the 1980s saw a piecemeal tightening up of legislation and greater activity by Customs and Excise and police, much of it targeted at lesbian and gay publications and bookshops. There were also a number of feminist-inspired attempts to restrict pornography by law. The first and most famous of these was the 'Page Three' Bill introduced into the House of Commons in 1986 by the Labour member Clare Short, which would have banned 'naked or partially naked women in provocative pages in newspapers' and fined offending publishers (such pictures were featured every day on page three of the *Sun* newspaper). In 1988, the Campaign Against Pornography (CAP) was officially launched at the House of Commons; some other feminists were inspired by the Dworkin–MacKinnon Ordinances to form the Campaign Against Pornography and Censorship (CPC), which argues that using the law to protect women from the harmful effects of pornography does not constitute censorship (Itzin, 1992).

Despite such activity, many feminists on both sides of the Atlantic are strongly opposed to any increase in legislative control and deeply suspicious of the political alliances that seem to have occurred between feminist anti-pornography campaigners and right-wing organisations. Some feminists are therefore campaigning against restrictions through organisations such as the Feminist Anti-Censorship Taskforce (FACT) in the United States and Feminists Against Censorship (FAC) in Britain.

176 *Feminist Debates*

Feminists, pornography and the law: an overview of the debates

The most militant campaigners against pornography are radical feminists, while many defenders of unrestricted sexual expression use liberal arguments. There is, however, no consistent or uncontested link between feminist attitudes to censorship and theoretical starting points, and each of the main feminist perspectives has been used to justify a range of competing conclusions.

Anti-censorship arguments

Liberal arguments against state intervention and in favour of an individual's right to express themselves freely provide an obvious starting-point for the anti-censorship case. The classic statement of the liberal position was given by the 19th-century philosopher John Stuart Mill, who argued in his famous essay *On Liberty* (1991) that society should only be allowed to restrict an individual's liberty in order to prevent harm to others; opinions or actions could not be outlawed simply because other people found them offensive, for this would not only be an intolerable restriction on individual freedom, but an impediment to human knowledge and progress. Today, belief in free speech is particularly strongly held in the United States, where there is no equivalent of British legislation against incitement to racial hatred. Many therefore agree with the American liberal feminist Nadine Strossen that both existing obscenity laws and feminist proposals for further restriction represent unacceptable violations of the First Amendment guarantee of free speech (Strossen, 1996).

Like many other anti-censorship feminists, Strossen argues that, far from harming women, the free availability of sexually explicit material represents a welcome source of information, expression and choice. She argues that any increase in censorship would signal a return to the sexual ignorance and repressiveness of the 1950s. What women need, she says, is not more censorship but less, and they need more open discussion as a means of developing their own erotica and combating dominant images of female sexuality. She also argues that pornography provides an outlet for male sexual needs, and that violent material represents a safety valve through which sadistic fantasies can be safely expressed; from this perspective, pornography positively protects women from men's sexual demands and the risk of sexual assault.

Not all opponents of censorship agree with Strossen that pornography is beneficial. For example, the British feminist Lynne Segal writes that 'It does distress most women, and it has always distressed me', and she agrees that 'When it celebrates sexist and dehumanising images of women, pornography is a legitimate target of attack by feminists' (Segal, 1987, pp. 108, 112). She does not, however, think that pornography is more dangerous than other forms of representation, such as romantic fiction – 'Here too we find a persistent worship of the strong, the powerful, the phallic male' (Segal, 1987, p. 113). She also refuses to believe either that silencing sexual expression can be in women's interests or that their oppression can be reduced to matters of sexuality. She therefore both argues like Strossen that we need more open and feminist led sexual discussion, and insists that an analysis of pornography and its effects cannot be isolated from the economic exploitation and vulnerability of women.

Segal is writing from within a socialist feminist tradition. A more explicitly Marxist analysis of pornography is provided by Sheila McGregor, who argues that it reflects the commercialisation and debasement of human relationships under capitalism, whereby people are alienated from their own bodies, and sexuality becomes a commodity rather than an expression of human connectedness and creativity. As such, pornography is 'a product of capitalist sexuality rather than a key component in structuring it', and therefore a symptom rather than a cause of the oppression of women (McGregor, 1989, p. 21. See also Foreman, 1978; Jaggar, 1983). This means that restrictive legislation cannot achieve meaningful change. Rather, pornography can most effectively be opposed by challenging the economic system in which sex has become a commercial transaction rather than an expression of human love, and in which some women are driven to selling their bodies as a means of economic survival. This approach also cautions us against seeing the production of pornography for women as a way forward, for the commodification of male bodies cannot be a solution for socialist feminists.

Although radical feminist analysis has been central to antipornography campaigns, its analysis of patriarchy has also been used to argue against opposing pornography by legal means. As discussed in Chapter 4, some claim that the law is inherently patriarchal, and that attempts to use it for feminist ends are likely to be counter-productive and to increase the power of the courts rather than of women. Many feminists are particularly reluctant to hand further powers on sexual matters to judges, some of whom have shown themselves completely lacking in understanding: statements made in court by British judges during the early 1990s included the remark that an 8-year-old victim of a sexual attack 'was not entirely an angel', the assertion that the rape by a man of a woman whom he had taken out for a meal was not 'the more serious type of rape – that is the rape of a total stranger' and the instruction to a rape jury that 'If she doesn't want it she only has to keep her legs shut' (*Guardian*, 10 June 1993, 11 August 1993). Feminist suspicion of the law also seems to many to have been confirmed by recent experience in Canada where, although obscenity legislation has been reinterpreted to outlaw material deemed 'degrading' or 'dehumanising' to women, the main target for an increase in censorship has been gay, lesbian and women's literature (Strossen, 1996, pp. 231–9).

Arguments for legal action against pornography

The liberal defence of individual freedom does not claim that this is absolute; rather, it argues that it can only be restricted to prevent harm to others. This means that if pornography can be shown to harm women, or if its manufacture involves coercion, liberal arguments can be used to demand its control. The language of citizenship can also be used to defend the right of women to be free from the intimidation and threat of sexual violence which some say pornography involves.

For Marxist feminists, the concept of social reproduction can provide a basis for arguing that pornography is not simply an ideological reflection of economic inequalities. Rather, it is a part of the conditions in which sexual relationships and biological reproduction take place; as such it can be contested in its own right. Although as we have seen in Chapters 4 and 5, many Marxist and socialist feminists are suspicious of using state institutions, many argue both that these can be seen as 'arenas of struggle' and that challenges to existing laws and practices can play an important role in contesting dominant male perceptions of reality, even when they do not achieve immediate practical results. This kind of analysis merges with the otherwise very different claims of radical anti-pornography campaigners that women must insist on using the law on their own terms.

The best known of these radical campaigners are Andrea Dworkin and Catherine MacKinnon, who claim that theirs is the only possible feminist analysis, and that their opponents are traitors to the feminist cause, or even in the pay of the pornography industry. They say that they do not oppose pornography because they are anti-sex. Rather, they say that they are opposed to sex*ism*, and they claim that because pornography eroticises subordination and violence it is the prime cause of women's oppression and of an epidemic of violence and hatred against them.

MacKinnon and Dworkin claim that arguments around free speech are irrelevant to the pornography debate, because pornography is not 'only words': to show a woman being mutilated or lying back with her legs open in a 'come and get me' pose is not to express an opinion, it is an act of oppression and discrimination against women in the same way as that a sign saying 'whites only' is an act of oppression and discrimination against black people. To outlaw pornography is not, therefore, to censor free expression, it is to prevent harm to women.

For MacKinnon and Dworkin, the demand for restrictions on pornography and sexual expression is not seen as a totalitarian extension of politics into personal life, but means of defending women from the political power that men already exercise there. Perhaps surprisingly, some of Dworkin and MacKinnon's liberal feminist opponents agree that sexuality is political. Indeed, it is precisely because she thinks this that liberal feminist Nadine Strossen is so strongly opposed to restricting the availability of sexual material, for she believes that this would amount to dangerous political censorship.

The middle ground

Partly because none of the theoretical starting-points provides an unequivocal answer, many feminists see the censorship issue as more complex than the certainty of leading protagonists might suggest, and some find themselves undecided, or occupying an uncomfortable middle ground. Many such feminists dislike pornography and feel that it harms women; however they see it as a symptom rather than the main cause of their oppression. Many who would like its availability to be restricted also fear the practical consequences of empowering a male-run legal system or entering into alliances with right-wing moralists who want to censor a wide range of erotic and educational material. Some feel that the link between pornography and sexual violence has not been proved, or that the extent of sexual violence has been exaggerated. Many such women are uneasy with an analysis which seems to define women as victims. Others wish to distance themselves from hostility to men, or to sex with men, seeing some campaigners as puritanical killjoys, who object to any form of sexual display or enjoyment, and want to take the fun out of life in general and sexual relations in particular. Such ambivalence is expressed by Myrna Kostash, who says that, rather than being consistent, she has 'flipped and flopped' on the censorship issue, and writes that:

> While I am deeply sympathetic to the impulse to, say, burn pornography in a big bonfire downtown, trash the video shops, string up the publishers and distributors, put my boyfriend in a political re-education camp whenever he buys Penthouse (and send my own fantasies there too), I can't act on it. (Kostash, 1993, p. 488)

This kind of inconsistency is reflected in disagreement and confusion over how pornography should be defined. It is necessary to analyse this before examining the disputed claim that pornography both harms women and is central to their oppression.

What is pornography?

This apparently simple question is fraught with theoretical significance. It is also of immediate practical importance for feminists advocating legal action, who are faced with the task of establishing a legally watertight definition.

Because there is no anti-pornography legislation in the United States or Britain, there is at present no legal definition. We do however have some less than helpful definitions of *obscenity* as something which 'appeals to the prurient interest in sex... [and]... lacks serious literary, artistic, political, or scientific value'(the United States Supreme Court's 1973 *Miller* ruling), or whose effect is 'to tend to deprave and corrupt' (the British 1959 Obscene Publications Act); in Britain a 1986 legal ruling also defined indecent material as that which 'an ordinary decent man or woman would find to be shocking, disgusting or revolting' (quoted in Merck, 1992, p. 91). There is, however, a more general public view of pornography as anything that depicts naked bodies or sexual activity; this is sometimes modified by a distinction between pornography and art, with the former aimed at sexual arousal while the latter is concerned with the portrayal of beauty and truth (put crudely, the former is said to provide masturbation material, while the latter appeals to intellectual and aesthetic sensibilities).

Many feminists have rejected the pornography/art distinction on the grounds that this merely disguises the sexual exploitation of women and legitimises their portrayal as objects of the male gaze. From this perspective, there is no inherent difference between a 'page three' nude and many of the famous pictures in art galleries. Some feminists have therefore campaigned not only against the depiction of women in contemporary art and literature but also against the public display of classical paintings which show women as passive sexual objects: for example, feminist protests in Pennsylvania University led to the removal of a Goya nude from a classroom wall (for a critical discussion of this incident, see Strossen, 1996).

Some feminists have, however, argued that pornography should be distinguished from erotica. According to this distinction, erotica is sexually arousing material based on the portrayal of mutual pleasure and equality rather than exploitation; such portrayal may be very explicit, but, far from damaging women, it can be a source of female power, knowledge and joy (see Lorde, 1984; Steinem, 1985). Pornography, in contrast, is said to involve sexual objectification, subordination and degradation, usually of women and children but sometimes of men. Other writers, however, deny that the distinction has any validity and claim that, like the pornography/art distinction, it is simply a way of legitimising personal preferences ('I like art, you like erotica, he likes pornography'), or policing sexual desires.

Andrea Dworkin and Catherine MacKinnon say that they accept the erotica/pornography distinction, and they argue that the central feature of pornography is its combination of sexual explicitness with the subordination and abuse of women; they argue that for material to be defined as pornographic it must therefore be both sexual *and* subordinating. This understanding, built on a conceptualisation of pornography as both cause and practice of oppression, was built into the legal definition used in the ordinances which they helped draft in the United States, and has been the model for anti-pornography campaigns elsewhere. Because it has been so influential, it is worth quoting in full the definition provided in the 1983 Minneapolis ordinance:

> Pornography means the graphic sexually explicit subordination of women through pictures and/or words that also includes one or more of the following: (i) women are presented dehumanized as sexual objects, things or commodities; or (ii) women are presented as sexual objects who enjoy humiliation or pain; or (iii) women are presented as sexual objects experiencing sexual pleasure in rape, incest or other sexual assault; or (iv) women are presented as sexual objects tied up or cut up or mutilated or bruised or physically hurt; or (v) women are presented in postures or positions of sexual submission, servility or display; or (vi) women's body parts – including but not limited to vaginas, breasts, or buttocks – are exhibited such that women are reduced to those parts; or (vii) women are presented being penetrated by objects or animals; or (viii) women are presented in scenarios of degradation, humiliation, injury, torture, shown as filthy or inferior, bleeding, bruised, or hurt in a context which makes these conditions sexual. (Quoted in Itzin, 1992, pp. 435–6)

The ordinance definition also includes 'the use of men, children and transsexuals in the place of women'.

Many supporters argue that this definition is aimed at the pornography industry and would not lead to significant restrictions on works of art or erotic material. However opponents such as Strossen claim that it is part of a puritanical agenda that is hostile to any kind of sexual expression. She argues that because the 'MacDworkinites' believe that free consent and genuinely equal sexual relations between men and women are virtually impossible in patriarchal society, they see almost any portrayal of heterosexual activity as a form of submission, humiliation or subordination. Like many others, she also points out that Dworkin and MacKinnon have formed political alliances with right-wing anti-feminist groups which are opposed to all forms of sexual expression outside marriage. For some such groups, any extra-marital or lesbian sex is inherently degrading, as is any suggestion that women enjoy sex for its own sake, rather than as a means of procreation. If such views were accepted, the ordinance definition would encompass a very wide range of material indeed, including much feminist literature; it would certainly include the depiction of lesbian sado-masochistic activity, which some 'sex radicals' claim provides a liberating exploration of sexual possibilities that subverts patriarchal assumptions (for critical discussion of the sex radical arguments, see Cooper, 1995).

The difficulty of establishing an objective definition of pornography is compounded by the complex nature of the relationship between the material that is being assessed, the purposes for which it was produced, and the context in which it is consumed. The attempt to produce such a definition seems to assume that the meaning of a picture, book or video is inherent in it, and that it is fixed and given. However, a post-modernist perspective helps us to see that meanings are shifting, fluctuating, and open to interpretation, and that the relationship between representation and meaning is far from straightforward (see Chapter 2).

Because the ordinance definitions concentrate on content rather than context, they imply that some works of feminist fiction which describe the sexual abuse of women must be legally defined as 'pornographic', despite the fact that their intention is to condemn rather than endorse women's subordination. Anti-pornography campaign material that cites examples of pornographic abuse could also fall foul of the legislation; indeed Dworkin's own work on pornography has been stopped by Canadian customs on the grounds that it 'illegally eroticized pain and bondage' (quoted in Strossen, 1996, p. 237. Strossen reports that Canadian customs seizures also included *Hot, Hotter, Hottest* – which turned out to be a cookery book using spices).

The meaning of material does not only change with the person using it, it can also vary with the circumstances in which an individual views or sees it. This means that a woman watching a sexually explicit film may experience it differently according to whether she is on her own, with female friends, with a trusted male partner or in a group of male strangers. It also means that a close-up photograph of a vagina could be used in a medical textbook or lecture as a necessary way of conveying knowledge to future doctors; if medical students photocopy the image and hand it round to their friends, it can acquire a very different significance. Similarly, Dworkin's novel *Mercy*, which describes the horror and unacceptability of rape, has provided inspiration for feminist activity; however her authorial intentions cannot prevent the book also being used as a source of sexual arousal. The meaning of a product can be further changed by knowledge of how and why it was produced. Thus the sexually explicit film *Deep Throat* was widely hailed in the early 1970s as an erotic breakthrough in which a sexy heroine, 'Linda Lovelace', was shown having a joyfully sensual time; however in her autobiography *Ordeal*, Linda Marchiono, the actress involved, has since revealed that she was brutally coerced into performing, so that 'every time someone watches that film they are watching me being raped' (quoted in *Everywoman*, 1988, p. 29).

All of this suggests that the question of definition is much more complex than some enthusiastic proponents of legislation would like to think, and that there is a very real danger that any attempts at legal restriction would be interpreted to include pro-feminist material. Whether or not the risks of legislation outweigh the gains depends in part upon an assessment of the harms that it is intended to prevent. It is to this highly contested area that we now turn.

Pornography, harm and the oppression of women

The belief that pornography harms women is built into Dworkin and MacKinnon's definition of pornography as material which subordinates women and, as we have seen, they believe that it is the central cause of oppression. Many other feminists do not go so far, but agree that pornography can harm women in a number of interconnected ways. The most commonly cited of these is the link between pornography and sexual violence; some writers see women's fear of this violence as a means of controlling women and sustaining male domination. Pornography is also said to distort human sexuality, and to maintain gender inequality by treating women as objects and sexualising their subordination. Others argue that it has further oppressed minority ethnic women by the exploitation of racial stereotypes; here Patricia Hill Collins argue that pornography has been central to the racially specific exploitation of black women, because whereas it reduces white women to sexual objects, it portrays black women as sexual animals (Collins, 1990. See also Forna, 1992).

Male sexual violence against women

The extent of the problem

Women's reluctance to report crimes of sexual violence has meant that official statistics on this are notoriously unreliable. However, the available evidence suggests that it is more widespread than most people realise. Surveys and research indicate that one in four women in Britain has experienced rape or attempted rape; that half of all girls experience some form of unwanted sexual experience (from flashing to rape) before they are 18; and that more than half of all women report sexual harassment in the workplace (for a summary of research findings see Labour Party Consultation, 1995). In the United States, Catherine MacKinnon has claimed that over 90 per cent of American women have been sexually assaulted or harassed at some point in their lives (MacKinnon, 1989b).

According to MacKinnon, such findings reveal 'the effectively unrestrained and systematic sexual aggression of one half of the population against the other half' (MacKinnon, 1989b, p. 332). The ubiquity of sexual violence and intimidation also suggests that much of it must be perpetrated by many apparently decent and ordinary men. This seems to have been confirmed by clinical tests which have, with rare exceptions, found that even rapists appear to be mentally 'healthy' and 'normal', rather than readily identifiable psychopaths. Studies also consistently show that women are most at risk from someone known to them, rather than from a stranger in a dark alleyway.

The recent research into sexual violence is itself partly the result of feminist analysis which has insisted that women's experiences be taken seriously, and which has helped to re-label unwelcome sexual attention as sexual harassment rather than harmless flirtation and to define rape as penetrative sex against a woman's wishes, whether or not she has consented to other forms of sexual activity or has agreed to penetrative sex in the past. Some feminists argue, however, that such changes have gone much too far, and that they have created a climate of hysteria and fear which disempowers, desexualises and infantilizes women and loses sight of the fun and joy of heterosexual encounters (see in particular Roiphe, 1993). They also complain that there has been an over-stretching of 'common sense' understandings of violence and rape, and that these trivialise the trauma involved in genuinely brutal and bloody assaults. Against this, their opponents claim that even apparently trivial incidents can be terrifying, and that these have to be understood in the context of a whole culture of sexual aggression and intimidation. Far from women rushing to the police at the suspicion of a wolf whistle or suggestive leer, they argue that many intimidating incidents go unreported because 'nothing happened', and that 'in the phrase "nothing happened" women's experience of terror is negated' (Radford, 1987, p. 33).

Violence and the maintenance of patriarchy

According to some feminists, male sexual violence against women is both a product of unequal power relations and a way of maintaining them. From this perspective, patriarchy rests ultimately on force, and women's fear of sexual assault works to the advantage of all men. This does not mean that all men are violent, but that all men benefit from the actions of those who are. Susan Brownmiller has notoriously argued that rape is 'nothing more or less than a conscious process of intimidation by which all men keep all women in a state of fear' (Brownmiller, 1977, p. 15). Some writers have also argued that the impersonal threat of violence purveyed through pornography has become particularly important in recent years because of the gains that women have made; as such it may represent a backlash against feminist demands (Faludi, 1992) or a shift from private to public patriarchy as women attempt to enter public life (Walby, 1990).

More specifically, men are said to gain because, although statistics suggest that young men are the social group most likely to be physically attacked on the streets, more women fear going out on their own and feel that 'using public space [is] perceived as using alien or occupied space' (McNeill, 1987, p. 108). To the extent that this fear restricts women's freedom of movement, it prevents them competing with men on an equal basis in employment and politics, while if they are uneasy about working late in half-empty offices or start demanding better lighting in the car park they may be seen as problem workers. Although women are in fact most at risk from men they know, many are offered protection by male friends or colleagues, or feel obliged to ask for it. The imbalance in power relations which this can produce is clear if we imagine a working environment in which women protectively enquire about the safety of their male colleagues, and insist on walking them to their car or bus stop. At a more personal level, men are also said to benefit because fear of male violence means that women seek a male partner to protect them from other men. The sense that she is safer with a man in the house who will also accompany her if she goes out can contribute to a woman's reluctance to leave an exploitative or unhappy marriage, or to push too hard for a more equal relationship. The result is male–female relationships based on dependency and subordination rather than equality.

Such views are, of course, fiercely disputed by many other feminists who refuse to believe that violence is as all-pervasive as this analysis suggests, that all men can be held responsible for the actions of a pathological minority or that many men do not want equal partnerships with women. Although definitions and analyses vary, all feminists can, however, agree that some forms of male sexual behaviour do constitute unacceptable violence. If pornography can be shown to cause such violence, it must therefore be condemned.

Pornography and violence: is there a link?

The claim that pornography somehow 'causes' sexual violence has been most clearly summed up in the slogan 'Pornography is the theory; rape is the practice'. At a general level, Dworkin and MacKinnon argue that our culture has become so saturated by degrading images of women that sexual violence has become normalised and legitimised, and women are seen as objects to be used for men's sexual gratification, rather than as human beings. In this context, sexual violence is not simply provoked by any one video, magazine or Internet site, but is the product of largely unquestioned and ubiquitous images: 'All women live in sexual objectification like fish live in water... all women live all the time under the shadow of sexual abuse' (MacKinnon, 1989b, p. 340).

Although this analysis may have a strong intuitive appeal, it is difficult to prove, and it is rejected by those, such as the young American writer Katie Roiphe, who assert that it bears no relation to their own experiences or to the reality of most sexual relationships (Roiphe, 1993). More substantive evidence cited in support of the alleged link between pornography and sexual violence comes mainly from the United States and takes three main forms.

The first consists of personal testimonies by rapists and victims of sexual violence, which claim that pornography provoked acts of sexual violence towards women or inspired particular forms of assault. This includes testimony from minority ethnic women who link their abuse to the portrayal of women of their group in pornographic material, and from women who say they have been coerced and abused in the production of pornography.

The second form of evidence involves laboratory experiments in which the penises of both convicted rapists and 'normal' men are wired up to monitoring equipment, and their sexual responses to different kinds of sexually explicit material measured. Here it has been found that 'healthy' men are, like rapists, aroused by rape scenes in which women are shown sexually excited by violence; unlike the rapists they are not aroused by brutality which the woman does not appear to enjoy.

The third kind of alleged evidence is the product of psychological and sociological research in which college students have been questioned about their attitudes to sexual violence before and after viewing pornographic material. These studies appear to show that even brief exposure to films in which women are shown enjoying violence can increase the belief that all women want or deserve to be raped, and produces a significant increase in the number of respondents who say that they would rape if they could get away with it. This suggests not only that such widely available films are likely to provoke violence, but that the sympathies of jurors, police officers and lawyers who have viewed this kind of material is likely to lie with the accused rather than with his victim.

Other feminists deny that the available evidence can be interpreted in this way, and accuse anti-pornographers of an inability to distinguish between fantasy and reality. They claim that sex offenders have in general seen less pornographic material than non-offenders. They insist that our emotional response to the personal testimonies of rape and pornography survivors should not mean that we uncritically accept their analysis of the causes of violence. They reject the view that all women who participate in the production of pornography are necessarily exploited, and argue that anti-pornography campaigners have silenced the voices of performers who enjoy their work and feel fully in control of what they are doing.

Opponents of censorship also say that campaigners have misused research data, and that some researchers have distanced themselves from feminist interpretations of their own work. In particular, they say that the damaging effects of pornographic material have been shown to be more than offset if an audience is 'de-briefed' by being provided with more accurate information about sexual violence; this suggests that wider discussion may be a better solution than censorship.

For some writers, historical and international comparison provides additional reasons for questioning the causal links between pornography and sexual violence. They point out that such violence is certainly not confined to societies with a large pornography industry. On the contrary, it is rife in China and in Muslim societies where pornography is completely illegal and is much less of a problem in Denmark and Sweden, where pornography is readily available. Here again, however, the evidence is inconclusive. The Swedish government's report to the 1995 Beijing Conference on women identified continuing violence against women as a serious problem, and in the same year a Swedish Commission on Violence Against Women reported that more research was needed into the correlation between violent pornography and crimes against women, as little was currently known.

It seems therefore that as Lynne Segal has commented, 'The fast-accumulating research on the effects of violent pornography is most notable only for its inconsistency' (Segal and McIntosh, 1992, p. 7). The uncertainty is compounded by the difficulties in defining pornography discussed earlier, so that it is frequently unclear what kind of material commentators are discussing, and it is at times almost impossible to distinguish pornography from other forms of cultural representation. For Dworkin and MacKinnon this is in a sense the point of their critique, as they claim that images of women's sexual subordination are so ubiquitous they are unrecognised. This claim in turn depends upon an analysis of the allegedly oppressive nature of virtually all heterosexual relationships in a patriarchal, pornographic society.

Pornography and sex: the basis of oppression?

Dworkin and MacKinnon's analysis taps into a long strand within feminist thought which has seen sex with men as unhealthy and disempowering for women. Although some early socialist writers praised the liberating effects of a freely expressed sexuality, the liberal tradition tended to see sex as dangerously disruptive of civilised society, involving a degrading surrender to 'animal appetites' and a loss of personal autonomy. Today, liberal arguments are still used to defend women's right to reject unwanted sexual advances; they are, however, also used to assert women's right to be sexually active in any way they choose, and to reject any attempt to impose moral restrictions, either by conventional moralists or by other feminists. From this perspective, women are entitled to assert and explore their own sexual needs in heterosexual or lesbian relationships; for some sex radicals and libertarians this can include sado-masochistic practices and pornography, which are defended both as a legitimate personal choice and as a way of destabilising social authority.

Radical feminists have generally denied that sexual preferences and practices can be purely personal. Many have, however, also rejected the claim that lesbian sado-masochism is really subversive, arguing rather that it is a product of patriarchy which mimics heterosexual abuse and power structures and endorses the degradation of women. They therefore argue both against such practices, and against their portrayal in pornographic material.

According to some radical feminists, all sex with men is inherently oppressive for women: not only is it unlikely to be satisfying, but it is said to undermine women's self-confidence and divert their energies from supporting other women (see Johnston, 1982). This means that celibacy can be seen as a positive and liberating choice (see Cline, 1993), while lesbianism is not simply a matter of personal preference, but is 'fundamentally a political statement representing the bonding of women against male supremacy' (Kitzinger, 1995, p. vii). In this context, the pornography industry is seen as a powerful means through which female sexuality is manipulated to deny the possibility of lesbianism and celibacy as valid sexual choices.

Although Dworkin and MacKinnon do not say that sex with men is necessarily and irrevocably oppressive, they claim that in practice in our patriarchal society it almost invariably is. They argue that the desires of both men and women are learned in the context of a pornographic culture in which male power and female submission have been eroticised, and that 'because intercourse so consistently expresses illegitimate power, unjust power, wrongful power, it is intrinsically an expression of the female's subordinate status, sometimes a celebration of that status' (Dworkin, 1983, p. 84). They therefore refuse to accept that there is a real distinction between rape and consensual sex, arguing that both are based on power rather than mutuality. They claim that some women's enjoyment of sex with men does not refute their argument; rather, it is a sign of pornography's success, through which women have internalised their own oppression.

From this perspective, the distortion of sexuality achieved through pornography's eroticisation of subordination and violence affects every area of life and is basic to women's oppression. Catherine MacKinnon suggests that this gives men an erotic as well as a material interest in the continuation of patriarchy, so that perhaps 'part of the male interest in keeping women down is the fact that it gets men up' (MacKinnon, 1989b, p. 335). At the same time, because sexual attractiveness in women has been linked to frail passivity, it may be difficult for a powerful or economically successful woman to appear attractive to men; this may mean that for heterosexual women, the need for male approval can work against their career or their involvement in feminist politics. Unlike a male trade unionist who does not need to worry about whether his boss or the public thinks him attractive, feminists are much more likely to be judged by their appearance; here recent research on attitudes to feminism has consistently found that it has a negative image linked to a perception of feminists as ugly and unattractive (Siann and Wilkinson, 1995). This means that the campaign against pornography can also be seen as a crusade against oppressive sexuality, and against the oppression produced in a culture which teaches men that women are there for their use and pleasure, and women that womanhood means submission and conformity to male desire.

Other feminists who share a concern with the effects of pornography on human sexuality and the status of women, nevertheless reject an analysis which they say fails to understand that human sexuality is far more complex and less immediately malleable than the crude reductionism of the anti-pornography movement suggests.

Lynne Segal, for example, has argued that, far from celebrating male domination, pornography both creates and reinforces male sexual insecurity and anxiety, and has contributed to a rise in male sexual problems (Segal, 1990a). Others similarly claim that the political attack on penetrative sex over-states its oppressive power by 'speak[ing] of the male sexual organ as if it held more power than a nuclear device, as if mere proximity to it were enough to ruin a woman forever', and they reject the idea that 'a few inches of wrinkly flesh' holds the key to social inequality (Assiter and Carol, 1993, p. 7).

Many feminists therefore also reject the view that heterosexual women should be seen as 'the bad girls who smoke in the changing room and go with men' (Campbell, 1982, p. 125), or that the practices of heterosexual sexuality cannot become more egalitarian and responsive to women's needs. Thus Stevi Jackson says that we must distinguish between heterosexuality as an oppressive institution, and heterosexual practice, experience and identity; she argues that because power is not exercised uniformly at the level of interpersonal relations, neither practice nor experience are wholly determined, and says that 'recently some of us have admitted – cautiously and defiantly – that even penetrative sex with men can be enjoyable, and that its pleasure is not merely eroticized submission' (Jackson, 1995, p. 22). Naomi Wolf similarly argues that feminists must stop denying the pleasures of sex with men and that 'The next phase of feminism must be about saying a sexual yes as well as a sexual no' (Wolf, 1993, p. 199).

Conclusions: debates and strategies for the 21st century

Feminist disagreements about pornography are unlikely to be resolved in the near future. It is, however, now possible to identify areas of consensus as well as difference, and, by disentangling levels of debate, to clarify the political choices that feminists face.

As a starting-point, most feminists now agree that sexuality is not simply a matter of personal preference, but is linked with wider social issues. They can also agree that if pornography contributes in any way to the oppression of women, it is to be opposed. This opposition is justified even if pornography is not the only or even the major cause of oppression. Whether or not feminists want actively to campaign against pornography will depend upon their assessment of the importance of its oppressive role, how convinced they are by the evidence against it and whether or not they think that it brings benefits as well as potential harms to women. They need not, however, see anti-pornography campaigns as an alternative to anti-racist or class politics, for they may agree that it contributes towards the exploitation of minority ethnic and/or working-class women, legitimising their abuse and creating a division between sexual and 'respectable' women. Some will conclude that anti-pornography campaigns must be the focus of feminist activity; others however will see pornography as a product of more important social and economic conditions, or argue that it is not pornography as such that is the problem, but the form which it currently takes. The harms which feminists identify will involve interconnected issues around sexual violence, the subordination of women through the eroticisation of inequality, and the distortion of human sexuality; they are, however, likely to continue to disagree about the nature and meaning of these.

Many feminists who agree that pornography is to a greater or lesser extent implicated in women's oppression will disagree over how it is to be opposed. For some, the solution will lie in legislation, and the MacKinnon–Dworkin model is likely to remain influential. Despite the claim that this is intended to empower women rather than the law, many feminists will remain reluctant to trust a patriarchal legal system; they will also be deeply suspicious of entering into alliance with right-wing moral conservatives, who may use the law for anti-feminist and repressive ends. Reluctance to censor pornography will also continue to be linked to the problem of producing a legally watertight definition, which is in turn linked to disagreements about what constitutes subordinating or oppressive material.

For some opponents of both pornography and restrictive legislation, the solution will lie with more open discussion, and with an insistence that men examine and justify their use of pornography. For some, this will include the development of erotic material for and by women, that recognises the validity of female desire and sexual pleasure. Disagreement is, however, likely to continue over whether sado-masochistic material is a legitimate form of sexual expression, and over whether female erotica is genuinely empowering, or the final triumph of capitalist alienation and commodification. Here some apparent disagreements about whether or not pornography can be beneficial to women can also be seen as disagreement over definitions: many feminists on both 'sides' agree both that sexual openness is desirable, and that the portrayal of sexual violence for the purpose of entertainment is not, but disagree about whether both should be labelled 'pornography'. Some will find post-modernist analyses of the complex relationship of language, reality, image, meaning and intent, a useful reminder of the problems involved in assuming that pornographic material can be readily defined, identified and isolated from other cultural artefacts.

Whatever the conclusions particular feminists reach, it is important they understand that there is no simple, one-way causal relationship between pornography, human sexuality and women's oppression. Rather, as in other areas, we are confronted with complex interaction and inter-relationships. This does not mean that political campaigns against pornography may not be justified. It does mean, however, that the elimination of pornography will not occur in isolation from other changes, and that even if it could, this would not end the oppression of women.

9
The problem of men

When I told a friend that this book was in danger of becoming too long, she suggested that I replace this chapter with a footnote explaining that although men are important, space is limited and unfortunately I cannot include everything. The 'problem of men' cannot, however, be solved so easily, for men will not simply go away or keep quiet while feminists get on with changing the world. Even those feminists who want to live separately from men cannot escape from their laws or the effects of their policy decisions, and men are obviously central to the lives of many women as fathers, sons, brothers, husbands, lovers, friends or colleagues. Most feminists have to work through their relationships with men on an immediate and personal basis, and feminist politics certainly cannot ignore their existence.

Feminists disagree profoundly as to how men fit into their analyses of inequality, strategies for change and visions of the future. These disagreements can at times reflect personal experience: some feminists have found in their relationships with men a source of practical and emotional support and strength, others find them a time-consuming, energy-sapping distraction, while for some they are a direct and immediate source of physical and emotional oppression. Feminist disagreements cannot, however, be reduced to personal experiences, but also stem from different theoretical starting-points. This chapter begins by applying these to three interconnected questions: whether men as well as women might benefit from greater equality between the sexes; whether we should see men as 'the enemy', or as potential allies and even potential feminists; and whether women-only organisations are either necessary or desirable. It links answers to these questions to recent theoretical developments, including a growing literature by men; as in other chapters it finds both that some areas of consensus are emerging and that hard choices still have to be made.

Theoretical starting-points

Liberalism

From a liberal feminist perspective, there is certainly no inherent or inevitable conflict of interests between women and men. The basis of this perspective is the claim that women and men have the same human qualities; this has been used to argue not only that women are entitled to the same rights as men, but that men too will gain if women's demands for equality are met. This argument was clearly expressed in the 19th century by the philosopher John Stuart Mill. In *The Subjection of Women* ([1869] 1983), Mill argued that ultimately everyone would benefit from living in a civilised society regulated according to principles of justice rather than injustice, that society as a whole would gain from being able to draw on the talents and abilities of all its members rather than confining half of them to the domestic sphere, and that the joys of a loving and equal relationship with a woman were far superior to the petty pleasures of domestic tyranny. Later writers have added to this the argument that men will also gain if women are more equal in the workplace, because husbands will no longer be expected to shoulder financial responsibilities on their own; rather than being threatened by women's financial independence, men therefore 'have nothing to lose but their coronaries' (Gloria Steinem, quoted in Ehrenreich, 1983, p. 100).

From the liberal perspective, therefore, the pursuit of gender equality is not part of a zero sum game, but one in which all can be winners and in which men's enlightened self-interest should combine with the requirements of justice to produce male support for feminist goals. This means that men can certainly be allies, and many liberal feminists see no problem in saying that men can also be feminists. At the same time, separatism and women-only groups seem to be ruled out; not only are they unnecessary, but they are a form of sexist discrimination against men. When the National Organisation for Women was set up in the United States in 1966, men were, therefore, eligible to join, and have always been about 10 per cent of its members. Because men are so powerful in public life, liberal feminists see male support as not only possible but also politically essential; men's support, both practical and emotional, will also often be necessary at a personal level. From this perspective, there is no inevitable 'problem of men'; the only problem is to convince men that sexist behaviour is contrary to their own real interests, and that the feminist cause is theirs as well.

Marxism and socialism

Marxist and socialist approaches also suggest that there is no basic conflict of interests between women and men. Socialist writers have long argued that working men and women should work together as comrades to create a socialist society in which all forms of subordination will be removed and relations between the sexes will no longer be debased by women's economic dependency. The enemy against which feminists must struggle is therefore not men, but the economic system: 'women's liberation is not aimed at men as a class enemy, but at the economic, social and sexual structures which allow men to dominate women and to legitimate this domination' (Ramazonoglu, 1989, p. 187).

Despite their commitment to the principle of gender equality, socialist men have in the past frequently treated it as something that could be postponed until 'after the revolution' (with a sub-text of 'Meanwhile, where's my dinner?'); indeed, the sexist behaviour of men in left-wing groups did much to inspire the development of radical feminism from the late 1960s (see Chapter 2). More recently, however, some socialist male writers have argued that in a capitalist economy men are not only exploited as workers, but also suffer as *men*. As such, they are forced into a breadwinning role and expected to conform to a model of masculinity which prevents them expressing their feelings or displaying emotion: 'The direct result is a high level of tension and anxiety; the indirect result is a high disease rate and early death' (Blood *et al.*, 1995, p. 159).

This analysis suggests that men as well as women have a vested interest in prioritising gender issues. Although a materialist analysis of knowledge suggests that men's relationship to feminist theory

198 *Feminist Debates*

cannot be the same as women's because it is not based in lived experience (see Chapter 2), it does not seem to preclude the possibility that men can be feminist supporters or even feminists, although not in the same way as women. Some socialist men argue that it also requires men as well as women to meet in single-sex groups to explore, on the basis of shared experiences, the ways in which dominant forms of masculinity have been constructed. By the mid-1970s, there were 20 to 30 such groups in Britain. In contrast to other kinds of men-only groups which have excluded women in order to maintain their subordination, these were inspired by a commitment to opposing sexism. As such, they shared the liberal feminist belief that a gender-equal society will be a better place for all, and that the interests of women and men are certainly not permanently opposed.

Radical feminism

A major problem with both liberal and socialist analyses is that they fail to explain why, if gender equality really is in their interests, so many men oppose it in practice, even when they claim to accept it in principle. In contrast, the radical feminist concept of patriarchy argues that, because men are systematically advantaged in the present system, they are unlikely to support significant change. According to this approach, the relationship between men and women is not simply one of inequality but of active oppression, and this is much more pervasive and deep-seated than the other approaches can see. The 1969 manifesto of the New York Redstockings provides an extreme example of this kind of analysis:

> Women are an oppressed class. Our oppression is total, affecting every facet of our lives. We are considered inferior beings whose only purpose is to enhance men's lives... We identify the agents of our oppression as men. All men receive economic, sexual, and psychological benefits from male supremacy. All men have oppressed women. (in Morgan, 1970, p. 598)

This analysis quite clearly identifies the enemy as men, and certainly rejects the view that men can be feminists. Indeed Marianne Hester has claimed that 'Whatever activities an anti-sexist man becomes involved in, and whatever opinions he chooses to hold as an anti-sexist man it appears that the motivation is egotistical and for his own enhancement', and she cites the admission by one such man that changes in men's behaviour constitute 'a cloak-and-dagger form of male chauvinism' designed to serve their own sexual ends (Hester, 1984, pp. 33, 37). From this perspective, women will certainly have to organise separately to defend their own interests against those of men, and any personal involvement with men will weaken the feminist cause.

Other feminists, however, argue that the analysis of men's patriarchal power cannot be so simple. Rather, it involves complex issues of structure and agency through which it may be possible to distinguish between male power and male persons, and to understand that the former is socially constructed rather than embodied in all biological men. Such an approach makes it possible to oppose patriarchy without assuming that all men are necessarily immune to the considerations of justice, denying the very possibility of non-exploitative relationships with men, or treating all forms of male support as automatically suspect. As such, it can appear to provide a comfortable solution for the majority of feminists, who continue to have personal, working and political relationships with men.

Nevertheless, even in its weakest form, the concept of patriarchy reminds us of the ways in which men are systematically privileged over women, so that even the kindest and gentlest of men may benefit from the oppressive and even violent actions of others, for these serve the function of maintaining male authority (for arguments in support of this, see Chapter 8). From this perspective, it is the depth and extent of male privilege that explains why apparently moderate feminist requests are so often resisted. Even if men are convinced of the justice of women's claims and even if they would gain from greater gender equality, it remains true that they will also lose, at least in the short term, for 'If women are to have more opportunities, more money, more time and more power than they do now, men will inevitably have less in relative terms, and will almost certainly have less in absolute terms as well' (Coote and Patullo, 1990, p. 24).

At a practical level, greater equality would mean for example that men would not only be unable to opt out of the more boring household chores, but that they would not be considered heroic for doing them, and that a male politician could not express his full commitment to increasing women's representation while exempting his own constituency. It would also mean that sexual attraction would no longer involve the eroticisation of male domination and female subordination, that women would cease to prioritise men's emotional and sexual needs above their own, and that they would no longer admire and flatter men simply because of their sex. Even more significantly, genuine equality would mean that men would no longer be taken as the starting-point for human experience, with women treated as an optional extra; men would therefore cease to be the measure of human worth against which women should be measured. Christine Battersby has recently defined patriarchy as 'that form of social organization which takes male bodies and life-patternings as both norm and ideal in the exercise of power' (Battersby, 1998, p. 15); this definition means that if patriarchy is to be ended, men must be displaced from their position at the centre of the human universe; far from 'business as usual plus a few women', the result would be a radical re-ordering of priorities and assumptions in all areas of life.

Anti-feminist arguments: the oppression of men

Some of these practical and theoretical changes are already beginning, and are provoking unease, anger and resentment on the part of many men. Because material, psychological and philosophical interests are at stake, such opposition goes beyond the resistance to a paradigm shift which would normally be expected on the part of those whose ways of thinking have been based upon the old. As Kate Millett said in *Sexual Politics* (see Chapter 2), a mark of patriarchy's success has been its invisibility, and many men are not even aware of the privileges their sex bestows. As these have come under threat, the response of some men has been to attack feminism for disturbing the natural order of things, and to claim that *men* are now the oppressed sex.

Anti-feminist writers like David Thomas (*Not Guilty*, 1993), Warren Farrell (*The Myth of Male Power*, 1994) and Neil Lyndon (*No More Sex War*, 1993) have claimed that men have to work harder than women, that affirmative action schemes discriminate against them in employment, that they are denied custodial or even access rights to their children, that divorce settlements require them to maintain former wives who choose not to work, that more men than women are victims of domestic violence, that men are falsely depicted as sexual predators, that malicious accusations of rape are automatically believed, that men are the victims of an anti-male culture in which they are the legitimate targets of sexist jokes, and that men are much more likely than women to kill themselves.

As the preceding chapters have shown, many of these allegations rest upon a clear distortion of reality: women continue to earn much less than men and to work longer hours overall, divorce leaves far more women than men in poverty, only a small fraction of rapes results in a conviction and women's refuges can accommodate only a fraction of the women who are trying to escape from domestic violence. Anti-feminist allegations of sexist discrimination against men also ignore the critical difference between employment practices, such as affirmative action, aimed at ending gender inequalities and those, such as reliance on informal networks, which have served to maintain them; they similarly fail to understand that jokes against men can subvert patriarchal inequalities, while jokes against women serve to legitimate and maintain them.

Nevertheless, some of the difficulties faced by men are very real. It is clearly not desirable that caring fathers should be denied access to their own children, that some men should be falsely accused of rape (see Cowling, 1995) or that increasing numbers of young men see suicide as the only solution to their problems. It also seems likely that when men are subject to domestic violence from a female partner they will find it particularly difficult to seek help.

Many men also feel resentment at a feminist analysis which seems to lump all men together as wife-beating rapists and which leaves no space for the recognition of loving tenderness between men and women. Such men resent being made to feel like a sexual predator if they walk down the same street as a woman at night or smile at children playing in a park; they may therefore feel that their lives have been poisoned by feminist propaganda. Well-intentioned men should however remember that the sexual abuse of women and children pre-dates feminism, and that women walking home at night have always known that any man is a potential threat, so that being able to ignore one's gender is a luxury which only men have previously enjoyed. Such men might also consider how the power balance between the sexes would be affected if we lived in a world in which well-meaning women offered to walk men home in order to protect them from female violence, and in which depiction of the sexual abuse of men by women was regularly shown as a form of entertainment.

Black feminism and post-modernism

As discussed in Chapters 2 and 3, black feminists have refused to see black men simply as enemies, and their primary political allegiance may at times lie with men of their ethnic group rather than with white women. Black feminism also reveals how, just as the meaning of being a woman is often very different for black and white women, so too is the meaning of being a man: for example, the idea that a man is the economic provider for his family was obviously meaningless for black male slaves, and is today irrelevant in communities characterised by high male unemployment and female-headed households. This means that although black men may be privileged by their gender, they also suffer as men in a society in which they cannot gain access to many of the attributes associated with dominant perceptions of successful masculinity.

Black feminism's insistence that men and women cannot be seen simply as two opposing groups has much in common with post-modernism's rejection of all unitary and closed categories. As Karlene Faith has said, 'The binary opposition model which necessitates belief in a singular Enemy – the family, the state, parents, capitalists, white people, straight people, the devil or whomever – does not square with Foucault's recognition of networks of interlinked power relations' (Faith, 1994, p. 47. It is tempting to add that neither does it square with common sense). From this perspective, not only masculinity and femininity, but also the very categories of 'man' and 'woman' and 'male' and 'female' are artificial constructs which disguise a multiplicity of fluid and shifting identities (for fuller discussion, see Chapters 2 and 3). This means that questions such as whether men are the enemies or potential allies of feminism simply dissolve, as neither 'man' nor 'feminism' has a stable meaning. It also implies that we all have an interest in transgressing boundaries and contesting the constricting categories of gender classification.

Men and feminist theory today

The theoretical starting-points which informed feminist debates in the early 1970s have been tempered both by practical experience and by ongoing developments in political theory. Today it is possible to identify four dominant and interconnected themes in relation to 'the man question', which transcend any one theoretical starting-point and attract a wide measure of agreement across the political spectrum of feminist thought. First, there is a growing recognition of the need to displace men as the norm against whom women are measured and in accordance with whose needs society is organised. Second, some feminists have moved from identifying and challenging the ways in which femininity is produced, to problematising masculinity as well. Third, the recognition that masculinity may be socially constructed is linked to a growing understanding that, just as feminists have to recognise differences among women, so we have to recognise differences among men. This does not mean simply that there are 'nice guys' and 'sexist pigs', or that men are divided by class and race; it also means that there may be competing models of masculinity in society at any one time, and that dominant forms may be experienced as oppressive by some men. Fourth, this in turn opens up the possibility that the way forward may be to welcome and strengthen non-oppressive forms of masculinity, and to attempt to move beyond the binary divisions of a gendered society.

Rejecting the male norm

As discussed above, many men are likely to find the idea that their sex should no longer be the automatic starting-point and measure of humanity profoundly threatening, and the mere assertion of the validity of a non-male perspective may feel to some men like female supremacism. In the short term it may indeed be necessary to insist on prioritising women's needs and perceptions if these are to be heard at all. However, as Kathy Ferguson has argued in *The Man Question*, 'Most versions of feminism reject the idea of simply reproducing phallocentric discourse or patriarchal society with women at the top' (Ferguson, 1993, p. 3), and many argue not that women should replace men in the centre, but that the idea of a centre should itself be abandoned. Such a move would avoid the danger of producing a new norm based on the experiences and interests of white, middle-class women and ignoring those of other groups. It would also avoid reaffirming the importance of gender differences, and opens up the possibility of a future in which 'partial identities and mobile subjectivities' could replace binary opposition (Ferguson, 1993, p. 158). The problem remains, however, of how this long-term dissolution of gender can be reconciled with the initial challenge to male hegemony.

A recurrent theme of this book has been the finding that legal rights and employment and political practices are frequently not gender neutral. Rather, they ignore women's traditional social responsibilities and reflect the specific needs, perceptions and priorities of people who cannot give birth, who have historically been absolved from many domestic and caring responsibilities, whose physical maintenance is taken care of by others, whose communication style is characteristically assertive or even combative, and who have been encouraged to repress their emotions. Simply extending male rights and opportunities to women cannot, therefore, produce equality; it is also now clear that society could not function if everyone behaved like men, and few people would welcome a world in which women acquired the attributes traditionally associated with masculinity, while men themselves remained unchanged.

As we saw in Chapter 6, the idea that men's behaviour must change has gone furthest in the Nordic nations, where equality policies since the late 1960s have been premised upon the need to increase men's role within the home, and educational programmes have been deliberately designed to challenge gender stereotypes from the earliest possible age. In Britain, similar arguments have been forcefully expressed by the Labour party politician Harriet Harman in *The Century Gap* (Harman, 1993). Here, Harman argues that women today want to be responsible parents who are also taken seriously at work, and they expect marriage to mean a partnership rather than an exchange of personal services in return for financial support. However, Harman says that such '21st-century women' are confronted with men and employers whose attitudes and practices are firmly stuck in the 20th century – hence the title of her book. Much as John Stuart Mill had earlier argued that it was in men's interest to give women the same rights as men, Harman argues that family-friendly employment practices and changes in domestic roles would benefit men and society as a whole:

When men take a full part in family life our homes will be less of a battleground. Marriage will become a relationship of democracy, rather than a power struggle. When women are able fully to participate in the world of work our economy will be revitalised. And when, in equal numbers with men, they walk the corridors of power, the entire political structure will be refreshed; the outside world will relate to it in new ways and democracy will come alive. (Harman, 1993, pp. 7–8)

However, men in general appear unconvinced. Even in Scandinavia, their domestic behaviour has been very slow to change, and male politicians have proved unwilling to share responsibility for family welfare issues. It seems that even the best-intentioned of partners or political leaders are unlikely to share the perception that they and their own behaviour are part of the problem that women face.

Masculinity in question

When men are no longer equated with humanity, their gender becomes visible. This makes it is possible to approach the analysis of economic, political or personal life from a viewpoint that recognises the gender-specific nature of male life-patterns and behaviour rather than seeing these as standard. This means, for example, that a gender analysis is central to an understanding of how political elites function, precisely because these have generally excluded women. Political scientists have, of course, not traditionally recognised this, and Terrell Carver has argued that they have thereby lost a whole dimension of understanding: he claims that not only is the 'abstract individual' not female, it is not really male either, for the concept ignores the reality of men's physical dependency on others, their actual or potential role as fathers and their domestic and sexual lives (Carver, 1996). It is therefore only when we understand that when we are studying politicians we are usually also studying men, that we can begin to understand their interests and behaviour, and the complex ways in which these are related both to their biological sex and to the social meanings and identities attached to this.

Since the 1970s, some feminist-influenced men have agreed on the need to question what it means to be a man. In addition to the formation of men's groups, this has led to a growth of academic writing by men about their own sex. Such writing generally accepts that society is male dominated and that men are part of the problem confronting women. Victor Seidler has therefore argued that although it is easier for male feminist supporters to focus on the oppression of women, because this 'can appeal to the archetypal vision of men as heroes on white horses, able to rescue women in distress' (Seidler, 1991, p. xiii), they must also focus on themselves and learn new ways of behaving if gender equality is to be achieved.

The men's collective of which Seidler was a member described the self-consciousness awareness by men of their masculinity as in a sense 'coming out' as men (Seidler, 1991, p. 17). This recognition that gender is about men as well as women produces a perspective on political and social behaviour that is radically different from conventional understandings. The implications of distinguishing between men and people in general are particularly clear in relation to criminal and socially disruptive behaviour. Conventional political and media discussion of 'rioters', 'violent teenagers', 'joy riders', 'child criminals', 'sex offenders' or 'child abusers' conceals the fact that such people are overwhelmingly men and boys rather than women and girls. In contrast, a recognition of gender not only identifies much anti-social activity as a problem of male behaviour, but enables us to explore the ways in which it is linked to 'normal' forms of masculinity.

Beatrix Campbell, in an investigation of the breakdown of law and order in some estates in Britain in the early 1990s, found that violent criminality did not simply represent a response to the problems of poverty and unemployment, but specifically *masculine* responses, with young men and women reacting to deprivation in very different ways: 'The lads got into trouble and the lasses got pregnant. The one was on the run, the other was trying to make relationships. The one was killing cars, the other was kissing a baby'; 'Crime and coercion are sustained by men. Solidarity and self-help are sustained by women. It is as stark as that'. She argues that the rioters and joy-riders do not express a deviant masculinity, but mainstream masculine values which are also held by the police forces which confront them and by 'the rowdy louts in the Palace of Westminster'. Similarly, she claims that the 'irresponsible' behaviour of young unemployed men who father children but do not care for them reflects the domestic absenteeism of 'respectable', middle-class men; the only difference, she says, is that whereas the former can use their employment to sanction their absence, in areas where few are in work 'Men's flight from fatherhood has no hiding place' (Campbell, 1993, pp. 201, 319, 313, 202).

Similar arguments have been developed by Lynne Segal in *Slow Motion. Changing Masculinities and Changing Men* (1990). In this, Segal claims that the criminal violence which characterises the behaviour of some groups of young men is a product of a society which 'constructs masculinity around ideas of dominance, social power and control over others, but then denies to some men any access to such prerogatives'. She further argues that we should not blame those who 'are brutalised within an underworld of fear and exploitation' but governments and organisations such as the International Monetary Fund, which 'never directly engage in acts of violence or physical force, but orchestrate the degradation and brutalisation of others' (Segal, 1990a, pp. 155–6, 270–1).

Some recent work on the sexual abuse of children similarly insists that, although a minority of abusers are women, abuse is often primarily about men's behaviour: it should therefore be understood as a product of dominant forms of masculinity, rather than either as an innate male attribute or the pathological behaviour of a deviant minority. From this perspective, the problem is the role of violence within 'normal' masculinities, and the ways in which male sexual arousal has become linked with both power and the erotisation of lesser physical strength and extreme youth. It is therefore only by challenging 'normal' masculine behaviour and expectations that we can tackle the problem of abuse (see Hearn, 1988).

It is clear that men as well as women can suffer from living in insecure families and in a violent society. Those in the most disadvantaged groups experience the effects most acutely: in the United States, homicide is the leading cause of death among young black men, more of whom were killed in 1987 (mainly by other young black men) than were killed abroad in the entire nine years of war in Vietnam (Dyson, 1995). If Campbell and Segal are correct, such violence is not the product of black or working-class culture, but of 'normal' masculine values, which are therefore profoundly damaging, not only to the life-chances and experiences of women, but to society as a whole. Campbell and Segal do not believe that these values are rooted in male biology or that men's anti-social behaviour is an inevitable product of their genes. The problem therefore becomes one of identifying the complex psychological, cultural and social processes through which masculinities are constructed, in order that these can be challenged and changed. Such changes would go far deeper than individual behaviour, and could not be disentangled from changes in power relationships and gender hierarchies at every level of society.

From masculinity to masculinities

The claim that masculinity is socially constructed almost inevitably leads to a recognition that it will vary both across time and within a given society. There is now a widespread recognition that although it makes sense to talk about dominant forms of masculinity, these are neither uncontested nor uniformly experienced. Clearly the meaning and experience of what it is to be a man can differ significantly between homosexuals and heterosexuals, black men and white men, old men and young men, rich men and poor men, and sick men and healthy men (while membership of these groups is both fluid and cross-cutting). Because members of these groups differ in their access to attributes of dominant masculinity, such as power and physical strength, they may experience these as oppressive; as Robert Connell has pointed out, the oppression of gays can also have a knock-on effect on effeminate or unassertive heterosexual men (Connell, 1987). At the same time, there has not been one clearly hegemonic ideal of masculinity. For example, the idea that 'a real man' is aggressive and sexually predatory has long co-existed with the idea that he is chivalrous, protective and 'gentlemanly' in his relationships both with women and with other men.

Today, this lack of one clear model of masculinity is particularly acute, as feminist critiques have combined with rapid social change to disrupt and challenge traditional assumptions. Thus the equation of masculinity with the role of family provider has little meaning in a society in which male unemployment, dual income families and single motherhood have all steadily increased. The idea that heterosexual men should be the sexual initiators of reluctant virgins is also difficult to sustain in a world in which young men are confronted with images of sexually confident, knowledgeable and assertive women, but in which some may also fear that any expression of sexual interest will be construed as harassment or even assault. The result has been a general climate of uncertainty about gender roles and behaviour, which some see as linked to a rise in male suicide, illness and psychological stress. Many commentators therefore share the concern expressed in 1995 by the Archbishop of York, Dr John Habgood, when he talked about 'a growing body of young men who feel they have no particular stake in society and who are regarded by women as not worth marrying' (*Daily Telegraph*, 8 March 1995).

Some men have reacted to these changes with a 'backlash' against feminism and a reassertion of misogyny and violence (see Faludi, 1992), and the American feminist Barbara Ehrenreich has argued that:

> Male culture seems to have abandoned the breadwinner role without overcoming the sexist attitudes that role has perpetuated: on the one hand, the expectation of female nurturance and submissive service as a matter of right; on the other hand, a misogynist contempt for women as 'parasites' and entrappers of men. (Ehrenreich, 1983, p. 182)

Other men have, however, changed in positive ways, and society today offers a range of masculine behaviours which include active fathering and the expression of emotion. The result is that 'A diversity of "masculinities" jostle to present themselves as the acceptable face of the new male order' (Segal, 1990a, p. 293); such diversity opens up the possibility of non-oppressive ways of being a man.

The reconstruction of masculinity

Accepting that a range of masculinities exists today, the problem for many feminists and feminist supporters is how to encourage and strengthen its positive forms while challenging its oppressive manifestations. Given that gender identity in our society is so basic to our sense of self, and so deeply embedded in our culture, social practices and interpersonal relationships, this is a highly complex task. As such, it will have to be tackled simultaneously at political, interpersonal and ideological levels, while changes in one area of life will interact with changes in others.

This becomes clear if we look at the role of fathers. Earlier images of a good father as provider and remote authority figure now coexist with the idea that 'real men' can cuddle babies, and that a good father is one who is involved with the practical and emotional care of his children from changing their nappies to taking them to school to advising them on relationship problems. As we have seen in Chapter 6, such changes in attitudes have only been translated into practice to a limited extent. Nevertheless, there has been a general trend towards greater parental involvement by men within two-parent families, and a minority now play at least as great a role as their partners.

Such changes are likely to have significant long-term effects both on the men involved and on the children for whom they care, and these may feed through into the wider society. Here some feminists have claimed that the experience of caring for children can give rise to particular ways of thinking and moralising based upon ideas of interconnection and responsibility, rather than abstract notions of justice and right (see Chapter 4). Sarah Ruddick has further argued that the practice of 'mothering' (which she says can be done by men) is based on the principle of 'preservative love' which is incompatible with military values, so that extending these values to men could encourage more peaceful resolution of political conflicts (Ruddick, 1990). Others claim that shared parenting could have important psychological effects upon a future generation of boys, who would not learn from an early age that they could only become men by denying the emotional and caring aspects of their personality (see in particular Chodorow, 1978; Dinnerstein, 1987 and the discussion in Chapter 6).

The greater involvement of men in childcare is however not simply a matter of cultural change or personal choice. Like other attempts at 'reconstructing masculinity', it cannot be isolated from its wider context, for:

> Beneath and beyond possibilities for personal change lies the whole web of interconnecting social, economic and political practices, public policies, welfare resources and understandings of sexuality which actually confer power upon men. (Segal, 1990a, p. 294)

What is a nice man to do?

The understanding that masculinity can be seen as a problem rather than a normal state of being, and that its dominant forms can often be harmful to men, has contributed to the development of critical work on gender by men. Much of this work attempts to establish points of contact between the experiences of men and women, and to develop new ways of relating to feminism that recognise the power that men have, but go beyond the politics of guilt. Robert Connell has argued that even white, middle-class, heterosexual men such as himself have additional reasons to detach themselves from the maintenance of a patriarchal system in which they are systematically privileged. Such men, he says, may want better lives for their wives, sisters, daughters and other women who are important to them; and they can recognise that large-scale changes are already occurring and that they cannot simply cling to the past. They can also come to see the ways in which their relationships with women are poisoned by an oppressive system; and, as people who 'are not excluded from the basic human capacity to share experiences, feelings and hopes', they can be motivated to work for change (Connell, 1987, p. xiii).

For some men, the exploration of masculinity involves a recognition that men have both repressed the emotional aspects of their personalities and depended upon women for emotional strength and support. From this perspective, a key role of anti-sexist men's groups is to enable men to discover their emotional needs and learn how to nurture each other. According to Seidler, such self-exploration cannot be separated from more overtly political change. As with women's consciousness-raising groups, however, there is a danger that such groups can become a form of personal therapy which concentrates on the individual while leaving structures of power intact. Many women have, moreover, learned to dread the 'new man' who has discovered the joys of discussing feelings, but only so long as they are his own, and who is as solipsistically unaware of the emotional needs of others as his unreconstructed predecessors. Although learning to provide and accept support from other men is a step forward, as Toril Moi has said, 'the underlying assumption here is that men require a fixed amount of support or "nurturing" no matter what, and that if women are not to provide it, then men must do so'; she says, however, that she would 'rather see men give up their excessive demands for support *tout court* and start practising the difficult art of supporting women instead' (Moi, 1989, p. 183).

However good their intentions, the pronouncements of pro-feminist men inevitably have a form of 'natural' authority which is still widely withheld from women. Other men may have less laudable reasons for endorsing feminist aims and/or studying masculinities.

For some, this can seem a way of furthering their academic career, or a means of attracting women. For others, it may be a way of reasserting control over an area of knowledge in which men have been excluded or marginalised; as such, men's academic study of feminism can be seen as a way of taming its raw power by presenting it as an abstract theory rather than a response to felt oppression.

More generally, although the problematisation and investigation of masculinities may be an important and valid response by men to feminism, it can easily degenerate into a 'look at ME!' example of what Diane Bell and Renate Klein have described as 'phallic drift': 'the powerful tendency for public discussion of gender issues to drift, inexorably, back to the male point of view' (Bell and Klein, 1996, p. 561). This is also true of the debate over whether or not men can be feminists, which can become an open-ended diversion from more substantive issues. As Moi (who thinks that, in principle, men can be feminists) says:

> If feminism is primarily the struggle against oppressive and exploitative patriarchal power structures, the important thing for men is not to spend their time worrying about definitions and essences ('am I really a feminist?'), but to take up a recognizable anti-patriarchal position. It is not enough simply to be interested in masculinity or in male sexuality or in gender differences. Such interests must in some way or other be developed as part of the anti-patriarchal struggle. (Moi, 1989, p. 184)

In other words, men's commitment to feminism is to be judged by their deeds rather than by their words, and the pursuit of a feminist label should not in itself be a goal.

Attempts by pro-feminist men to translate their beliefs into action have in the past included the provision of crèches at women's conferences and support for women's abortion rights, as well as changes in their personal relationships and behaviour within the home. There has, however, been no mass men's movement demanding paternity leave or a radical reappraisal of pay and employment to recognise the importance of caring and domestic work; although some men have acknowledged the harmful effects of pornography on their own sexuality (see for example Kimmel, 1990), this has not been translated into serious political action.

Sustained commitment to feminist goals is frequently difficult and wearying for women, and it is even more so for men, who frequently find it hard to tread a middle way between masochistic, paralysing guilt and smug self-righteousness, or between providing support for women and taking over from them. An important starting-point must, however, be the recognition that men's relationship with feminism cannot be straightforward, and that 'To respond to feminism is to forego mastery... Feminism makes things unsafe for men, unsettles assumed positions, undoes given identities' (Heath, 1989, p. 6). It also seems likely that any man who claims not to be frightened by feminism has simply failed to understand its implications.

Conclusions

This chapter opened by asking whether men can benefit from greater equality between the sexes, whether they should be seen as 'the enemy' or as potential allies or even feminists, and whether women-only organisations are either necessary or desirable. The above discussions suggest that men could indeed benefit from living in a society in which women were not simply given the same rights as men, but in which dominant male attributes, life-patterns and models of masculinity were no longer the norm. Many men are also not immune to the appeals of reason and justice, and would agree with John Stuart Mill's belief that it is infinitely preferable that 'the most universal and pervading of all human relations [be] regulated by justice instead of injustice' ([1869] 1983, p. 148).

A sense of justice is however a perishable flower, and the alleged benefits of feminist change can appear intangible and uncertain to men who frequently do not recognise the extent of their privileges, see little reason to adjust their immediate political priorities or modes of behaviour, and cannot imagine the loss of their own centrality. This does not mean that men can be lumped together as undifferentiated enemies; it is, however, important to recognise the ways in which the nicest of men can benefit from the overtly oppressive or discriminatory practices of others; because their failure to oppose such practices can itself be seen as a form of connivance, the distinction between male power and male persons is frequently difficult to sustain.

Whether or not men can ever really be feminists remains in dispute. Female feminists and anti-sexist men can, however, perhaps agree that the question is at best of secondary importance; many will also concede that, whatever labels we use, men's relationship to feminism will continue to be different from women's as long as society remains organised on hierarchical gender lines.

Although most men fail to understand the full implications of a commitment to feminism, a minority have made genuine attempts to change their behaviour and to support feminist women. Some feminists have recently attacked others for mocking or rejecting such well-intentioned men. Thus Naomi Wolf insists that 'If a man wants to be a feminist, he should not have to lay down his basic self-respect' (Wolf, 1993, p. 203), while Yvonne Roberts criticises the reaction of some feminists to anti sexist men in the early 1980s:

> If help was offered running crèches at a women's conference, it was conceived as men trying to take over. If a man suggested bottle-feeding instead of breastfeeding so that he could take his share of sleepless nights, this was male manipulation; if a man attempted to open up discussions on fathering and mothering, he was accused of distracting women from the 'real fight' – their own. If a man was open about his feelings as a father, it was regarded as embarrassingly wet: the wimp effect in sexual politics. (Roberts, 1992, p. 7).

The suggestion that feminists should learn to be more tactful and understanding in their dealings with men can seem very irritating to those who fail to see why we should indulge men's need for praise or show gratitude when they undertake work that women have done unremarked for centuries. Given the realities of both political power and personal relationships such tact may, however, at times be strategically necessary: men may be the problem, but they will have to be part of the solution as well, and women will at times have to work with them if they are to achieve the changes in social and political policy that gender equality requires.

This becomes even clearer if we accept that, as argued in Chapter 3, different forms of oppression interact and overlap with each other, and that an effective 'politics of solidarity' requires alliances between different groups as well as a recognition of group-specific needs and interests. In this context, the situation of those white, heterosexual, middle-class and able-bodied women who claim to oppose racism, discrimination against lesbians, poverty and the denial of rights to disabled people has parallels with that of anti-sexist men. Like men, privileged women cannot directly share the experiences of women in other social groups, they cannot easily appreciate the enormity of rejecting the 'normality' of their own situation, and few translate their stated commitments into political priorities or significant life-style changes. Disabled feminists such as Jenny Morris have attacked the insensitive and disablist assumptions of able-bodied feminists (Morris, 1991); her criticisms may also have the unintended effect of enabling such women to empathise with the experiences of men who think they are opposed to sexism, but who find themselves attacked by the women they are trying to 'help'.

Although feminists will at times have to work with men to achieve social and political changes, the need for single-sex activities and organisations remains, at least for the foreseeable future. It seems simply unrealistic to expect men to keep women's needs firmly and consistently in focus, and the strength that a woman-only space can provide is a necessary counter to the colonising effects of 'phallic drift' in mixed groups. Recognition of this need now goes well beyond the anti-male hostility of radical separatists, and is endorsed by such 'mainstream' writers as Naomi Wolf, who refuses to see men as the enemy, but advocates women-only groups and networks through which women can share knowledge, resources and skills (Wolf, 1993).

Paradoxically, the need for single-sex groups can sometimes be more important for heterosexual women than for lesbians: although the latter may be the particular targets of male aggression in mixed organisations, they do not experience the same disempowering effects of an ingrained need to appear attractive in a society in which attractiveness for women is associated with compliance and passivity, and for men with assertiveness and strength. For a minority of women, separatism will extend into their personal life; for most it will be limited to a woman-only space in a life that includes men.

The above discussion assumes that gender interests are not permanently and irrevocably opposed, and it leaves open the possibility that 'man' and 'woman' are not fixed and closed categories. It therefore assumes that the anti-social personality traits and modes of behaviour currently associated with masculinity are not determined by biology, and that, even if men's hormones and/or genes predispose them to aggressive behaviour and a low level of communicative skills, these can be significantly modified by their social environment. It also suggests that more positive aspects of masculinity, such as courage and assertiveness, can be acquired by women. As such, it is inherently optimistic, and it rejects the view that society could only be rescued from the destructive effects of masculinity by massive programmes of testosterone reduction, or that cloning could produce a final solution to the 'problem of men'.

10
Conclusions

When I started writing this book, I was worried that theoretical debates would remain stubbornly separate from more immediate and down-to-earth concerns, and that my aim of using feminist theory to clarify debates over political strategy would be impossible to realise. It was therefore with some relief that I found that recurrent themes did emerge, as discussion of one set of issues naturally fed into and enriched discussion of others, at both theoretical and more practical levels.

The related themes of *interconnection*, *interaction* and *interdependence* provide a unifying starting-point for my conclusions. Throughout this book, I have found myself repeatedly arguing that no one issue can be understood or solved in isolation, for changes have a cumulative effect, and progress in one area can be both dependent upon and a precondition for progress in others. This is clear if we look at the example of abortion, discussed more fully in Chapter 7. Many feminists have seen access to legal abortion as both important in itself and as a prerequisite for full participation in employment and the free expression of sexuality, so that women's ability to make their own reproductive decisions is causally linked to other improvements in their lives. Women's reproductive decisions are, however, also a product of other factors, including their economic situation, the extent to which childcare responsibilities are shared within the home or with the state, the status of disabled people, and patterns of sexual behaviour. This means that a woman who has an abortion because she cannot afford to have a baby, because inadequate childcare and maternity leave mean that she has to choose between children and a career, because ante-natal tests have detected fetal abnormalities, or because she is pregnant as a

218 *Feminist Debates*

result of coercive sex, is not really in control of her own fertility. For such a woman, genuine reproductive choice would mean far more than legal abortion, and would require changes in employment practices, family responsibilities, attitudes to disability and sexual expectations. This in turn means that the 'politics of reproduction' could be understood as including feminist campaigns for better pay and prospects for female workers, for family-friendly employment practices that would enable fathers as well as mothers to combine employment and caring responsibilities, for better social support for disabled people and their carers, and against the portrayal of women as passive sex objects to be used by men.

It is an awareness of such interconnections that makes patriarchy a meaningful concept, linking apparently separate or coincidental incidences of male power and privilege, and revealing their systematic and structural nature. The concept of patriarchy therefore enables feminists to identify the ways in which male power may be exercised within the family and sexual relationships, and to see that issues around domestic violence, the division of household chores or the consumption of pornography are not simply private concerns, but are part of the processes through which dominant relations of power are reflected, reproduced or challenged. From this perspective, the distinction between private and public dissolves, and 'the personal is political'.

Although the concept of patriarchy has at times been used in oversimplified ways, this can be avoided if we also recognise that patriarchy interacts with other systems of oppression. At a practical level, this means that 'feminist issues' are linked with other social and political questions. The British Labour party politician Clare Short has written that:

> The beauty of the women's agenda is that it is necessarily generous and egalitarian. Because women do most of the caring, have on average lower incomes and less wealth, are missing from institutions of power and too often suffer from violence and sexual assault – the changes that will satisfy their demand for equality will create a society which will provide more support for carers, be less unequal, distribute power more fairly and be less violent and brutal. (Short, 1995a, p. 2)

However, the feminist agenda will only be 'necessarily generous and egalitarian' if it includes all groups of women. It is important that it does not become the mouthpiece of a privileged minority who are able to buy themselves out of caring responsibilities, and whose claim to speak on behalf of all women sounds hollow to those whose class or ethnic identity seems at least as important a source of oppression as their sex. As discussed in Chapters 2 and 3, if feminism treats the experiences of the most disadvantaged as central starting-points, it almost automatically reveals the interactive nature of different forms of oppression, and the ways in which gender, race, class and other oppressions are experienced differently in different social groups. It can therefore understand both that, as Short says, measures which benefit women will lead to a more generally just society, and that feminist goals are bound up with other 'progressive' social measures.

A focus on interconnection can also be interpreted as a shift away from narrow individualism to a political perspective which understands that humans are part of society and that they do not exist in isolation from one another. This means in particular that claims for 'rights' gain their meaning and effectiveness from their social context rather than as abstract statements of entitlement: thus, for example, although the legal right to abortion is of clear symbolic importance, it has little direct impact on women's lives unless it is also readily available and affordable.

This perspective also means that care and responsibility are recognised as essential to human survival. At the most obvious physical level, we are all dependent upon the care of others when we are babies, and also often at later stages in our lives; although many adults, particularly men, can appear to function as independent members of society, they are, in fact, frequently dependent upon the domestic and emotional care provided by relatives and friends, usually female. A perspective that recognises this can therefore also recognise the social importance of work that is frequently unpaid, and the ways in which this affects the roles played by men and women in economic and political life. As such, it rejects the conventional distinction between public and private life, and again argues that these are essentially interconnected.

The realities of human reproduction provide further reasons for rejecting theories based upon extreme individualism, for there is a sense in which a pregnant woman embodies the essentially interactive nature of human rights and is a living refutation of any theory that ignores the reality of human interdependence. It is therefore

220 Feminist Debates

unsurprising that, as discussed in Chapter 7, feminist attempts to invoke the language of individual rights have run into particular difficulties when used to demand access abortion. As a number of feminist commentators have said, such difficulties are at the heart of feminist problems with an individualistic approach to rights:

> The problems that arise with claiming individual rights for women over reproductive decisions are not chance. They arise from the contradictions within liberal theory over the status of women as individuals, which in turn arises from liberal theory's inability to cope with the inherently social activity of reproduction. This is a failure which cannot be dismissed as trivial because reproduction is necessary to the survival of society. (Himmelweit, 1988, p. 49)

Such discussion provides a good example of the links between apparently esoteric theoretical debate and practical political issues. It reminds us both that good feminist theory cannot be plucked out of the air or based on an uncritical acceptance of existing male paradigms, and that the aim of theory is to provide political guidance. In the case of abortion, it shows the dangers of getting sucked into an inappropriate discourse which can distort feminist demands into narrowly individualistic and apparently selfish claims; it therefore suggests that re-framing the issue from the basis of women's perceptions and experiences can be both empowering and politically expedient. Theory and practice are, therefore, inherently interconnected.

Finally, the theme of interconnection also arises from discussion of the 'competing feminist perspectives' which were identified in Chapter 2, and which I have drawn on throughout the book. It should now be clear that although their starting-points are distinct, the different perspectives have increasingly merged into and fed off one another. This means that today feminist understanding should be able to move beyond any kind of rigid classification, and can draw on insights wherever they are to be found. An identification of underlying assumptions can however clarify debates by showing how disagreement on one level often conceals consensus on another. It can, therefore, allow feminists to build on agreements and work towards shared goals, rather than focusing on their differences.

During the course of this book I have frequently been critical of some of the assumptions underlying a liberal approach, particularly its uncritical acceptance of male norms and its tendency to see issues in abstract and individualistic terms which lose sight of structural and collective inequalities. Liberal values have, however, often provided an important and liberating starting-point for the articulation of feminist demands, and the basic claim that women should be treated as full members of the human race remains important whenever this is questioned. My conclusion that we must recognise the importance and cumulative effects of small-scale reforms is also very much in line with liberal thinking, as is my belief in the need for dialogue, diversity and debate within feminist politics and thought.

Socialist, radical and black feminist approaches have the advantage of recognising the wider social context within which specific debates occur. Marxism may be particularly useful in helping us to conceptualise and understand the ways in which women's situation is linked both to the economic organisation of society and to wider historical processes; as discussed above, radical feminism contributes the invaluable concept of patriarchy. In the past, these approaches have at times produced over-simplistic generalisations, naive talk of overthrowing capitalism or patriarchy and intolerance towards feminists who do not toe the 'party line'. Here liberalism's insistence on open discussion provides a useful corrective, as do black and/or disabled feminist perspectives, for these highlight the interactive effects of different forms of oppression, rather than attempting to reduce these to one single cause. Recognition of differences is of course in line with much post-modernist thinking. Most feminists continue to be suspicious of its allegedly de-politicising effects and its apparently deliberate obscurity; I have, however, found that its analysis of the power of language to structure perceptions and debates, and of the fluid and constructed nature of gender identity, can provide useful tools for more down-to-earth discussion.

An insistence on recognising the complexity and interconnectedness of feminist concerns is not intended to produce a paralysis of political will by suggesting that it is impossible to establish priorities or to change anything without at the same time changing everything else. On the contrary, it means that feminists do not have to reach universal agreement on priorities before doing anything, but can become engaged in the forms of action which appear most practical or relevant to their particular situation and stage in life. This means for instance that it will be mainly young women who will focus on reproduction and childcare provision, but that issues around pension entitlements will become more interesting to them as they get older. It also suggests that although some white women may support them, black women are more likely to prioritise anti-racist campaigns. These different forms of activity can draw strength from an awareness of their knock-on effects, and through the development of both temporary and longer lasting alliances and support networks, which would enable grass-roots political or workplace campaigners to draw on the experience and resources of those feminists who have broken into more powerful positions.

Such an analysis is not based upon a dewy-eyed assertion of women's essential 'niceness' or of universal sisterhood. It does, however, depend upon the beliefs that solidarity is possible between people who are disadvantaged in different ways, and that activity is only feminist if it aims at improving the situation of women in general, rather than a select few. As discussed in Chapters 2 and 3, a politics based on solidarity does not pretend that the interests of all women are identical; it does, however, recognise the ways in which they can gain by supporting each other, and retains the idea of sisterhood as a goal towards which we can work.

The understanding that even small-scale changes can have incremental effects means that it is not necessary to take on the whole world in order to make a difference to women's lives. As the previous chapters have shown, important feminist gains have been made in recent years, and have helped establish the foundations for further progress. The process of converting the vicious circle of oppression and disadvantage into a virtuous circle of progress can be engaged with at almost any point, so that apparently disconnected activities can have a multiplier effect, producing a feminist politics which is greater than the sum of its parts. In this context, feminists debates will continue and some no doubt will be bitter. It should however be possible to identify and build upon areas of agreement rather than simply focusing on disputes. So long as we can talk to each other, diversity and disagreement can be seen as sources of strength and vitality; rather than a sign of feminism's decline, they show that it is still alive.

Further reading

Chapter 1

For global overviews of the situation of women in the mid-1990s, see United Nations (1995 and 1996), Wetzel (1993) and International Labour Organization (1995).
On attitudes to feminism, see Wolf (1993), Faludi (1992), Siann and Wilkinson (1995) and Walter (1998).
On recent feminism and feminist movements, see Kaplan (1992), Rowbotham (1992), Bystydzienski (1992), Kauffman (1993), Griffin 1995, Oakley and Mitchell (1997) and readings for Chapter 2.

Chapter 2

For overviews and analyses of feminist theory, see Bryson (1992), Coole (1993 and 1994), Whelehan (1995) and Evans (1995).
For feminist use of liberal theory, see Richards (1982) and Okin (1990). For now standard criticisms of liberal individualism, see Jaggar (1983) and Eisenstein (1981), but see also Slomp (1995) and Nash (1998) for more nuanced discussion. On the philosophical implications of taking women as the norm, see Battersby (1998).
For recent feminist defences of socialism and/or attempts to use Marxist concepts see Segal, (1991), Vogel (1995), Davis (1995), Giminez (1991), Brenner and Laslett (1996), Bryson (1995) and the discussion of class in Chapter 3.
For recent defences of radical feminism, see Richardson (1997) and Bell and Klein (1996); for a recent criticism of the concept of patriarchy, see Pollert (1996).
On black feminism, see Collins (1990), Davis (1982, 1990), hooks (1981, 1984), Mirza (1997b) and the readings for Chapter 3.
Nicholson (1990) provides a good collection of articles on the relationship between post-modernism and feminism. See also Weedon (1987) for a clear introduction and Jones (1993) and Assiter (1996) for critical analyses.

224 *Feminist Debates*

Chapter 3

On the interaction of gender, race and class, see Brah (1996), recent editions of *Gender and Society*, and the collections edited by James and Busia (1993), Anderson and Collins (1995) and Chow, Wilkinson and Zinn (1996).

For further discussion of the problem of terminology and the complex nature of racial identity, see Nain (1991), Marable (1995), Liu (1994), Bhavnani and Coulson (1986), Simmonds (1997) and Foster-Carter (1987).

On the racial identity of white women, see Ruiz and Dubois (1994), McIntosh (1995), Frankenberg (1993a and 1993b), Ware (1992), Smith, (1995) and Wekker (1995).

Chapter 4

For histories of the movement to legal rights, see Banks (1986), Carter (1988) and Gregory (1987).

On feminist legal theory, see Smart (1989, 1995), Kingdom (1991), Frug (1992), O'Donovan (1985a), Edwards (1985), MacKinnon (1993b), Olsen (1995) and Lacey (1991, 1993).

For discussion of the ideas of Carol Gilligan, see Pollitt (1995), Noddings (1984); Dubois *et al.* (1984), the January 1989 volume of *Ethics*, Sevenhuijson (1998); Addelson (1991, 1993) and Bubeck (1995).

Chapter 5

For discussion of the public/private dichotomy, see Pateman (1987, 1989), Phillips (1991), Ramsay (1997) and Lister (1997).

On women's participation in informal politics and the neglect of this in malestream political analysis, see Galloway and Robertson (1991), Sapiro (1990), Collins (1990), West and Blumberg (1990), Norris (1991), Lister (1997), Chanan (1992), Campbell (1984, 1993), Coote and Patullo (1990), Randall (1987) and Hersch (1991).

For feminist discussion of the British welfare state, see Dale and Foster (1986), Williams (1989) and Pascall (1996). On the United States, see Sapiro (1990), Fraser (1987), Gordon (1990) and Nelson (1990). See also the discussions in Barrett (1986), Pringle and Watson (1992), Dominelli (1991), Ungerson and Kember (1997) and Sainsbury (1996). On the coercive use of welfare see Bryan *et al.* (1985), Mama (1989) and Simpson (1991).

On feminist theories of the state, see Watson (1990) and Hoffman (1998).

On municipal feminism, see Breugel and Kean (1995), Forbes (1996) and Stokes (1995, 1998).

On electoral politics in the United States, see Meuller (1988), Boles (1991), Bendyna and Lake (1994), Clark and Clark (1996), Burrell (1994), Cook *et al.* (1994) and Duke (1996). On Britain, see Lovenduski and Norris (1996),

Norris and Lovenduski (1995), Stephenson (1998) and *Towards Equality* (the journal of the Fawcett Society).

For key early contributions to the debate on women and the Scandinavian welfare states, see Haavio-Mannila *et al.* (1985), Hernes (1987), Holter (1984), Sassoon (1987), Jones and Jonasdottir (1988) and Dahlerup (1988). For more recent discussion see Karvonen and Selle (1995), and also Siim (1991), Skejeie (1991), Leira (1992, 1993) and Stark (1997). For overviews, see Bryson (1996b), Chapman (1993) and Kaplan (1992).

On the effects of proportional representation, see Norris (1985), Phillips (1991) and Barkman (1995).

On the debate over whether women have shared interests, see Cockburn (1996), Costain (1998a, 1998b), Diamond and Harstock (1981), Sapiro (1981), Pringle and Watson (1992), Jonasdottir (1988) and Sainsbury (1988).

Chapter 6

For global overviews of changes in family structure and women's labour market participation, see Blumberg (1991), Stockman *et al.* (1995) and the references for Chapter 1. On the United States, see also Sapiro (1990), Rosenberg (1992) and Bryson (1996c). On Britain, see Innes (1995), Lewis (1992) Bryson and Lister (1994), Bradshaw and Millar, (1991) and Figes (1994).

On black families and employment see the references on black feminism and race in Chapters 2 and 3, Westwood and Bhachu (1988) and Davidson (1997). For minority ethnic women in Britain, see also Commission for Racial Equality (1997). For the perspectives of disabled women, see Morris, J. (1991, 1995, 1996), Londsdale (1990), Begum (1992) and Boylan (1991).

On the unequal distribution of household responsibilities and financial resources, see Brannen and Wilson (1987), Gershuny (1996), Benn (1998), Pahl (1989), Blumberg (1991), Vogler and Pahl (1994). For the claim that men's family role has nevertheless increased, see Burgess, (1997); for the finding that women often feel financially better off after separation see Maclean (1991) and Bradshaw and Millar (1991).

For international comparison of policies on lone parent families, see Bradshaw *et al.* (1996); for feminist perspectives, see Lewis (1997) and Silva (1996). For anti-feminist attacks on lone parenthood, see Murray (1990), Halsey (1992), Morgan P. (1995) and Dennis and Erdus (1993).

For recent feminist discussion of motherhood, see Freely (1996), Figes (1998) and Benn (1998).

For international comparisons of women's employment situation, see Davidson and Cooper, (1992), Rees (1992), Adler and Izraeli (1994), Jacobs (1994), Jenson *et al.* (1988), Meulders *et al.* (1993), Maier (1991) and Walby (1996). On the United States, see also Jocobsen (1994), Fuchs (1988) and Milkman (1995). On Britain, see Paci and Joshi (1996), Sly *et al.* (1997) and, for the particularly bad situation of homeworkers, Tate (1994).

For a controversial attack on feminist analyses of women's employment situation, see Hakim (1995) and the reply by Ginn *et al.* (1996).

226 Feminist Debates

On the debate over affirmative action, see Bacchi (1996), Jaggar (1994c, Part II) and Johnson (1996).

On the length of the working day and its effect on family life, and on feminist demands for shorter hours, 'family friendly' employment and an increase in men's family role, see Marsh (1991b), Witherspoon and Prior (1991/2), Wilkinson (1997), Stockman *et al.* (1995), Mulgan and Wilkinson, (1995), Ferri and Smith (1996), Walter (1998), Benn (1998), Lister (1997), Friedan (1997) and Hochschild (1997).

For details of parental leave provision in all EU countries, see Dulk *et al.* (1996). On Scandinavian provision see the references for the Scandinavian welfare states in Chapter 5. On the claim that Swedish men are at last increasing their role in the home, see Wilkinson (1997) and the National Report by the Government of Sweden (1994), but for a less optimistic view, see Newell (1996).

Chapter 7

For comparative material on earlier campaigns for birth control and the situation today, see Banks (1986), Francombe (1986) and Lovenduski and Outshoorn (1986). On the United States see Craig and O'Brien (1993), Goggin (1993), Staggenborg (1991) and O'Connor (1996). On Britain, see Lovenduski and Randall (1993) and Sheeran (1987).

For evidence of coercive birth control, including forced sterilisation, in the United States see Roberts (1995), Davis (1993) and Ross (1993). On Britain see Bryan *et al.* (1985), Nain (1991) and Bhavnani and Coulson (1986).

On the activities of the fetal rights movement in the United States see Condit (1995), Strickland and Whicker (1995), Schroedel and Peretz (1995), Pollitt (1995), Faludi (1992) and Krum (1997).

For discussion of reproductive issues from a liberal perspective, see Richards (1982) and Warren (1991). For socialist feminist perspectives, see Himmelweit (1988), Petchesky (1990), Gimenez (1991), Jaggar (1994a) and Seal (1990). On disability issues see Morris (1991), Bailey (1996) and Kaplan (1994). For radical feminist perspectives see Firestone (1979), O'Brien (1981 and 1989), MacKinnon (1989a) and Badinter (1989). For radical feminist critiques of reproductive technology, see Arditti *et al.* (1984), Dworkin (1983), Corea (1985), Stanworth (1987), Hynes (1989), Rowland (1992, 1997), Woliver (1991), Boling (1995) and Raymond (1989).

For discussion of feminist criticisms of 'rights' in relation to reproductive issues, see Rowland (1992, 1997), Himmelweit (1988), Fox-Genovese (1991), Kingdom (1991), Poovey (1992), Shaver (1993), Shrage (1994) and Shanley (1995). For application of 'ethic of care' arguments to abortion, see McDonnell (1984), Baier (1986), Luker (1984), Colker (1992), Neitz (1981), and the further reading on Gilligan in Chapter 4.

On public attitudes to abortion in the United States and the beliefs that underlie these, see Craig and O'Brien (1993), Goggin (1993), Luker (1984), Ginsburg (1989), Tribe, (1990), Schnell (1993) and O'Connor (1996).

Further reading 227

On attempts to find a common ground with opponents of abortion, see Ginsburg (1989), Davis (1993), Poovey (1992), Shrage, (1994), Colker (1992) and the newsletters of *Common Ground* and *Catholics for a Free Choice*.

Chapter 8

For overviews of the debates on pornography, see Ryan (1992) and Cloonan (undated). Chester and Dickey (1988) provide a good selection of competing views. For key anti-pornography writings see Griffin (1981), Dworkin (1981), Kappeler, (1986), MacKinnon (1994), Itzin (1992), Russell (1993) and Easton (1994). For anti-censorship (but not always pro-pornography) arguments see Segal and McIntosh (1992), Assiter and Carol (1993), Strossen (1996) and Smith (1993).

On the MacKinnon–Dworkin ordinances, see Kelly (1988), Lacey (1993), Rodgerson and Semple (1990) and Merck (1992). For British initiatives see Benn (1988), Wilson (1992) and Itzin (1992, Appendix 1).

On the extent of male sexual violence and its alleged role in maintaining patriarchy, see Hester, Kelly and Radford (1996), Hanmer and Maynard M. (1987), Featherstone, Fawcett, and Toft (1994) and Corrin (1996).

For a good overview of recent debates on sexuality, see Whelehan (1995). See also Cooper (1995), Grant (1993) and Maynard and Purvis (1995). For feminist criticisms of lesbian sado-masochism, see Jeffreys (1990), Itzin (1992) and Lorde (1984). For arguments that sex with men is oppressive and that lesbianism can be liberating, see Rich (1980), Johnston (1982), Faderman (1991), Hester (1992), Jeffreys (1990) and Anderson (1994).

Chapter 9

Whelehan (1995) provides a good overview. For key feminist discussions of men and masculinity, see Ehrenreich (1983), Segal (1990a), Ferguson (1993) and Campbell (1993). Jardine and Smith (1989) is a good collection with both male and female contributors.

Roberts (1992) provides a sympathetic and factually based rebuttal of anti-feminist arguments and allegations.

For contributions by men, see Carver (1996), Morra and Smith (1995), the series of *Critical Studies on Men and Masculinities* edited by Jeff Hearn, the *Male Order* series edited by Victor Seidler (both Routledge) and the collection of articles from the influential socialist, anti-sexist men's magazine, *Achilles Heel*, edited by Seidler (1991).

Bibliography

Abdo, N. (1994) 'Nationalism and Feminism: Palestinian Women and the Intifada – No Going Back?', in V.M. Moghadam (ed.) *Gender and National Identity. Women and Politics in Muslim Societies* (London: Zed Books).
Abrar, S. (1996) 'Feminist Intervention and Local Domestic Violence Policy', in J. Lovenduski and P. Norris (eds).
Addelson, K. (1991) *Impure Thoughts. Essays on Philosophy, Feminism and Ethics* (Philadelphia: Temple University Press).
Addelson, K. (1993) 'Knowers/Doers and Their Moral Problems', in L. Allcoff and E. Potter (eds).
Adler, N. and Izraeli, D. (eds) (1994) *Competitive Frontiers. Women Managers in a Global Economy* (Oxford: Blackwell).
Aitkenhead, D. (1997) 'A carefree abortion can be embarrassing', *Guardian* 14 March.
Ali, Y. (1996) Contribution to *Feminising Politics*, a Conference organised by Charter 88 and the Centre for Women's Studies at the University of Kent at Canterbury, held in Birkbeck College, London.
Allcoff, L. and Potter, E. (eds) (1993) *Feminist Epistemologies* (London: Routledge).
Allen, J. (1990) 'Does Feminism Need a Theory of the State?', in S. Watson (ed.).
Amos, V. and Parmar, P. (1984) 'Challenging Imperial Feminism', *Feminist Review* **17**.
Amott, T. (1995) 'Shortchanged: Restructuring Women's Work', in M. Anderson and P. Collins (eds).
Amott, T. and Matthaei, J. (1991) *Race, Gender and Work. A Multi-Cultural Economic History of Women in the United States* (New York: Black Rose Books).
Anderson, J. (1994) 'Separatism, Feminism and the Betrayal of Reform', *Signs* **19**(2).
Anderson, M. (1993) 'From the Editor', *Gender and Society* **7**(2).
Anderson, M. (1996) 'Foreword', in E. Chow, D. Wilkinson and M. Zinn (eds).
Anderson, M. and Collins, P. (eds) (1995) *Race, Class and Gender. An Anthology* (London: Wadsworth).
Andrews, G. (ed.) (1991) *Citizenship* (London: Lawrence & Wishart).
Ang-Lydgate, M., Corrin, C. and Henry, M. (eds) (1997) *Desperately Seeking Sisterhood. Still Challenging and Building* (London: Taylor & Francis).

Anthias, F. and Yuval-Davis, N. (1992) *Racialized Boundaries. Race, Nation, Gender, Colour and Class and the Anti-racist Struggle* (London: Routledge).
Arber, S. and Ginn, J. (1990) 'The Meaning of Informal Care: Gender and the Contribution of Elderly People', *Ageing and Society* **10**.
Arditti, R., Klein, R. and Minden, S. (eds) (1984) *Test-tube Woman* (London: Pandora Press).
Assiter, A. (1996) *Enlightened Women. Modernist Feminism in a Postmodern Age* (London: Routledge).
Assiter, A. and Carol, A. (eds) (1993) *Bad Girls and Dirty Pictures. The Challenge to Reclaim Feminism* (London: Pluto Press).
Bacchi, C. (1990) *Same Difference. Feminism and Sexual Difference* (London: Allen & Unwin).
Bacchi, C. (1991) 'Pregnancy, the Law and the Meaning of Equality', in E. Meehan and S. Sevenhuijsen (eds).
Bacchi, C. (1996) *The Politics of Affirmative Action* (London: Sage).
Badinter, E. (1989) *Man/Woman. The One is the Other* (London: Collins Harvill).
Baier, A. (1986) 'Trust and AntiTrust', *Ethics* **96**.
Bailey, R. (1996) 'Prenatal Testing and the Prevention of Impairment: A Woman's Right To Choose?', in J. Morris (ed.).
Banks, O. (1986) *Faces of Feminism* (Oxford: Basil Blackwell).
Barkman, K. (1995) 'Politics and Gender: The Need for Electoral Reform', *Politics* **15**(3).
Barnett, B. (1993) 'Invisible Southern Black Women Leaders in the Civil Rights Movement: The Triple Constraints of Gender, Race, and Class', *Gender and Society* **7**(2).
Barrett, M. (1986) *Women's Oppression Today. Problems in Marxist Feminist Analysis* (London: Verso).
Barrett, M. (1988) *Women's Oppression Today. The Marxist/Feminist Encounter* (London: Verso).
Barrett, M. and McIntosh, M. (1982) *The Anti-Social Family* (London: Verso).
Barrett, M. and McIntosh, M. (1985) 'Ethnocentrism and Socialist–Feminist Theory', *Feminist Review* **20**.
Barrett, M. and Phillips, A. (eds) (1992) *Destabilizing Theory. Contemporary Feminist Debates* (Cambridge: Polity Press).
Bashevkin, S. (ed.) (1985) *Women and Politics in Western Europe* (London: Frank Cass).
Battersby, C. (1998) *The Phenomenal Woman: Feminist Transitions and Metaphysical Traditions* (Cambridge: Polity Press).
Bawdon, F. (1995) 'Babes and Arms', *Guardian* 3 August.
Begum, N. (1992) 'Disabled Women and the Feminist Agenda', *Feminist Review* **4**.
Bell, D. and Klein, R. (eds) (1996) *Radically Speaking: Feminism Reclaimed* (London: Zed Books).
Bendyna, M. and Lake, C. (1994) 'Gender and Voting in the 1992 Presidential Election', in E. Cook, S. Thomas and C. Wilcox (eds).
Benhabib, S. and Cornell, D. (eds) (1987) *Feminism as Critique* (Cambridge: Polity Press).
Benn, M. (1988) 'Page 3 and the Campaign Against It', in G. Chester and J. Dickey (eds).

Benn, M. (1997) 'Yes, But is there a Philosophy to Welfare-to-Work?', *Guardian* 3 June.
Benn, M. (1998) *Madonna and Child. Towards a New Politics of Motherhood* (London: Jonathan Cape).
Bennett, C. (1993) 'Ordinary Madness', *Guardian* 20 January.
Berger, M. (1988) 'Whatever Happened to "A Woman's Right to Choose"?' *Feminist Review* **29**.
Bhavnani, K. and Coulson, M. (1986) 'Transforming Socialist Feminism: The Challenge of Racism', *Feminist Review* **23**.
Blood, P., Tuttle, A. and Lakey, G. (1995) 'Understanding and Fighting Sexism: A Call to Men', in M. Anderson and P. Collins (eds).
Blumberg, R. (ed.) (1991) *Gender, Family and Economy. The Triple Overlap* (London: Sage).
Boetcher, J. and Scheman, N. (1994) 'Separatism re-viewed: Introduction', *Signs* **19**(2).
Boles, J. (1991) *American Feminism: New Issues for a Mature Movement. The Annals of the American Academy of Political and Social Science* (London: Sage).
Boling, P. (ed.) (1995) *Expecting Trouble. Surrogacy, Fetal Abuse and New Reproductive Technologies* (Oxford: Westview Press).
Boneparth, E. and Stoper, E. (eds) (1988) *Women, Power and Policy. Towards the Year 2,000* (New York and Oxford: Pergamon Press).
Bonk, K. (1988), 'The selling of the "gender gap": the role of organized feminism', in C. Meuller (ed.).
Bookman, A. and Morgan, S. (eds) (1988) *Women and the Politics of Empowerment* (Philadelphia: Temple University Press).
Bottomley, A. and Conaghan, J. (eds) (1993) *Feminist Theory and Legal Strategy* (Oxford: Blackwell).
Boutros-Ghali, B. (1996) 'Introduction' to United Nations Department of Public Information.
Boylan, E. (1991) *Women and Disability* (London: Zed Books).
Bradshaw, J. and Millar, J. (1991) *Lone Parent Families in the UK* (London: HMSO Department of Social Security Research Report).
Bradshaw, J., Kennedy, S., Kilkey, M., Hutton, S., Corden, S., Eardley, T., Holmes, H. and Neale, J. (1996) *The Employment of Lone Parents: A Comparison of Policy in 20 Countries* (London: Family Policy Studies Centre).
Brah, A. (1993) 'Re-framing Europe: En-gendered Racisms, Ethnicities and Nationalisms in Contemporary Western Europe', *Feminist Review* **45**.
Brah, A. (1996) *Cartographies of Diaspora* (London: Routledge).
Brannen, J. and Moss, P. (1991) *Managing Mothers. Dual Earner Households after Maternity Leave* (London: Unwin Hyman).
Brannen, J. and Wilson, G. (eds) (1987) *Give and Take in Families: Studies of Resource Allocation* (London: Unwin Hyman).
Bray, R. (1995) 'Taking Side Against Ourselves', in M. Anderson and P. Collins (eds).
Brenner, J. (1993) 'The Best of Times, The Worst of Times: US Feminism Today', *New Left Review* **200**.
Brenner, J. and Laslett, B. (1996) 'Gender, Social Reproduction and Women's

Self-Organization: Considering the U.S. Welfare State', in E. Chow, D. Wilkinson and M. Zinn (eds).
Breugel, I. (1996) 'Whose Myths are They Anyway?: A Comment', *British Journal of Sociology* **47**(1).
Breugel, I. and Kean, H. (1995) 'The Moment of Municipal Feminism: Gender and Class in 1980s' Local Government', *Critical Social Policy* **44/45**.
Brewer, R. (1993) 'Theorizing Race, Class and Gender. The New Scholarship of Black Feminist Intellectuals and Black Women's Labour', in S. James and A. Busia (eds).
Brophy, J. and Smart, C. (eds) (1985) *Women-in-law. Explorations in Law, Family and Sexuality* (London: Routledge & Kegan Paul).
Brownmiller, S. (1977) *Against Our Will* (Harmondsworth: Penguin).
Brunt, R. (1990) 'The Politics of Identity', in S. Hall and M. Jacques (eds) *New Times* (London: Lawrence & Wishart).
Bryan, B., Dadzie, S. and Scaffe, S. (1985) *The Heart of the Race: Black Women's Lives in Britain* (London: Virago).
Bryson, V. (1992) *Feminist Political Theory: An Introduction* (Basingstoke: Macmillan).
Bryson, V. (1995) 'Adjusting the Lenses: Feminist Analyses and Marxism at the End of the Twentieth Century', *Contemporary Politics* **1**(1).
Bryson, V. (1996a) 'Women and Citizenship: Some Lessons from Israel', *Political Studies* **44**(4).
Bryson, V. (1996b) *The Citizenship of Women in Scandinavia* (Huddersfield: University of Huddersfield Politics Departmental Paper).
Bryson, V. (1996c) *The Citizenship of Women in the United States* (Huddersfield: University of Huddersfield Politics Departmental Paper).
Bryson, V. (1998) 'Citizen Warriors, Workers and Mothers: Women and Democracy in Israel', in N. Charles and H. Hintjens (eds) *Gender, Ethnicity and Political Ideologies* (London: Routledge).
Bryson, V. and Lister, R. (1994) *Women, Citizenship and Social Policy* (Bradford: Bradford University Applied Social Studies/Joseph Rowntree Foundation).
Bubeck, D. (1995) *Care, Gender and Justice* (Oxford: Clarendon Press).
Buckley, M. (1989) *Women and Ideology in the Soviet Union* (London: Harvester Wheatsheaf).
Bulbeck, C. (1988) *One World Women's Movement* (London: Pluto Press).
Burgess, A. (1997) *Fatherhood Reclaimed. The Making of the Modern Father* (London: Vermilion).
Burghes, L. (1996) 'Debates on Disruption: What Happens to the Children of Lone Parents', in E. Silva (ed.).
Burrell, B. (1994) 'Women in American Politics', in G. Peele, C. Bailey, B. Cain and B. Peters (eds) *Developments in American Politics* (Basingstoke: Macmillan).
Butler, J. (1990) *Gender Trouble. Feminism and the Subversion of Identity* (London: Routledge).
Butler, J. and Scott, J. (eds) (1992) *Feminists Theorize the Political* (London: Routledge).
Bystydzienski, J. (ed.) (1992) *Women Transforming Politics. Worldwide*

Strategies for Empowerment (Bloomington and Indianapolis: Indiana University Press).
Campbell, B. (1982) 'A Feminist Sexual Politics: Now You See It, Now You Don't', in M. Evans (ed.).
Campbell, B. (1984) *Wigan Pier Revisited. Poverty and Politics in the 1980s* (London: Virago).
Campbell, B. (1987) *The Iron Ladies. Why Do Women Vote Tory?* (London: Virago).
Campbell, B. (1993) *Goliath. Britain's Dangerous Places* (London: Methuen).
Carter, A. (1988) *The Politics of Women's Rights* (London: Longman).
Carver, T. (1996) *Gender is Not a Synonym for Women* (Colorado: Lynne Rieder).
Catholics for a Free Choice (1993) 'Special Anniversary Issue', *Conscience. A Newsjournal of Prochoice Catholic Opinion* **XIV**(1 & 2).
Central Statistical Office (1995) *Social Focus on Women* (London: HMSO).
Chanan, G. (1992) *Out of the Shadows. Local Community Action and the European Community* (Dublin: European Foundation for the Improvement of Living and Working Conditions).
Chapman, J. (1987) 'Adult Socialization and Out-Group Politicization: An Empirical Study of Consciousness-Raising', *Journal of Political Science* **17**(3).
Chapman, J. (1991) *The Political Versus the Personal: Participatory Democracy and Feminism* (Strathclyde Papers on Government and Politics, No. 81).
Chapman, J. (1993) *Politics, Feminism and the Reformation of Gender* (London: Routledge).
Chazan, N. (1993) 'Israeli Women and Peace Activism', in B. Swirski and M.R. Safir (eds) *Calling the Equality Bluff. Women in Israel* (New York and London: Teachers College Press Athene Series).
Chester, G. and Dickey, J. (eds) (1988) *Feminism and Censorship: The Current Debate* (Bridport, Dorset: Prism Press).
Chisholm, D. (1993) 'Violence against Violence against Women: An Avant-garde for the times', in A. Kroker and M. Kroker (eds).
Chodorow, N. (1978) *The Reproduction of Mothering. Psychoanalysis and the Sociology of Gender* (London: University of California Press).
Chow, E. (1993) 'The Feminist Movement: Where Are All the Asian American Women?', in A. Jaggar and P. Rothenberg (eds).
Chow, E., Wilkinson, D. and Zinn, M. (eds) (1996) *Race, Class and Gender. Common Bonds, Different Voices* (London: Sage).
Clark, C. and Clark, J. (1996) 'Whither the Gender Gap?', in L. Duke (ed.).
Clarke, K. (1990) *Black and Ethnic Minority Women in Britain: A Review of Demographic and Employment Patterns* (Manchester, EOC Research Department: unpublished).
Cline, S. (1993) *Women, Celibacy and Passion* (London: André Deutsch Ltd).
Cloonan, M. (undated) *No Limits? Pornography and John Stuart Mill's Concept of 'Harm'* (York: University of York Case Studies for Politics No. 6).
Cockburn, C. (1991) *In the Way of Women. Men's Resistance to Sex Equality in Organizations* (Basingstoke: Macmillan).
Cockburn, C. (1995) 'Women in Black', *Women Against Fundamentalism* **7**.

Cockburn, C. (1996) 'Strategies for Gender Democracy: Strengthening the Representation of Trade Union Women in the European Social Dialogue', *European Journal of Women's Studies* **3**(1).
Cole, L. (1992) *My Baby, My Body, My Choice. A Study of Abortion* (Maidenhead: Lloyd Cole).
Colker, R. (1992) *Abortion and Dialogue. Pro-choice, Pro-life and American Law* (Bloomington and Indianapolis: Indiana University Press).
Collier, R. (1995) *Combatting Sexual Harassment in the Workplace* (Buckingham: Open University Press).
Collins, P. (1989) 'The Social Construction of Black Feminist Thought', *Signs* **14**(4).
Collins, P. (1990) *Black Feminist Thought* (London: Routledge).
Collins, P. (1995) 'Symposium on West and Fenstermaker's "Doing Difference"', *Gender and Society* **9**(4).
Commission for Racial Equality (1997) *Factsheet. Ethnic Minority Women* (London: Commission for Racial Equality).
Commission of the European Communities (1991) *Women and Men of Europe Today. Attitudes towards Europe and Politics* (Brussels: Women of Europe Supplements 35).
Common Ground (1995) 'News From the Common Ground Network for Life and Choice' (Washington: Common Ground).
Condit, D. (1995) 'Fetal Personhood: Political Identity under Construction', in P. Boling (ed.).
Connell, R.W. (1987) *Gender and Power* (Cambridge: Polity).
Connell, R.W. (1994) 'The State, Gender and Sexual Politics: Theory and Appraisal', in H. Radtke and H. Stam (eds).
Cook, A., Lorwin, V. and Daniels, A. (eds) (1984) *Women and Trade Unions in Eleven Industrialised Countries* (Philadelphia: Temple University Press).
Cook, E., Thomas, S. and Wilcox, C. (eds) (1994) *The Year of the Woman. Myths and Realities* (Boulder, Colorado: Westview Press).
Coole, D. (1993) *Women in Political Theory* (London: Harvester Wheatsheaf).
Coole, D. (1994) 'Whither Feminisms?', *Political Studies* **42**(1).
Cooper, D. (1995) *Power in Struggle. Feminism, Sexuality and the State* (Buckingham: Open University Press).
Coote, A. and Campbell, B. (1987) *Sweet Freedom. The Struggle for Women's Liberation* (Oxford: Blackwell).
Coote, A. and Patullo, P. (1990) *Power and Prejudice* (London: Weidenfeld and Nicolson).
Coote, A., Harman, H. and Hewitt, P. (1990) *The Family Way. A New Approach to Policy-Making* (London: Institute for Public Policy Research).
Copper, B. (1994) 'The Radical Potential in Lesbian Mothering of Daughters', in A. Jaggar (ed.).
Corea, G. (1989) 'Who May Have Children and Who May Not', in H.P. Hynes (ed.).
Corea, G. (ed.) (1985) *Man-Made Woman. How New Reproductive Technologies Affect Women* (London: Hutchinson).
Cornell, D. (1992) 'Gender, Sex, and Equivalent Rights', in J. Butler and J. Scott (eds).

Corrin, C. (1992) *Superwomen and the Double Burden. Women's Experience of Change in Central and Eastern Europe and the former Soviet Union* (London: Scarlet Press).
Corrin, C. (ed.) (1996) *Women in A Violent World. Feminist Analyses and Resistance Across 'Europe'* (Edinburgh: Edinburgh University Press).
Cosgrove, K. (1996) 'No Man has the Right', in C. Corrin (ed.).
Costain, A. (1988a) 'Representing Women: The Transition from Social Movement to Interest Group', in E. Boneparth and E. Stoper (eds).
Costain, A. (1988b) 'Women's Claims as a Special Interest' in C. Meuller (ed.).
Cott, N. (1987) *The Grounding of Modern Feminism* (New Haven: Yale University Press).
Cowling, M. (1995) 'Date Rape and Consent', *Contemporary Politics* **1**(2).
Craig, B. and O'Brien, D. (1993) *Abortion and American Politics* (New Jersey: Chatham House).
Crenshaw, K. (1993) 'Whose Story is it Anyway? Feminist and Anti-racist Appraisals of Anita Hill', in T. Morrison (ed.).
Crime and Criminal Justice Unit, Research and Statistics Directorate (1994) *Aspects of Crime: Gender* (London: Home Office).
Crompton, R. and Mann, M. (eds) (1986) *Gender and Stratification* (Cambridge: Polity Press).
Crowley, H. and Himmelweit, S. (eds) (1992) *Knowing Women. Feminism and Knowledge* (Cambridge: Polity Press).
Currie, E. *et al.* (eds) (1990) *What Women Want* (London: Sidgewick & Jackson).
Dahlerup, D. (ed.) (1986) *The New Women's Movement. Feminism and Political Power in Europe and the USA* (London: Sage).
Dahlerup, D. (1988) 'From a Small to a Large Minority: Women in Scandinavian Politics', *Scandinavian Political Studies* **11**(4).
Dale, J. and Foster, P. (1986) *Feminists and State Welfare* (London: Routledge & Kegan Paul).
Dalley, G. (1988) *Ideologies of Caring. Rethinking Community and Collectivism* (Basingstoke: Macmillan).
Daly, M. (1978) *Gyn/ecology. The Metaethics of Radical Feminism* (Boston: Beacon Press).
Davidson, M. (1997) *The Black and Ethnic Minority Woman Manager. Cracking the Concrete Ceiling* (London: Paul Chapman).
Davidson, M. and Cooper, C. (1992) *Shattering the Glass Ceiling. The Woman Manager* (London: Paul Chapman).
Davis, A. (1982) *Women, Race and Class* (London: Women's Press).
Davis, A. (1990) *Women, Culture and Politics* (London: Women's Press).
Davis, A. (1993) 'Outcast Mothers and Surrogates: Racism and Reproductive Politics in the Nineties', in L. Kauffman (ed.).
Davis, M. (1995) 'Towards a Theory of Marxism and Oppression', *Contemporary Politics* **1**(2).
Davis, N. (1993) 'The Abortion Debate: The Search for Common Ground, Parts 1 and 2', *Ethics* **103**.
Delphy, C. (1984) *Close to Home. A Materialist Analysis of Women's Oppression* (London: Hutchinson).

Delphy, C. and Leonard, D. (1992) *Familiar Exploitation. A New Analysis of Marriage in Contemporary Western Societies* (Cambridge: Polity Press).
Dennis, N. and Erdus, G. (1992) *Families without Fatherhood* (London: Institute of Economic Affairs).
Deutchman, I. (1996) 'Feminist Theory and the Politics of Empowerment', in L. Duke (ed.).
Dex, S. and Shaw, L. (1986) *British and American Women at Work. Do Equal Opportunities Policies Matter?* (Basingstoke: Macmillan).
Dex, S., Lissenburgh, S. and Taylor, M. (1994) *Women and Low Pay: Identifying the Issues* (Manchester: Equal Opportunities Commission).
Diamond, I. and Harstock, N. (1981) 'Beyond Interests in Politics: A Commentary on Virginia Sapiro's "When are Interests Interesting? The Problems of Political Representation of Women"', *American Political Science Review* **75**(2).
Dinnerstein, D. (1987) *The Rocking of the Table and the Ruling of the World* (London: Women's Press).
Dione, E. (1995) 'Welfare Rights and Wrongs', *Washington Post*, March, reprinted in *Guardian* 23 March.
Dominelli, L. (1991) *Women Across Continents. Feminist Comparative Social Policy* (London: Harvester Wheatsheaf).
D'Silva, B. (1996) 'A Case of Mistaken Identity', *Guardian* 29 August.
Dubois, E. (1981) *Elizabeth Cady Stanton and Susan B. Anthony: Correspondence, Writings, Speeches* with a critical commentary by E. Dubois (New York: Schocken Books).
Dubois, E., Dunlop, M., Gilligan, C., MacKinnon, C. and Menkel-Meadow, C. (1984) 'Feminist Discourse, Moral Values, and the Law – A Conversation', reprinted in F. Olsen (ed.).
Duke, L. (ed.) (1996) *Women in Politics. Outsiders or Insiders?* (New Jersey: Simon and Schuster).
Dulk, L., Doorne-Huiskes, A. and Schippes, J. (1996) 'Work–family arrangements and gender inequality in Europe', *Women in Management Review* **11**(5).
Dworkin, A. (1974) *Women Hating* (New York: E.P. Dutton).
Dworkin, A. (1981) *Pornography: Men Possessing Women* (London: Women's Press).
Dworkin, A. (1982) *Our Blood. Prophecies and Discourses on Sexual Politics* (London: Women's Press).
Dworkin, A. (1983) *Right-Wing Women. The Politics of Domesticated Feminism* (London: Women's Press).
Dworkin, A. (1988) *Letters from a War Zone* (London: Secker & Warburg).
Dworkin, A. (1997) *Life and Death* (New York and London: Free Press).
Dyson, M. (1995) 'The Plight of Black Men', in M. Anderson and P. Collins (eds).
Easton, S. (1994) *The Problem of Pornography. Regulation and the Right to Free Speech* (London: Routledge).
Eduards, M., Halsaa, B. and Skejeie, H. (1985) 'Equality: How Equal? Public Equality Policies in the Nordic Countries', in E. Haavio-Mannila *et al.* (eds).
Edwards, S. (ed.) (1985) *Gender, Sex and the Law* (London: Croom Helm).
Ehrenreich, B. (1983) *The Heart of Men. American Dreams and the Flight from*

Commitment (Garden City, New York: Anchor Press/Doubleday).
Einhorn, B. (1993) *Cinderella Goes to Market* (London: Verso).
Eisenstein, H. (1984) *Contemporary Feminist Thought* (London: Unwin).
Eisenstein, H. (1991) *Gender Shock. Practising Feminism on Two Continents* (Boston: Beacon Press).
Eisenstein, Z. (1981) *The Radical Future of Liberal Feminism* (London: Longman).
Eisenstein, Z. (1994) *The Color of Gender* (London: University of California Press).
Eisiedel, E. (1992) 'The Experimental Research Evidence: Effects of Pornography on the "Average Individual"', in C. Itzin (ed.).
Ellis, E. (1988) *Sex Discrimination Law* (Aldershot: Gower).
Employment Department Group (1994) *Report of the United Kingdom and Northern Ireland to the United Nations Fourth World Conference on Women – Beijing 1995* (London: Employment Department Group).
Enloe, C. (1996) *The Morning After. Sexual Politics and the End of the Cold War* (Berkeley and Los Angeles: University of California Press).
Equal Opportunities Commission (1995) *The Lifecycle of Inequality. Women and Men in Britain: 1995* (Manchester: Equal Opportunities Commission).
Equal Opportunities Commission (1996) *Facts About Women and Men in Great Britain* (Manchester: Equal Opportunities Commission).
Equal Opportunities Commission (1998) *Consultation. Equality in the 21st Century: A New Approach* (Manchester: Equal Opportunities Commission).
Evans, J. (1995) *Feminist Theory Today. An Introduction to Second-Wave Feminism* (London: Sage).
Evans, M. (ed.) (1982) *The Woman Question* (Oxford: Fontana).
Evans, R. (1977) *The Feminists: Women's Emancipation Movements in Europe, America and Australasia 1840–1920* (London: Croom Helm).
Evans, S. (1980) *Personal Politics. The Roots of Women's Liberation in the Civil Rights Movement and the New Left* (New York: Vintage Books).
Everywoman (1988) *Pornography and Sexual Violence. Evidence of the Links* (London: Everywoman).
Fact Sheets on Sweden (1997) *The Financial Circumstances of Swedish Households* (Stockholm: Swedish Institute).
Faderman, L. (1991) *Surpassing the Love of Man. Romantic Friendship and Love between Women from the Renaissance to the Present* (London: Women's Press).
Faith, K. (1994) 'Resistance: Lessons from Foucault and Feminism', in H. Radtke and H. Stam (eds).
Faludi, S. (1992) *Backlash. The Undeclared War against Women* (London: Chatto & Windus).
Farganis, S. (1994) *Situating Feminism. From Thought to Action* (London: Sage).
Farrell, W. (1994) *The Myth of Male Power* (London: Fourth Estate).
Featherstone, B., Fawcett, B. and Toft, C. (eds) (1994) *Violence, Gender and Social Work* (Bradford: University of Bradford).
Feminist Review (1984) Many Voices, One Chant. Black Feminist Perspectives, *Feminist Review* **17**.

Ferguson, K. (1993) *The Man Question* (Berkeley: University of California Press).
Ferri, E. and Smith, K. (1996) *Parenting in the 1990s* (London: Family Policy Studies Centre).
Figes, K. (1994) *Because of Her Sex. The Myth of Equality for Women in Britain* (London: Macmillan).
Figes, K. (1998) *Life After Birth. What Even Your Friends Won't Tell You About Motherhood* (London: Viking).
Firestone, S. (1979) *The Dialectic of Sex* (London: Women's Press).
Forbes, I. (1996) 'The Privatisation of Sex Equality Policy', in J. Lovenduski and P. Norris (eds).
Foreman, A. (1978) *Femininity as Alienation* (London: Pluto Press).
Forna, A. (1992) 'Pornography and Racism: Sexuality, Oppression and Inciting Hatred', in C. Itzin (ed.).
Forna, A. (1996) 'Sisters in Arms: Women are Marching too', *Independent on Sunday* 20 January.
Foster-Carter, O. (1987) 'Ethnicity: The Fourth Burden of Black Women – Political Activism', *Critical Social Policy* **20**.
Foucault, M. (1980) *Power/Knowledge. Selected Interviews and Other Writings 1972–1977* edited by C. Gordon (London: Harvester Wheatsheaf).
Fox-Genovese, E. (1991) *Feminism Without Illusions. A Critique of Individualism* (London: University of North Carolina Press).
Fraad, H., Resnick, S. and Wolff, R. (1994) *Bringing It All Back Home. Class, Gender and Power in the Modern Household* (London: Pluto Press).
Francombe, C. (1986) *Abortion Practice in Britain and the United States* (London: Allen & Unwin).
Frankenberg, R. (1993a) 'Growing up White: Feminism, Racism and the Social Geography of Childhood', *Feminist Review* **45**.
Frankenberg, R. (1993b) *White Women, Race Matters. The Social Construction of Whiteness* (Minneapolis: University of Minnesota Press).
Frankovic, K. (1988) 'The Ferraro Factor: The Women's Movement, the Polls and the Press', in C. Meuller (ed.).
Fraser, N. (1987) 'Women, Welfare and the Politics of Needs Interpretation', *Hypatia* **2**(2).
Frazer, E., Hornsby, J. and Lovibond, S. (eds) (1992) *Ethics: A Feminist Reader* (Oxford: Blackwell).
Freedland, J. (1995) 'Demon at the Heart of Black America' *Guardian* 14 October.
Freely, M. (1996) *What About Us? An Open Letter to The Mothers Feminism Forgot* (London: Bloomsbury).
French, M. (1994) 'Power/Sex', in H. Radtke and H. Stam (eds).
Friedan, B. (1986) *The Feminine Mystique* (Harmondsworth: Penguin Books).
Friedan, B. (1997) *Beyond Gender. The New Politics of Work and Family* (Washington: The Woodrow Wilson Center Press).
Frug, M. (1992) *Postmodern Legal Feminism* (London: Routledge).
Fuchs, V. (1988) *Women's Quest for Economic Equality* (Cambridge, Mass. and London: Harvard University Press).
Galloway, K. and Robertson, J. (1991) 'Introduction: A Woman's Claim of Right for Scotland', in Women's Claim of Right Group (ed.).

Gama, K. de (1993) 'A Brave New World? Rights Discourse and the Politics of Reproductive Autonomy', in A. Bottomley and J. Conaghan (eds).
Gardiner, J. (1997) *Gender, Care and Economics* (Basingstoke: Macmillan).
Gatens, M. (1991) *Feminism and Philosophy* (Cambridge: Polity Press).
Gender and Society (1991) 'Special Issue on Marxism and Feminism', *Gender and Society* **5**(3).
Gershuny, J. (1996) 'Family hours', *Independent on Sunday* 29 December.
Giddings, P. (1994) 'The Last Taboo', in V. Ruiz and E. Dubois (eds).
Gilligan, C. (1982) *In a Different Voice* (London: Harvard University Press).
Gilligan, C. (1997) 'Getting Civilized?', in A. Oakley and J. Mitchell (eds).
Gimenez, M. (1991) 'The Mode of Reproduction in Transition: A Marxist–Feminist Analysis of the Effects of Reproductive Technology', *Gender and Society* **5**(3).
Ginn, J., Brannen, J., Dex, S., Moss, P., Roberts, C., Arber, S., Dale, A., Elias, P., Pahl, J. and Rubery, J. (1996) 'Feminist Fallacies: A Reply to Hakim on Women's Employment', *British Journal of Sociology* **47**(1).
Ginsburg, F. (1989) *Contested Lives. The Abortion Debate in an American Community* (Berkeley: University of California Press).
Githens, M., Norris, P. and Lovenduski, J. (1994) *Different Roles, Different Voices. Women and Politics in the United States and Europe* (New York: HarperCollins).
Glendinning, C. and Millar, J. (eds) (1992) *Women and Poverty in Britain* (Brighton: Wheatsheaf).
Goggin, M. (ed.) (1993) *Understanding the New Politics of Abortion* (London: Sage).
Gordon, L. (ed.) (1990) *Women, The State, and Welfare* (Madison, Wisconsin: University of Wisconsin Press).
Grant, J. (1993) *Fundamental Feminism. Contesting the Core Concepts of Feminist Theory* (London: Routledge).
Grant, L. (1993) *Sexing the Millennium* (London: HarperCollins).
Green, E., Hebron, S. and Woodward, D. (1987) 'Women, Leisure and Social Control', in J. Hanmer and M. Maynard (eds).
Green, E., Hebron, S. and Woodward, D. (1990) *Women's Leisure, What Leisure?* (Basingstoke: Macmillan).
Greer, G. (1971) *The Female Eunuch* (London: Paladin).
Gregory, J. (1987) *Sex, Race and the Law. Legislating for Equality* (London: Sage).
Grewal, S., Kay, J., Landor, G., Lewis, G. and Parmaar, P. (eds) (1988) *Charting the Journey. Writings by Black and Third World Women* (London: Sheba Feminist Publishers).
Griffin, G. (ed.) (1995) *Feminist Activism in the 1990s* (London: Taylor and Francis).
Griffin, S. (1981) *Pornography and Silence: Culture's Revenge against Nature* (London: Women's Press).
Grossman, D. (1993) *Sleeping on a Wire. Conversations with Palestinians in Israel* (London: Picador).
Haavio-Mannila, E., Dahlerup, D., Eduards, M. *et al.* (eds) (1985) *Unfinished Democracy. Women in Nordic Politics* (Oxford: Pergamon Press).

Hakim, C. (1995) 'Five Feminist Myths about Women's Employment', *British Journal of Sociology* **46**(3).
Hakim, C. (1996) 'The Sexual Division of Labour and Women's Heterogeneity', *British Journal of Sociology* **47**(1).
Halsey, A. (1992) 'Foreword' to N. Dennis and G. Erdos.
Hanmer, J. and Maynard, M. (eds) (1987) *Women, Violence and Social Control* (Basingstoke: Macmillan).
Harding, L. (1996) '"Parental Responsibility": The Reassertion of Private Patriarchy?', in E. Silva (ed.).
Harding, S. (1986) *The Science Question in Feminism* (Ithaca: Cornell University Press).
Harding, S. (1991) *Whose Science? Whose Knowledge? Thinking from Women's Lives* (Ithaca: Cornell University Press).
Harman, H. (1993) *The Century Gap* (London: Vermilion).
Harrison, B. (1983) *Our Right to Choose. Toward a New Ethic of Abortion* (Boston: Beacon Press).
Harstock, N. (1985) *Money, Sex and Power. Towards a Feminist Historical Materialism* (Boston: Northeastern University Press).
Hart, V. (1994) *Bound by our Constitution. Women, Workers and the Minimum Wage* (New Jersey: Princeton University Press).
Hartmann, H. (1986) 'The Unhappy Marriage of Marxism and Feminism: Towards a More Progressive Union', in L. Sargent (ed.).
Hearn, J. (1988) 'Commentary, Child Abuse: Violence and Sexualities Towards Young Children', *Sociology* **22**(4).
Hearn, J. and Morgan, D. (eds) (1990) *Men, Masculinities and Social Theory* (London: Unwin Hyman).
Heath, S. (1989) 'Men in Feminism: Men and Feminist Theory', in A. Jardine and P. Smith (eds).
Heise, L. (1989) 'The Global War Against Women', reprinted in A. Jaggar and P. Rothenberg (eds).
Hernes, H. (1987) *Welfare State and Woman Power. Essays in State Feminism* (Oslo: Norwegian University Press).
Hersch, M. (1991) 'Women in Campaigning Groups in Central Scotland', in Women's Claim of Right Group (ed.).
Hester, M. (1984) 'Anti-sexist Men: A Case of Cloak-and-Dagger Chauvinism', *Women's Studies International Forum* **7**(1).
Hester, M. (1992) *Lewd Women and Wicked Witches. A Study of the Dynamics of Male Domination* (London: Routledge).
Hester, M., Kelly, L. and Radford, J. (eds) (1996) *Women, Violence and Male Power* (Buckingham: Open University Press).
Hewlett, S. (1988) *A Lesser Life. The Myth of Women's Liberation* (London: Sphere).
Himmelweit, S. (1988) 'More than "A Woman's Right to Choose"?', *Feminist Review* **29**.
Hirsch, M. and Fox Keller, E. (1990) *Conflicts in Feminism* (London: Routledge).
Hochschild, A. (1997) *The Time Bind. When Work Becomes Home and Home Becomes Work* (New York: Metropolitan Books, Henry Hold).

Hoff, J. (1994) 'Comparative Analysis of Abortion in Ireland, Poland and the United States', *Women's Studies International Forum* **17**(6).
Hoffman, J. (1995) 'Are States Patriarchal?', *Contemporary Political Studies* **2**.
Hoffman, J. (1998) 'Is there a Case for a Feminist Critique of the State?', *Contemporary Politics* **2**(4).
Holter, H. (ed.) (1984) *Patriarchy in a Welfare Society* (Norway: Universitetsforlaget).
hooks, bell (1981) *Ain't I a Woman. Black Women and Feminism* (Boston: South End Press).
hooks, bell (1984) *Feminist Theory: From Margin to Center* (Boston: South End Press).
hooks, bell (1991) *Yearning. Race, Gender and Cultural Politics* (London: Turnaround).
Hull, G., Scott, P. and Smith, B. (eds) (1982) *All the Women are White, All the Blacks are Men, But Some of Us Are Brave. Black Women's Studies* (New York: Feminist Press).
Hursthouse, R. (1987) *Beginning Lives* (Oxford: Blackwell).
Hynes, H. (ed.) (1989) *Reconstructing Babylon. Women and Western Technology* (London: Earthscan).
Innes, S. (1995) *Making It Work. Women, Change and Challenge in the 90s* (London: Chatto & Windus).
Institute of Management (undated) *The Key to the Men's Club* (London: Institute of Management/BhS).
International Labour Organization (1995) *Gender Equality at Work: Strategies Towards the Twenty First Century. An ILO Contribution to the Fourth Conference on Women* (Geneva: International Labour Organisation).
Itzin, C. (ed.) (1992) *Pornography. Women, Violence and Civil Liberties* (Oxford: Oxford University Press).
Jackson, S. (ed.) (1993) *Women's Studies. A Reader* (London: Harvester Wheatsheaf).
Jackson, S. (1995) 'Gender and Heterosexuality: A Materialist Feminist Analysis', in M. Maynard and J. Purvis (eds).
Jackson, S. (1996) *Christine Delphy* (London: Sage).
Jacobs, J. (ed.) (1994) *Gender Inequality at Work* (London: Sage).
Jacobson, J. (1994) 'The Global Politics of Abortion', in A. Jaggar (ed.).
Jaffe, F., Lindheim, B. and Lee, P. (1981) *Abortion Politics, Private Morality and Public Policy* (New York: McGraw-Hill).
Jaggar, A. (1983) *Feminist Politics and Human Nature* (Brighton: Harvester).
Jaggar, A. (1994a) 'Abortion and a Woman's Right to Decide', in A. Jaggar (ed.).
Jaggar, A. (1994b) 'Introduction: Living with Contradictions', in A. Jaggar (ed.).
Jaggar, A. (ed.) (1994c) *Living with Contradictions. Controversies in Feminist Social Ethics* (Boulder: Westview Press).
Jaggar, A. and Rothenberg, P. (1993) 'Introduction', in A. Jaggar and P. Rothenberg (eds).
Jaggar, A. and Rothenberg, P. (eds) (1993) *Feminist Frameworks. Alternative Theoretical Accounts of the Relations between Women and Men* (New York: McGraw-Hill).

James, S. (1993) 'Mothering. A Possible Black Feminist Link to Social Transformation?', in S. James and A. Busia (eds).
James, S. and Busia, A. (eds) (1993) *Theorizing Black Feminisms. The Visionary Pragmatism of Black Women* (London: Routledge).
Jankowska, H. (1993) 'The Reproductive Rights Campaign in Poland' *Women's Studies International Forum* **16**(3).
Jardine, A. and Smith, P. (eds) (1989) *Men in Feminism* (London: Routledge).
Jeffreys, S. (1990) *Anticlimax* (London: Women's Press).
Jenson, J., Hagen, E. and Reddy, C. (eds) (1988) *Feminization of the Labour Force. Paradoxes and Promises* (Cambridge: Polity).
Jocobson, J. (1994) *The Economics of Gender* (Oxford: Blackwell).
Joeres, R. and Scheman, N. (1994) 'Separatism Re-viewed: Introduction', *Signs* **19**(2).
Johnson, R. (1996) 'Affirmative Action as a Woman's Issue', in L. Duke (ed.).
Johnston, J. (1982) 'Lesbian Nation: The Feminist Solution', in M. Evans (ed.).
Jonasdottir, A. (1988) 'On the Concept of Interests, Women's Interests and the Limitations of Interest Theory', in K. Jones and A. Jonasdottir (eds).
Jones, K. (1990) 'Citizenship in a Woman-friendly Policy', *Signs* **15**(4).
Jones, K. (1993) *Compassionate Authority. Democracy and the Representation of Women* (London: Routledge).
Jones, K. and Jonasdottir, A. (eds) (1988) *The Political Interests of Gender. Developing Theory and Research with a Human Face* (London: Sage).
Jordan, J. (1995) 'A New Politics of Sexuality', in M. Anderson and P. Collins (eds).
Joshi, H. and Davies, H. (1996) 'Financial Dependency on Men: Have Women Born in 1958 Broken Free?', *Policy Studies* **17**(1).
Kalb, D. (1996) 'Women of Freshman Class Not Easily Labeled', *Congressional Quarterly Weekly Report* **54**(49).
Kaplan, D. (1994) 'Disability Rights Perspectives on Reproductive Technologies and Public Policy', in A. Jaggar (ed.).
Kaplan, G. (1992) *Contemporary West European Feminism* (London: UCL Press).
Kappeler, S. (1986) *The Pornography of Representation* (Cambridge: Polity Press).
Karvonen, L. (1995) 'Trade Unions and the Feminization of the Labour Market in Scandinavia', in L. Karvonen and P. Selle (eds).
Karvonen, L. and Selle, P. (eds) (1995) *Women in Nordic Politics. Closing the Gap* (Aldershot: Dartmouth).
Kauffman, L. (ed.) (1989) *Gender and Theory. Dialogues in Feminist Criticism* (Oxford: Blackwell).
Kauffman, L. (ed.) (1993) *American Feminist Thought at Century's End. A Reader* (Oxford: Blackwell).
Kay, H. (1995) 'Equality and Difference: The Case of Pregnancy', in F. Olsen (ed.).
Kazi, H. (1986) 'The Beginning of a Debate Long Due: Some Observations on "Ethnocentricism and Socialist–Feminist Theory"', *Feminist Review* **22**.
Kelly, L. (1988) 'The U.S. Ordinances: Censorship or Radical Law Reform?', in G. Chester and J. Dickey (eds).

Kennedy, H. (1992) *Eve was Framed. Women and British Justice* (London: Vintage).
Kenski, H. (1988) 'The Gender Factor in a Changing Electorate', in C. Meuller (ed.).
Ketting, E. and Praag, P. (1986) 'The Marginal Relevance of Legislation Relating to Abortion', in J. Lovenduski and J. Outshoorn (eds).
Khodyreva, N. (1996) 'Sexism and Sexual Abuse in Russia', in C. Corrin (ed.).
Kimmel, M. (1990) *Guilty Pleasures. Pornography in Men's Lives* (New York: Crown).
King, D. (1993) 'Multiple Jeopardy: The Context of a Black Feminist Ideology', in A. Jaggar and P. Rothenberg (eds).
Kingdom, E. (1991) *What's Wrong with Rights? Problems for Feminist Politics of Law* (Edinburgh: Edinburgh University Press).
Kitzinger, C. (1995) *The Social Construction of Lesbianism* (London: Sage).
Kooiman, J. (1993) *Modern Governance. New Government Society Interactions* (London: Sage).
Kostash, M. (1993) 'Second Thoughts', in A. Jaggar and P. Rothenberg (eds).
Kroker, A. and Kroker, M. (eds) (1993) *The Last Sex. Feminism and Outlaw Bodies* (Basingstoke: Macmillan).
Krum, S. (1997) 'A Deadly Addiction', *Guardian* 7 August.
Labour Party Consultation on the Elimination of Domestic and Sexual Violence Against Women (1995) *Peace at Home* (London: Labour Party).
Labour Research Department (1991) *Women in Trade Unions. Action for Equality* (London: Labour Research Department).
Lacey, N. (1991) 'Legislation Against Sex Discrimination: Question from a Feminist Perspective', in C. McCrudden (ed.).
Lacey, N. (1993) 'Feminist Theory and Legal Strategy', in A. Bottomley and J. Conaghan (eds).
Landry, D. and Maclean, G. (1993) *Materialist Feminisms* (Oxford: Blackwell).
Larrabee, J. (ed.) (1993) *An Ethic of Care* (London: Routledge)..
Lavalette, M. and Kennedy, J. (1996) *Solidarity on the Waterfront* (Liverpool: Liver Press).
Lees, S. (1986) 'Sex, Race and Culture: Feminism and the Limits of Cultural Pluralism', *Feminist Review* 22.
Lees, S. (1993) *Sugar and Spice. Sexuality and Adolescent Girls* (Harmondsworth: Penguin).
Lees, S. (1996) *Carnal Knowledge. Rape on Trial* (London: Hamish Hamilton).
Leira, A. (1989) *Models of Motherhood. Welfare State Policies and Everyday Practices: The Scandinavian Experience* (Oslo: Institute for Social Research).
Leira, A. (1992) *Welfare States and Working Mothers* (Cambridge: Cambridge University Press).
Leira, A. (1993) 'Mothers, Markets and the State: A Scandinavian "Model"?', *Journal of Sociology* 22(3).
Lerner, G. (1993) 'Reconceptualising Differences among Women', in A. Jaggar and P. Rothenberg (eds).
Lewis, J. (1992) *Women in Britain since 1945* (Oxford: Blackwell).
Lewis, J. (ed.) (1997) *Lone Mothers in European Welfare Regimes* (London: Jessica Kingsley).

Lister, R. (1990) 'Women, Economic Dependency and Citizenship', *Journal of Social Policy* **19**(4).
Lister, R. (1992) *Women's Economic Dependency and Social Security* (Manchester: Equal Opportunities Commission).
Lister, R. (1997) *Citizenship. Feminist Perspectives* (Basingstoke: Macmillan).
Liu, T. (1994) 'Teaching the Differences among Women from a Historical Perspective: Rethinking Race and Gender as Social Categories', in V. Ruiz and E. Dubois (eds).
Londsdale, S. (1990) *Women and Disability. The Experience of Physical Disability Among Women* (Basingstoke: Macmillan).
Lorber, J. (1991) 'Dismantling the Noah's Ark', in J. Lorber and S. Farrell (eds).
Lorber, J. and Farrell, S. (eds) (1991) *The Social Construction of Gender* (London: Sage).
Lorde, A. (1984) *Sister Outsider. Essays and Speeches* (New York: Crossing Press).
Lorde, A. (1992) 'Age, Race, Class and Sex: Women Redefining Difference', from 'Sister Outsider' (1984) reprinted in E. Frazer, J. Hornsby and S. Lovibond (eds).
Lovenduski, J. (1986) *Women and European Politics. Contemporary Feminism and Public Policy* (Brighton: Harvester Press).
Lovenduski, J. and Hills, J. (eds) (1981) *The Politics of the Second Electorate. Women and Public Participation* (London: Routledge & Kegan Paul).
Lovenduski, J. and Norris, P. (eds) (1996) *Women in Politics* (Oxford: Oxford University Press).
Lovenduski, J. and Outshoorn, J. (eds) (1986) *The New Politics of Abortion* (London: Sage).
Lovenduski, J. and Randall, V. (1993) *Contemporary Feminist Politics. Women and Power in Britain* (Oxford: Oxford University Press).
Luker, K. (1984) *Abortion and the Politics of Motherhood* (Berkeley: University of California Press).
Lutz, A., Phoenix, A. and Yuval-Davis, N. (eds) (1995) *Crossfires. Nationalism, Racism and Gender in Europe* (London: Pluto Press).
Lutz, A., Phoenix, A. and Yuval-Davis, N. (1995) 'Introduction. Nationalism, Racism and Gender: European Crossfires', in A. Lutz, A. Phoenix and N. Yuval-Davis (eds).
Lyndon, N. (1993) *No More Sex War. The Failures of Feminism* (London: Mandarin).
McCrudden, C. (ed.) (1991) *Anti-Discrimination Law* (Aldershot: Dartmouth).
McDonagh, E. (1996) *Breaking the Abortion Deadlock. From Choice to Consent* (Oxford: Oxford University Press).
McDonnell, K. (1984) *Not an Easy Choice. A Feminist Re-examines Abortion* (Toronto: Women's Press).
McGregor, S. (1989) 'Rape, Pornography and Capitalism', *International Socialism* **45**.
McIntosh, M. (1992) 'Liberalism and the Contradictions of Sexual Politics', in L. Segal and M. McIntosh (eds).
McIntosh, M. (1996) 'Social Anxieties about Lone Motherhood and Ideologies of the Family: Two Sides of the Same Coin', in E. Silva (ed.).

McIntosh, P. (1995) 'White Privilege and Male Privilege: A Personal Account of Coming to See Correspondence through Work in Women's Studies', in M. Anderson and P. Collins (eds).
McKay, D. (1993) *American Politics and Society* (Oxford: Blackwell).
Mackay, F. (1996) 'The Zero Tolerance Campaign: Setting the Agenda', in J. Lovenduski and P. Norris (eds).
MacKinnon, C. (1983) 'Feminism, Marxism, Method and the State. Towards Feminist Jurisprudence', *Signs* **8**(4).
MacKinnon C. (1989a) *Towards a Feminist Theory of the State* (London: Harvard University Press).
MacKinnon, C. (1989b) 'Sexuality, Pornography and Method: Pleasure under Patriarchy', *Ethics* **99**(2).
MacKinnon, C. (1993a) 'On Collaboration', part of a speech given at the National Conference on Women and the Law, New York 1985, reprinted in S. Jackson (ed.).
MacKinnon, C. (1993b) 'Reflections on Sex Equality Under Law', in L. Kauffman (ed.).
MacKinnon, C. (1993c) 'Sex Equality: Difference and Dominance, in A. Jaggar and P. Rothenberg (eds).
MacKinnon, C. (1994) *Only Words* (London: HarperCollins).
Maclean, M. (1991) *Surviving Divorce. Women's Resources after Separation* (Basingstoke: Macmillan).
McNeill, S. (1987) 'Flashing: Its Effect on Women', in J. Hanmer and M. Maynard (eds).
Maier, F. (1991) 'Part-time Work, Social Security Protections and Labour Law: An International Comparison', *Policy and Politics:* **19**(1).
Mama, A. (1989) 'Violence against Black Women: Gender, Race and State Responses', *Feminist Review* **32**.
Mandell, N. (ed.) (1995) *Feminist Issues. Race, Class and Sexuality* (Scarborough, Ontario: Prentice Hall Canada).
Manning, N. (ed.) *Social Policy Review 1990–91* (London: Longman).
Mansbridge, J. (1986) *Why We Lost the ERA* (Chicago and London: University of Chicago Press).
Marable, M. (1995) 'Beyond Racial Identity Politics: Towards a Liberation Theory for Multicultural Democracy', in M. Anderson and P. Collins (eds).
Marsh, C. (1991a) 'The Right to Work: Justice in the Distribution of Employment', in N. Manning (ed.).
Marsh, C. (1991b) *Hours of Work of Women and Men in Britain* (Manchester: Equal Opportunities Commission).
Marshall, J. (1995) 'Working at Senior Management Level: Some of the Issues for Women', *Women in Management Review* **10**(3).
Martin, E. (1996) 'Women within the Judicial System: Changing Roles', in L. Duke (ed.).
Maynard, M. and Purvis, J. (eds) (1995) *Hetero(sexual) Politics* (London: Taylor and Francis).
Meehan, E. (1985) *Women's Rights at Work: Campaigns and Policy in Britain and the US* (Basingstoke: Macmillan).
Meehan, E. (1993) *Citizenship and the European Community* (London: Sage).

Meehan, E. and Collins, E. (1996) 'Women, the European Union and Britain', in J. Lovenduski and P. Norris (eds).
Meehan, E. and Sevenhuijsen, S. (eds) (1991) *Equality Politics and Gender* (London: Sage).
Mendelson, J. (1988) 'The Ballot-box Revolution: The Drive to Register Women', in C. Meuller (ed.).
Merck, M. (1992) 'From Minneapolis to Westminster', in L. Segal and M. McIntosh (eds).
Metcalf, H. and Leighton, P. (1989) *The Under-Utilization of Women in the Labour Market* (Brighton: Institute of Manpower Studies).
Meulders, D., Plasman, R. and Stricht, V. (1993) *Position of Women in the Labour Market in the European Community* (Aldershot: Dartmouth).
Meuller, C. (1988) *The Politics of the Gender Gap* (London: Sage).
Miliband, R. (1977) *Marxism and Politics* (Oxford: Oxford University Press).
Mill, J.S. ([1869] 1983) *The Subjection of Women* (London:Virago).
Mill, J.S. (1991) *On Liberty and Other Essays*, edited and with an introduction by John Gray (Oxford: Oxford University Press).
Milkman, R. (1995) 'Economic Inequality among Women', *British Journal of Industrial Relations* **33**(4).
Millett, K. (1985) *Sexual Politics* (London: Virago).
Millns, S. (1996) 'Legislative Constructions of Motherhood', in J. Lovenduski and P. Norris (eds).
Minnow, M. (1990) 'Adjudicating Differences: Conflicts among Feminist Lawyers', in M. Hirsch and E. Fox Keller.
Mirza, H. (1986) 'The Dilemma of Socialist Feminism: A Case for Black Feminism', *Feminist Review* **22**.
Mirza, H. (1997a) 'Introduction: Mapping a Geneology of Black British feminism', in H. Mirza (ed.).
Mirza, H. (ed.) (1997b) *Black British Feminism. A Reader* (London: Routledge).
Mitchell, H. (1977) *The Hard Way Up* (London: Virago).
Mitchell, J. (1971) *Women's Estate* (Harmondsworth: Penguin).
Mitchell, J. (1974) *Psychoanalysis and Feminism* (London: Allen Lane).
Mitchell, J. (1984) *Women: The Longest Revolution* (London: Virago).
Moi, T. (1989) 'Men against Patriarchy', in L. Kauffman (ed.).
Molyneux, M. (1979) 'Beyond the Domestic Labour Debate', *New Left Review* **116**.
Moraga, C. (1993) 'From a Long Line of Vendidas: Chicanas and Feminism', in A. Jaggar and P. Rothenberg (eds).
Moraga, C. and Anzaldua, G. (1983) *This Bridge Called My Back: Writings by Radical Women of Color* (New York: Kitchen Table, Women of Color Press).
Moran-Ellis, J. (1996) 'Close to Home: The Experience of Researching Child Sexual Abuse', in M. Hester *et al.* (eds).
Morgan, D. (1992) *Discovering Men* (London: Routledge).
Morgan, J. (1995) 'Feminist Theory', in F. Olsen (ed.).
Morgan, P. (1995) *Farewell to the Family? Public Policy and Family Breakdown in Britain and the USA* (London: Institute of Economic Affairs).
Morgan, R. (1993) *The Word of a Woman. Selected Prose 1968–1992* (London: Virago).

Morgan, R. (1996) 'Light Bulbs, Radishes and the Politics of the 21st Century', in D. Bell and R. Klein (eds).
Morgan, R. (ed.) (1970) *Sisterhood is Powerful. An Anthology of Writing from the Women's Liberation Movement* (New York: Vintage).
Morra, N. and Smith, M. (1995) 'Men in Feminism: Reinterpreting Masculinity and Feminity', in N. Mandell (ed.)
Morris, J. (1991) *Pride against Prejudice* (Harmondsworth: Penguin).
Morris, J. (1995) 'Creating a Space for Absent Voices: Disabled Women's Experience of Receiving Assistance with Daily Living Activities', *Feminist Review* **51**.
Morris, J. (ed.) (1996) *Encounters with Strangers. Feminism and Disability* (London: Women's Press).
Morris, L. (1994) *Dangerous Classes. The Underclass and Social Citizenship* (London: Routledge).
Morrison, T. (ed.) (1993) *Race-ing Justice, En-gendering Power. Essays on Anita Hill, Clarence Thomas and the Construction of Social Reality* (London: Chatto & Windus).
Mossman, M. (1995) 'The Paradox of Feminist Engagement with Law', in N. Mandell (ed.).
Mulgan, G. and Wilkinson, H. (1995) *The Time Squeeze* (London: Demos).
Murray, C. (1984) *Losing Ground: American Social Policy, 1950–1980* (New York: Basic Books).
Murray, C. (1990) *The Emerging British Underclass* (London: IEA Health and Welfare Unit, Choice in Welfare Series No. 2).
Murray, C. (1994) *Underclass: The Crisis Deepens*, with commentaries by Pete Alcock, Miriam David, Melanie Phillips and Sue Slipman (London: Institute of Economic Affairs).
Nain, G. (1991) 'Black Women, Sexism and Racism: Black or Antiracist Feminism', *Feminist Review* **37**.
Najjar, O. (1992) 'Between Nationalism and Feminism: The Palestinian Answer', in J. Bystydzienski (ed.)
Narasimham, S. (1993) 'The Unwanted Sex', *New Internationalist* **240**.
Narayan, U. (1995) 'The "Gift" of a Child: Commercial Surrogacy, Gift Surrogacy, and Motherhood', in P. Boling (ed.).
Nash, K. (1997) 'The Feminist Critique of Liberal Individualism', *Journal of Political Ideologies* **2**(1).
Nash, K. (1998) *Universal Difference: Feminism and the Liberal Undecidability of 'Women'* (Basingstoke: Macmillan).
National Report by the Government of Sweden for the Fourth World Conference on Women in Beijing 1995 (1994) *Shared Power Responsibility* (Stockholm).
Neitz, M. (1981) 'Family, State and God: Ideologies of the Right-to-Life Movement', *Sociological Analysis* **42**(3).
Nelson, B. (1984) 'Women's Poverty and Women's Citizenship: Some Political Consequences of Economic Marginality', *Signs* **10**(2).
Nelson, B. (1990) 'The Origins of the Two-Channel Welfare State: Workmen's Compensation and Mothers' Aid', in L. Gordon (ed.).
Nelson, S. (1987) *Incest. Fact and Myth* (Trowbridge, Wiltshire: Redwood Burn).
Neustatter, A. (1995) 'Howling Wolf', *Guardian* 10 October.

Neustatter, A., with Newson, G. (1986) *Mixed Feelings. The Experience of Abortion* (London: Pluto Press).
New, C. and David, M. (1995) *For the Children's Sake. Making Childcare more than Women's Business* (Harmondsworth: Penguin).
Newell, S. (1996) '"The superwoman syndrome": a comparison of the "heroine" in Denmark and the UK', *Women in Management Review* **11**(5).
Nicholson, L. (ed.) (1990) *Feminism/Postmodernism* (London: Routledge).
Noddings, N. (1984) *Caring. A Feminine Approach to Ethics and Moral Education* (London: University of California Press).
Norris, P. (1985) 'Women's Legislative Participation in Western Europe', in S. Bashevkin (ed.).
Norris, P. (1987) *Politics and Sexual Equality. The Comparative Position of Women in Western Democracies* (London: Wheatsheaf).
Norris, P. (1991) 'Gender Difference in Political Participation in Britain: Traditional, Radical and Revisionist Models', *Government and Opposition* **26**(111).
Norris, P. and Lovenduski, J. (1995) *Political Recruitment. Gender, Race and Class in the British Parliament* (Cambridge: Cambridge University Press).
Oakley, A. (1997) 'A Brief History of Gender', in A. Oakley and J. Mitchell (eds).
Oakley, A. and Mitchell, J. (eds) (1997) *Who's Afraid of Feminism? Seeing Through the Backlash* (London: Hamish Hamilton).
O'Brien, M. (1981) *The Politics of Reproduction* (London and Henley: Routledge & Kegan Paul).
O'Brien, M. (1989) *Reproducing the World. Essays in Feminist Theory* (London: Westview Press).
O'Connor, K. (1996a) 'Women's Rights and Legal Wrongs: The U.S. Supreme Court and Sex Discrimination', in L. Duke (ed.).
O'Connor, K. (1996b) *No Neutral Ground? Abortion Politics in an Age of Absolutes* (London: Westview Press).
O'Donovan, K, (1985a) *Sexual Divisions in Law* (London: Weidenfeld & Nicolson).
O'Donovan, K. (1985b) 'Transsexual Troubles: The Discrepancy between Legal and Social Categories', in S. Edwards (ed.).
O'Donovan, K. and Szyszczak, E. (1988) *Equality and Sex Discrimination Law* (Oxford: Blackwell).
Okin, S. (1990) *Justice, Gender and the Family* (New York: Basic Books).
Olsen, F. (ed.) (1995) *Feminist Legal Theory I: Foundations and Outlooks* (Aldershot: Dartmouth).
Overall, C. (1987) *Ethics and Human Reproduction. A Feminist Analysis* (London: Allen & Unwin).
Paci, P. and Joshi, H. (1996) *Wage Differentials Between Men and Women. Evidence from Cohort Studies* (London: Department for Education and Employment).
Pahl, J. (1989) *Money and Marriage* (London: Macmillan).
Pannick, D. (1985) *Sex Discrimination Law* (Oxford: Clarendon Press).
Parker, G. (1990) *With Due Care and Attention. A Review of Research on Informal Care* (London: Family Policy Studies Centre, Occasional Paper No. 2).

Pascall, G. (1996) *Social Policy. A New Feminist Analysis* (London: Routledge).
Pateman, C. (1987) 'Feminist Critiques of the Public/Private Dichotomy', in A. Phillips (ed.).
Pateman, C. (1988) *The Sexual Contract* (London: Polity Press).
Pateman, C. (1988/1989) 'The Patriarchal Welfare State', first published in A. Gutmann (ed.) (1988) *Democracy and the Welfare State* (Princeton: Princeton University Press).
Pateman, C. (1989) *The Disorder of Women. Democracy, Feminism and Political Theory* (Cambridge: Polity Press).
Pennington, S. and Westover, B. (1989) *A Hidden Workforce. Homeworkers in England 1850–1935* (Basingstoke: Macmillan).
Perrigo, S. (1996) 'Women and Change in the Labour Party 1976–1995', in J. Lovenduski and P. Norris (eds).
Petchesky, R.(1990) *Abortion and Women's Choice. The State, Sexuality, and Reproductive Freedom* (Boston: Northeastern University Press).
Phillips, A. (1987a) *Divided Loyalties. Dilemmas of Sex and Class* (London: Virago).
Phillips, A. (ed.) (1987b) *Feminism and Equality* (Oxford: Blackwell).
Phillips, A. (1991) *Engendering Democracy* (Cambridge: Polity Press).
Phillips, A. (1993) *Democracy and Difference* (Cambridge: Polity Press).
Phillips, A. (1995) *The Politics of Presence* (Oxford: Clarendon Press).
Phillips, A. and Taylor, B. (1986b) 'Sex and Skill', in Feminist Review (ed.) *Waged Work: A Reader* (London: Virago).
Phoenix, A. (1996) 'Social Constructions of Lone Motherhood', in E. Silva (ed.).
Pollert, A. (1996) 'Gender and Class Revisited; or, The Poverty of "Patriarchy"', *Sociology* **30**(4).
Pollitt, K. (1995) *Reasonable Creatures. Essays on Women and Feminism* (London: Vintage).
Poovey, M. (1992) 'The Abortion Question and the Death of Man', in J. Butler and J. Scott (eds).
Pope, J. (1992) 'The Emergence of a Joint Israeli–Palestinian Women's Peace Movement During the Intifada', in H. Afshar (ed.) *Women in the Middle East* (Basingstoke: Macmillan).
Porter, E. (1991) *Women and Moral Identity* (London: Allen & Unwin).
Pringle, R. and Watson, S. (1992) '"Women's Interests" and the Post-structuralist State', in M. Barrett and A. Phillips (eds).
Radford, J. (1987) 'Policing Male Violence – Policing Women', in J. Hanmer and M. Maynard (eds).
Radford, J. and Kelly, L. (1995) 'Self Preservation: Feminist Activism and Feminist Jurisprudence', in M. Maynard and J. Purvis (eds).
Radtke, H. and Stam, H. (1994) *Power/Gender. Social Relations in Theory and Practice* (London: Sage).
Ramazanoglu, C. (1986) 'Ethnocentricity and Socialist Feminist Theory: a Response to Barrett and McIntosh', *Feminist Review* **22**.
Ramazanoglu, C. (1989) *Feminism and the Contradictions of Oppression* (London: Routledge).
Ramsay, M. (1997) *What's Wrong with Liberalism? A Radical Critique of Liberal Political Philosophy* (London: Leicester University Press).

Randall, V. (1987) *Women and Politics* (Basingstoke: Macmillan).
Randall, V. (1996) 'Feminism and Child Daycare', *Journal of Social Policy* **25**(4).
Rathzel, N. (1995) 'Nationalism and Gender in West Europe: The German Case', in H. Lutz, A. Phoenix and N. Yuval-Davis (eds).
Raymond, J. (1989) 'The International Traffic in Women: Women Used in Systems of Surrogacy and Reproduction', in H. Hynes (ed.).
Rees, T. (1992) *Women and the Labour Market* (London: Routledge).
Relations Review and Report (1991) *Twenty Years of Increasing Opportunities for Women?* Report No. 500.
Renzetti, C. and Curran, J. (1992) *Women, Men and Society* (London: Allyn and Bacon).
Rich, A. (1977) *Of Woman Born. Motherhood as Experience and Institution* (London: Virago).
Rich, A. (1980) 'Compulsory Heterosexuality and Lesbian Existence', *Signs* **5**(4).
Richards, J. (1982) *The Sceptical Feminist* (Harmondsworth: Penguin).
Richardson, D. (1997) 'Deconstructing Feminist Critiques of Radical Feminism', in M. Ang-Lydgate, C. Corrin and M. Henry (eds).
Richardson, D. and Robinson, V. (eds) (1993) *Introducing Women's Studies* (Basingstoke: Macmillan).
Roberts, D. (1995) 'Racism and Patriarchy in the Meaning of Motherhood', in F. Olsen (ed.)
Roberts, Y. (1992) *Mad About Women* (London: Virago).
Roberts, Y. (1995) 'Is this Modern Justice?', *Guardian* 7 December.
Robson, A. (1993) 'Rape: Weapon of War', *New Internationalist* **244**.
Rodgerson, G. and Semple, L. (1990) 'Who Watches the Watchwomen?: Feminists Against Censorship', *Feminist Review* **36**.
Rogers, B. (1983) *52% Getting Women's Power into Politics* (London: Women's Press).
Roiphe, K. (1993) *The Morning After. Sex, Fear and Feminism* (London: Hamish Hamilton).
Roll, J. (1991) 'One in Ten: Lone Parent Families in the European Community', in N. Manning (ed.).
Rosenberg, R. (1992) *Divided Lives. American Women in the Twentieth Century* (Harmondsworth: Penguin).
Roseneil, S. and Mann, K. (1996) 'Unpalatable Choices and Independent Families. Lone Mothers and the Underclass Debate', in E. Silva (ed.).
Rosenfeld, R. and Kalleberg, A. (1990) 'A Cross-national Comparison of the Gender Gap in Income', *American Journal of Sociology* **96**(1).
Ross, L. (1993) 'African–American Women and Abortion 1800–1970', in S. James and A. Busia (eds).
Rowbotham, S. (1992) *Women in Movement. Feminism and Social Action* (London: Routledge).
Rowbotham, S., Segal, L. and Wainwright, H. (1979) *Beyond the Fragments. Feminism and the Making of Socialism* (London: Merlin Press).
Rowland, R. (1992) *Living Laboratories. Women and Reproductive Technologies* (Bloomington and Indianapolis: Indiana University Press).

Rowland, R. (1997) 'The Politics of Relationship: Reproductive and Genetic Screening Technology', in M. Ang-Lydgate, C. Corrin and S. Millsom (eds).
Ruddick, S. (1990) *Maternal Thinking. Towards a Politics of Peace* (London: Women's Press).
Ruggie, M. (1984) *The State and Working Women. A Comparative Study of Britain and Sweden* (Princeton, New Jersey: Princeton University Press).
Ruiz, V. and Dubois, E. (eds) (1994) *Unequal Sisters. A Multi-cultural Reader in U.S. Women's History* (London: Routledge).
Rumbold, A. (1991) 'Introduction' to Conservative Research Department *A Britain Without Barriers. The Conservative Record for Women* (London: Conservative Party).
Russell, D. (1993) *Making Violence Sexy. Feminist Views on Pornography* (Buckingham: Open University Press).
Ryan, B. (1992) *Feminism and the Women's Movement* (London: Routledge).
Sainsbury, D. (1988) 'The Scandinavian Model and Women's Interests: The Issues of Universalism and Corporatism', *Scandinavian Political Studies* **11**(4).
Sainsbury, D. (ed.) (1996) *Gendering Welfare States* (London: Sage).
Sapiro, V. (1981) 'When are Interests Interesting? The Problem of Political Representation of Women', *American Political Science Review* **75**(2).
Sapiro, V. (1990) *Women in American Society. An Introduction to Women's Studies* (London: Mayfield).
Sargent, L. (ed.) (1986) *The Unhappy Marriage of Marxism and Feminism. A Debate on Class and Patriarchy* (London: Pluto Press).
Sassoon, A. (ed.) (1987) *Women and the State* (London: Hutchinson).
Schneir, M. (ed.) (1972) *Feminism: The Essential Historical Writings* (New York: Vintage).
Schnell, F. (1993) 'The Foundations of Abortion Attitudes' in M. Goggin (ed.).
Schroedel, J. and Peretz, P. (1995) 'A Gender Analysis of Policy Formation: The Case of Fetal Abuse', in P. Boling (ed.).
Scott, J. (1993) 'Deconstructing Equality-Versus-Difference: or, the Uses of Poststructuralist Theory for Feminism', in A. Bottomley and J. Conaghan (eds).
Seal, V. (1990) *Whose Choice? Working Class Women and the Control of Fertility* (London: Fortress).
Sedley, S. (1991) 'Charter 88: Wrongs and Rights', in G. Andrews (ed.).
Segal, L. (1987) *Is the Future Female? Troubled Thoughts on Contemporary Feminism* (London: Virago).
Segal, L. (1990a) *Slow Motion: Changing Masculinities and Changing Men* (London: Virago).
Segal, L. (1990b) 'Pornography and Violence: What the "Experts" Really Say', *Feminist Review* **36**.
Segal, L. (1991) 'Whose Left? Socialism, Feminism and the Future', *New Left Review* **185**.
Segal, L. and McIntosh, M. (eds) (1992) *Sex Exposed. Sexuality and the Pornography Debate* (London: Virago).
Seidler, V. (1991) 'Men, Feminism and Power', in J. Hearn and D. Morgan (eds).
Seidler, V. (ed.) (1991) *The Achilles Heel Reader. Men, Sexual Politics and Socialism* (London: Routledge).

Shanley, M. (1995) '"Surrogate Mothering" and Women's Freedom: A Critique of Contracts for Human Reproduction', in P. Boling (ed.).
Shaver, S. (1993) 'Body Rights, Social Rights and the Liberal Welfare State', *Critical Social Policy* 39.
Sheeran, P. (1987) *Women, Society, the State and Abortion. A Structuralist Analysis* (New York: Praeger).
Short, C. (1995a) *Labour's Strategy for Women* (London: House of Commons).
Short, C. (1995b) 'Foreword' to Labour Party Consultation on the Elimination of Domestic and Sexual Violence Against Women.
Short, C. (1996) 'Women and the Labour Party, in J. Lovenduski and P. Norris (eds).
Shrage, L. (1994) *Moral Dilemmas of Feminism. Prostitution, Adultery and Abortion* (London: Routledge).
Siann, G. and Wilkinson, H. (1995) *Gender, Feminism and the Future* (London: Demos).
Siddiqui, S. (1996) 'Domestic Violence in Asian Communities: The Experience of Southall Black Sisters', in C. Corrin (ed.).
Siim, B. (1987) 'The Scandinavian Welfare States – Towards Sexual Equality or a New Kind of Male Domination?' *Acta Sociologica* **30**(3/4).
Siim, B. (1991) 'Welfare State, Gender Politics and Equality Policies – Women's Citizenship in the Scandinavian Welfare States', in E. Meehan and S. Sevenhuijsen (eds).
Siltanen, J. and Stanworth, M. (eds) (1984) *Women and the Public Sphere. A Critique of Sociology and Politics* (London: Hutchinson).
Silva, E. (ed.) (1996) *Good Enough Mothering? Feminist Perspectives on Lone Motherhood* (London: Routledge).
Simmonds, F. (1997) 'Who Are the Sisters? Difference, Feminism and Friendship', in M. Ang-Lydgate, C. Corrin and M. Henry (eds).
Simpson, N. (1991) 'Equal Treatment? – Black Claimants and Social Security', *Benefits* September.
Skejeie, H. (1991) 'The Uneven Advance of Norwegian Women', *New Left Review* **187**.
Sklar, H. (1995) 'The Upperclass and Mothers N the Hood', in M. Anderson and P. Collins (eds).
Slomp, G. (1995) 'The Silence of the Limbs', *Contemporary Political Studies* **1** (Belfast: The Political Studies Association of the United Kingdom).
Sly, F., Price, A. and Risdon, A. (1997) 'Women in the Labour Market: Results from the Spring 1996 Labour Force Survey', *Labour Market Trends* **105**(3).
Smart, C. (1984) *The Ties that Bind. Law, Marriage and the Reproduction of Patriarchal Relationships* (London: Routledge & Kegan Paul).
Smart, C. (1989) *Feminism and the Power of Law* (London: Routledge).
Smart, C. (1995) *Law, Crime and Sexuality. Essays in Feminism* (London: Sage).
Smith, A. (1993) 'What is Pornography?: An Analysis of the Policy Statement of the Campaign Against Pornography and Censorship', *Feminist Review* 43.
Smith, B. (1995) 'Crossing the Great Divide. Race, Class and Gender in Southern Women's Organizing, 1979–1991', *Gender and Society* **9**(6).
Smith, V. (1987) 'The Circular Trap: Women and Part-time Work', in A. Sassoon (ed.).

Social Trends (1992) Volume 22 (London: HMSO Central Statistical Office).
Soper, K. (1991) 'Postmodernism and its Discontents', *Feminist Review* **39**.
Southall Black Sisters (1990) *Against the Grain: A Celebration of Survival and Struggle. Southall Black Sisters 1979–1989* (London: Southall Black Sisters).
Spelman, E. (1988) *Inessential Woman. Problems of Exclusion in Feminist Thought* (Boston: Beacon Press).
Spender, D. (1985) *Man Made Language* (London, Routledge & Kegan Paul).
Squires, J. (1996) 'Quotas for Women: Fair Representation?', in J. Lovenduski and P. Norris (eds).
Stacey, J. (1993) 'Untangling Feminist Theory', in D. Richardson and V. Robinson (eds).
Staggenborg, S. (1991) *The Pro-Choice Movement. Organization and Activism in the Abortion Conflict* (Oxford: Oxford University Press).
Stanworth, M. (ed.) (1987) *Reproductive Technologies* (Oxford: Polity Press).
Stark, A. (1997) 'Combatting the Backlash: How Swedish Women Won the War', in A. Oakley and J. Mitchell (eds).
Steinem, G. (1985) 'Erotica vs. Pornography', in *Outrageous Acts and Everyday Rebellions* (London: Fontana).
Stephenson, M. (1998) *Women, Politics and the Media during the 1997 General Election* (London: Fawcett).
Stockman, N., Bonney, N. and Xuewen, S. (1995) *Women's Work in East and West. The Dual Burden of Employment and Family Life* (London: UCL Press).
Stokes, W. (1995) 'Women and Political Representation', Paper presented at the Political Studies Association Conference, York.
Stokes, W. (1998) 'Feminist Democracy: The Case for Women's Committees', *Contemporary Politics* **4**(1).
Strickland, R. and Whicker, N. (1995) 'Fetal Endangerment Versus Fetal Welfare', in P. Boling (ed.).
Strossen, N. (1996) *Defending Pornography. Free Speech, Sex, and the Fight for Women's Rights* (London: Abacus).
Sumner, L.W. (1981) *Abortion and Moral Theory* (New Jersey: Princeton University Press).
Tate, J. (1994) 'Homeworking in West Yorkshire', in S. Rowbotham and S. Mitter (eds) *Dignity and Daily Bread* (London: Routledge).
Thomas, D. (1993) *Not Guilty. Men: The Case for the Defence* (London: Weidenfeld & Nicolson).
Thompson, J. (1984) 'A Defence of Abortion', *Philosophy and Public Affairs* **1**(1).
Thompson, J. (1996) 'The Family and Medical Leave Act: A Policy for Families', in L. Duke (ed.).
Thorogood, Nicki (1987) 'Race, Class and Gender: The Politics of Housework', in J. Brannen and G. Wilson (eds).
Tong, R. (1989) *Feminist Thought. A Comprehensive Introduction* (London: Unwin Hyman).
Travis, A. (1996) 'Old School Tie Still Counts in Recruitment of Judges' *Guardian* 27 June.
Travis, A. (1998) 'The Usual Suspects', *Guardian* 25 February.
Tribe, L. (1990) *Abortion: The Clash of Absolutes* (New York: Norton).

Tronto, J. (1993) 'Beyond Gender Difference to a Theory of Care', in J. Larrabee (ed.).
Ungerson, C. and Kember, M. (eds) (1997) *Women and Social Policy. A Reader* (Basingstoke: Macmillan).
United Nations (1991a) *Women. Challenges to the Year 2,000* (New York: United Nations).
United Nations (1991b) *The World's Women. Trends and Statistics 1970–1990* (New York: United Nations).
United Nations (1995) *From Nairobi to Beijing. Second Review and Appraisal of the Implementation of the Nairobi Forward-Looking Strategies for the Advancement of Women. Report of the Secretary-General* (New York: United Nations).
United Nations Department of Public Information (1996) *Platform for Action and the Beijing Declaration* (New York: United Nations).
Violence Against Children Study Group (1989) *Taking Child Abuse Seriously* (London: Unwin Hyman).
Vogel, L. (1983) *Marxism and the Oppression of Women* (London: Pluto Press).
Vogel, L. (1995) *Woman Questions. Essays for a Materialist Feminism* (London: Pluto Press).
Vogler, C. and Pahl, J. (1994) 'Money, Power and Inequality within Marriage', *Sociological Review* **42**(2).
Voronina, O. (1989) 'Women in a "Man's Society"', *Soviet Sociology* **28**(2).
Walby, S. (1986a) 'Gender, Class and Stratification. Towards a New Approach', in R. Crompton and M. Mann (eds).
Walby, S. (1986b) *Patriarchy at Work. Patriarchal and Capitalist Relations in Employment* (Cambridge: Polity Press).
Walby, S. (1990) *Theorizing Patriarchy* (Oxford: Blackwell).
Walby, S. (1996) 'Comparative Analysis of Gender Relations in Employment in Western Europe', *Women in Management Review* **11**(5).
Walker, A. (1993) *Possessing the Secret of Joy* (London: Vintage).
Walker, J. (1995) *The Cost of Communication Breakdown* (Newcastle Upon Tyne: University of Newcastle Upon Tyne, Relate Centre for Family Studies).
Walter, N. (1998) *The New Feminism* (London: Little, Brown and Company).
Ward, C., Dale, A. and Joshi, H. (1996) 'Combining Employment with Childcare: An Escape from Dependency?', *Journal of Social Policy* **25**(2).
Ware, V. (1992) *Beyond the Pale. White Women, Racism and History* (London: Verso).
Warren, M. (1991) 'On the Moral and Legal Status of Abortion', in J. White (ed.) *Contemporary Moral Problems* (Minneapolis: West Publishing Company).
Watson, S. (ed.) (1990) *Playing the State. Australian Feminist Intervention* (London: Verso).
Weedon, C. (1987) *Feminist Practice and Poststructuralist Theory* (Oxford: Blackwell).
Wekker, G. (1995) 'After the Last Sky, Where do the Birds Fly? What Can European Women learn from Anti-Racist Struggles in the United States?', in H. Lutz, A. Phoenix and N. Yuval-Davis (eds).
West, C. and Zimmerman, D. (1991) 'Doing Gender', in J. Lorber and S. Farrell (eds).

West, G. and Blumberg, L. (eds) (1990) *Women and Social Protest* (Oxford: Oxford University Press).
Westwood, S. and Bhachu, P. (eds) (1988) *Enterprising Women. Ethnicity, Economy, Gender Relations* (London: Routledge).
Wetzel, J. (1993) *The World of Women. In Pursuit of Human Rights* (Basingstoke: Macmillan).
Whelehan, I. (1995) *Modern Feminist Thought. From Second Wave to 'Post-Feminism'* (Edinburgh: Edinburgh University Press).
Wilkinson, H. (1994) *No Turning Back. Generations and the Genderquake* (London: Demos).
Wilkinson, H. (1997) *Time Out. The Costs and Benefits of Paid Parental Leave* (London: Demos).
Williams, B. (1979) *Report of the Committee on Obscenity and Film Censorship* (London: HMSO Cmnd 7772).
Williams, F. (1989) *Social Policy: A Critical Introduction* (Cambridge: Polity Press).
Williams, S. (1997) 'Doing the Dirty Work', *Guardian* 15 January.
Willis, L. and Daisley, J. (1990) *Springboard. Women's Development Workbook* (Stroud: Hawthorn Press).
Wilson, A. (1991) Review of Southall Black Sisters *Against the Grain: A Celebration of Survival and Struggle*, *Feminist Review* **39**.
Wilson, E. (1977) *Women and the Welfare State* (London: Tavistock).
Wilson, E. (1992) 'Feminist Fundamentalism. The Shifting Politics of Sex and Censorship', in L. Segal and M. McIntosh (eds).
Witherspoon, S. and Prior, G. (1991/2) 'Working Mothers: Free to Choose?', in R. Jowell, L. Brasil and B. Taylor (eds) *British Social Attitudes* (Aldershot: Dartmouth).
Wolf, N. (1990) *The Beauty Myth* (London: Vintage).
Wolf, N. (1993) *Fire with Fire. The New Female Power and How it will Change the 21st Century* (London: Chatto & Windus).
Wolf, N. (1995a) 'Our Bodies, Our Souls', *New Statesman and Society* 20 October.
Wolf, N. (1995b) 'The Lady's not for Turning' *Guardian* 16 October.
Wolf, N. (1997) *Promiscuities. A Secret History of Female Desire* (London: Chatto & Windus).
Wolf-Devine, C. (1989) 'Abortion and the "Feminine Voice"', *Public Affairs Quarterly* **3**(3).
Woliver, L. (1991) 'The Influence of Technology on the Politics of Motherhood. An Overview of the United States', *Women's Studies International Forum* **14**(5).
Women's Claim of Right Group (ed.) (1991) *A Women's Claim of Right in Scotland* (Edinburgh: Polygon).
Women's National Commission (undated) *Women in the 90s* (London: Women's National Commission).
Wood, E. (1995) *Democracy Against Capitalism. Renewing Historical Materialism* (Cambridge: Cambridge University Press).
Young, I. (1987) 'Impartiality and the Civic Public: Some Implications of Feminist Critiques of Moral and Political Theory', in S. Benhabib and D. Cornell (eds).

Young, I. (1990) *Justice and the Politics of Difference* (Princeton: Princeton University Press).
Yuval-Davis, N. (1985) 'Front and Rear: The Sexual Division of Labour in the Israeli Army', *Feminist Studies* **11**(3).
Yuval-Davis, N. (1989) 'National Reproduction and the Demographic Race in Israel', in N. Yuval-Davis and F. Anthias (eds).
Yuval-Davis, N. (1991) 'The Citizenship Debate: Women, Ethnic Processes and the State', *Feminist Review* **39**.
Yuval-Davis, N. and Anthias, F. (eds) (1989) *Women–Nation–State* (London: Macmillan).
Zaleweski, M. (1991) 'The Debauching of Feminist Theory/The Penetration of the Postmodern', *Politics* **11**(1).
Zaleweski, M. (1996) *Feminist Theory After Postmodernism: Theorising Prenatal Screening and Diagnosis* (Aberystwyth: University of Wales PhD thesis).
Zartov, D. (1995) 'Gender, Orientalism and the History of Ethnic Hatred in the Former Yugoslavia', in H. Lutz, A. Phoenix and N. Yuval-Davis (eds).
Zinn, M. (1996) 'Family, Feminism and Race in America', in E. Chow *et al.* (ed.).

Index

A
300 Group, 117
able-bodied feminists, 215
abortion, 2, 4, 217–18, 219
  competing feminist perspectives on, 11, 21, 28, 155–9, 166
  and disability, 153, 156–7, 170, 217, 218
  and ethic of care, 166–8
  of female fetuses, 153, 159
  feminist ambivalence towards, 7, 149, 160–1, 161–3, 167, 168–9, 171
  feminist demands for legal access, 1, 11, 28, 69, 148, 149, 217
  laws, 149–52
  and patriarchy, 82, 158, 161, 167
  rates, 150–2, 169
  see also Abortion Act; abortion rights; contraception; reproductive rights
Abortion Act, 151
abortion rights, 11, 106, 149, 161–6, 167, 220
  absolute, 149, 155, 161
  problems with rights claims, 160–4, 219–20
  'sliding scale', 165–6, 168
  see also abortion; Abortion Act; reproductive rights; 'a woman's right to choose'
affirmative action, 6, 14, 74, 75, 77, 200, 201
  in legal profession, 73, 85
  and race, 87
  see also merit; quotas; positive action; positive discrimination
African-American men, 67–8, 70
  see also black men

African-American women, 24, 68, 70
  and employment, 139
  as heads of families, 124
  see also black women
Afro-Caribbean boys, 88
Afro-Caribbean women, 67, 98
  and employment, 139
  as heads of families, 124
  see also black women
Aitkenhead, D., 163
Ali, Y., 94
alienation, 17, 22–3, 63, 157, 193
Angelou, M., 70
anorexia, 70–1
ante-natal screening, 152, 153, 170, 217
  see also reproductive technology
Anthony, S., 11
anti-censorship arguments and campaigns, 175, 176–8, 188–9, 193
  see also pornography
anti-feminist men, 200–2
  see also 'backlash' against feminism
anti-pornography arguments and campaigns, 1, 174–5, 176, 178, 179, 182–3, 184–5, 187–8, 189, 190–2, 193, 194
  see also pornography
anti-racist feminism, 8
anti-sexist men, 198–9, 211, 214, 215
  see also men's groups; pro-feminist men
arranged marriage, 54, 70
artificial insemination by donor (AID), 128, 153
  see also fertility treatment; reproductive technology; sperm donors

art/pornography distinction, 181, 182
Asian women in Britain, 67
  see also black women
Astell, M., 10
Australia, 102, 108
autonomy, 11, 38, 155, 159, 160, 165, 190

B
Bacchi, C., 75, 76
'backlash' against feminism, 144, 186, 209
  see also anti-feminist men
Bangladesh, 51
Barrett, M., 100, 126
Battersby, C., 200
Beijing World Conference on Women, 2, 4, 125, 189
Bell, D., 212
benefit system, 131, 138
Benn, M., 130
biological bases of sex difference, 31, 44, 47–8, 49, 87, 215–16
birth control, coercive, 54, 64, 148, 150–1, 158
  see also eugenics; sterilisation, forced
births outside marriage, 123
black as a category, 51
black families, 129, 133
black feminists, black feminism, 8, 9, 31, 32–6, 40, 42, 61, 133, 221
  and men, 60, 67–8, 70, 202
  and employment, 140
  and reproductive rights, 148, 157–8
  see also African-American women; Afro-Caribbean women; Asian women; black women
black men, 45, 104
  and homicide, 207

and the legal system, 73, 76
and masculinity, 202
sexism of, 32, 68
and sexual violence and rape, 53, 60, 80
see also African-American men; Afro-Caribbean boys
black women, 43, 103, 107
centrality to feminism, 34–6, 61, 212
education and employment, 137–8, 139
and gender stereotypes, 50, 53
political activity, 59, 67, 70, 93, 222
and reproductive rights, 54, 64, 148, 157–8
and separatism, 6, 69, 71
sexual exploitation of, 53, 184–5, 188, 193
voters, 106
see also African-American women; Afro-Caribbean women; Asian women; women of colour
Blair, T., 121
Brazil, 152
breadwinner, male, 57, 70, 83, 98, 101, 123, 140–1, 197, 202, 208, 209
Britain, 2, 3, 13, 17, 198, 206
abortion and reproductive issues, 54, 150, 151–2, 153, 154, 156–7, 166, 168
family, 124, 125
ethnic groups in, 51, 52
law, legal system, 73, 75, 77, 78–81, 83, 84, 86–7
politics, 93, 96, 102, 103–5, 108–9, 110, 113, 114, 117–18, 119–21, 122
pornography debates, industry and legislation, 173–4, 175, 180–1

women's employment, 75, 77, 135, 136, 137, 138, 139, 144, 145, 146
Brownmiller, S., 186
Bubeck, D., 57
bureaucratic feminism, 102
see also femocrats
Bush, G., 76, 107

C
California, 154
Campaign Against Pornography (CAP), 175
Campaign Against Pornography and Censorship (CAPC), 175
Campbell, B., 104, 120, 206–7, 207
Canada,
Charter of Rights and Freedoms, 74
obscenity and pornography regulations, 175, 178, 1830
capitalism, capitalist economy, 18, 22, 24
and childcare, 133
and exploitation, 16, 17, 55, 140 197
and patriarchy, 20, 21, 62, 98, 140
and sexuality, 177
and women's oppression, 16, 17, 20, 55, 62, 63
care, as a 'womanly quality', 12, 48, 81, 113, 128, 142, 160
see also childcare; domestic and caring work; ethic of care; mothers, motherhood and mothering
career breaks, 142
see also family-friendly employment
carer's income, 130
Carver, T., 205
Ceaucesco, N., 54
celibacy, 190
censorship and pornography, 7, 172, 174–5, 176–80, 180–1, 182–3, 184, 189, 193

child abuse, 84, 206, 207
see also pornography, child
childbearing/women's reproductive role, importance of, 12–13, 47, 76
and women's oppression, 56, 159
see also mothers, motherhood and mothering
childcare, 43, 106, 117, 138, 147, 221
and abortion, 157, 167, 217–18
costs, 144, 146
and disabled women, 129
men and women's responsibilities for, 47, 76, 83, 124, 128, 209–10
public provision/responsibility 14, 47, 77, 85, 97, 132–3, 144, 146, 157, 167, 217
see also care; domestic and caring work; fathers; mothers, motherhood and mothering
child custody, 87, 88, 200, 201
Child Support Agency, 131
child support laws, 83
China, 18, 189
Chodorow, N., 128
citizens/citizenship, 11, 91, 94–5, 122, 127, 143, 147
and care, 95, 132
and pornography, 178
and reproductive rights, 95, 155, 156, 168, 170
citizen's income, 131
civil rights movement, 26, 32
Clarence Thomas hearings, 67–8, 107
class, 6, 15, 23, 29, 35, 38, 61–5, 138
definitions, 55–6
interests, 16, 55, 120, 141
struggle, 18, 21, 24, 62

and women, 55–6
see also women as a class
Clinton, B., 105, 106, 107, 150
cloning, 153
see also reproductive technology
Cockburn, C., 145
Colker, R., 164
Collins, P., 34, 65, 184–5
'common sense', 9, 13, 15, 90, 160
communism, communist societies, 17, 18, 19, 39, 54, 55, 62
see also eastern Europe; Soviet Union; China; Marxism, Marxist feminism
community politics/informal politics, 59, 67, 69, 72–4, 90–91, 98–9, 99–100
and municipal feminism, 103–4
'concrete ceiling', 138
Connell, R., 208, 211
consciousness-raising, 26–7, 211
Conservative party, 93, 108, 116, 120, 121
contraception, 2, 4, 21, 54, 149–52, 169
see also abortion; birth control; reproductive rights
Coole, D., 43
Coote, A., 104
corporate bodies/corporatism, 14, 109, 110, 111
crime and masculinity, 206–8
criminal law, 78–80
cultural feminism, 8, 28, 39

D

Daly, M., 39
Davis, A., 34, 60, 70, 157–8
Delphy, C., 56
Democratic party, 106, 116
demographic competition, 53–4
Denmark, 189
Depo Provera, 151
see also birth control, coercive; contraception; eugenics
'designer babies', 152, 159, 170
see also reproductive technology
difference feminism, 48
Dinnerstein, D., 128
disability/people with disabilities,
ante-natal tests for, 152
attitudes towards, 65–6, 156, 169, 170, 218
and care, 132, 144
and employment, 138–9
and gender identity, 50, 65–6
as grounds for abortion, 153, 156–7, 170, 217
and oppression, 65–6, 215
as a standpoint, 57
disability feminism, 8, 9, 215
disabled women, 34, 43, 66, 67
and coercive birth control, 148
right to be mothers, 1, 66, 129, 148, 156
right to family life, 128–9
and women's committees, 103, 104
discrimination,
against disabled people, 138–9
against men, 74, 75, 119, 121, 144, 196, 200, 201
against women,
in employment, 138, 140, 141, 142–3, 144
in politics, 115, 117
and pregnancy, 74, 75
racial 87
see also racism
divorce, 87, 123, 145
financial consequences of, 74, 124, 200, 201
financial responsibilities after, 74
rise in, 123, 130
Dole, R., 105, 137
'domestic absenteeism', 206–7
see also childcare; domestic and caring work; fathers
domestic and caring work, and disabled women, 129
and gender identity, 134
importance of, 12–3, 20, 76, 126, 129–30, 142, 147, 219
men and women's unequal responsibilities for, 3, 6, 17, 58, 91–2, 101, 124, 127, 130, 133–4, 143, 145, 146, 169, 199, 205, 212, 218
state support for, 111
and women's exploitation, 56–7
see also care; childcare; domestic labour debate
domestic labour debate, 20, 21
domestic violence, 2–3, 43, 122, 125
and the law, 78, 79, 83, 86, 130
and male power, 127, 218
men as victims of, 200, 201
in minority communities, 54, 67, 129
see also sexual violence; violence against women; Zero Tolerance campaign
Dworkin, A., 174, 179, 181–2, 183, 184, 187, 189, 190–1
see also MacKinnon–Dworkin Ordinances

E

eastern Europe, 14, 18, 54
see also communism, communist societies
eco-feminism, 128

Edinburgh District Council, 104–5
education, 88, 137, 139
  and patriarchy 27
  women's attainments, 135, 139
  women's former exclusion from, 10, 72, 86
  women's right to, 9, 10, 135
egg donors, 154
  see also in vitro fertilisation; reproductive technology
Ehrenreich, B., 209
elderly people, 129, 132
elections/electoral politics, 105–9, 116–19
  see also electoral systems; gender gap in voting; politics; vote
electoral systems, 111, 118–19
EMILY's List, 116–17
EMILY's List UK, 117
employment,
  law, 74–8, 84–5, 135, 144
  male, 135, 137
  women's right to, 9, 11, 135, 139
  see also alienation; equal pay legislation; European Community e. regulations; family-friendly e.; hours of work; minimum wage; part-time work; women workers/women's e.
Engels, F., 20, 62, 63
Equal Opportunities Commission, 3, 84–5, 88
equal opportunities policies, 137, 142
  see also merit
equal pay legislation, 77
Equal Rights Amendment (ERA), 74
erotic material, the erotic, 1, 176, 180, 193
  distinguished from pornography, 181, 182

essentialism, 23, 29, 31, 36, 48, 113–14
ethic of care, 81, 128, 166–8, 210
ethnicity, 52
  see also race
ethnic conflict and gender, 52–4
ethnic identity, 57, 62
eugenics, 7, 59, 170
  see also birth control, coercive; disability as grounds for abortion
Europe, 16, 33
European Community employment regulations, 73, 137
European elections, 121

F
Faith, K., 202
false universalism, 6, 24, 29, 32, 33, 34, 40
family,
  changes in 123–5, 133, 145
  competing feminist perspectives on, 125–29
  ongoing feminist debates, 129–35
  and patriarchy, 56–7, 28, 127, 131, 169, 218
  see also domestic and caring work; fathers; mothers, motherhood and mothering
family-friendly employment, 76–7, 85, 111, 132, 134, 136, 143, 145, 146, 169
  see also maternity leave; parental leave; paternity leave
Family and Medical Leave Act, 76, 107
fathers, 88, 205, 209–10, 214, 218
  and abortion, 163
  absent, 145, 206–7
  age of, 154
  financial responsibilities, 83, 131

  see also childcare; domestic and caring work; domestic absenteeism; paternity leave
Farrakhan, L., 70
Farrell, W., 200
Fawcett Society, 109
female headed households, 3, 202
femininity, 46, 47, 134, 202
  and disabled women, 66
  and politics, 42, 115–16
  see also gender; 'womanly qualities'/ 'womanly values'
feminism,
  continuing importance of, 5
  definitions, 5, 45
  and elitism, 2, 6, 24, 29, 40, 55, 59–61, 122, 140, 218–19
  and racism 2, 5, 6, 23–4, 29, 32–4, 40, 59–61, 67, 68
  young women's attitude to, 1–2
  see also feminist politics; women's movement
Feminist Anti–Censorship Taskforce (FACT), 175
Feminist International Network of Resistance to Reproductive and Genetic Engineering (FINRRAGE), 159
  see also reproductive technology
feminist politics, 5, 27, 30–1, 40, 43–4, 71, 122, 221–2
  see also personal is political; women's movement
Feminists Against Censorship (FAC), 175
femocrats, 110
  see also bureaucratic feminism
Ferguson, K., 203
Ferraro, G., 106

260 Feminist Debates

fertility treatment, 4, 128, 153, 154, 159, 170
  age limits, 154
  see also reproductive technology
fetal rights movement, 150, 161, 163–4
  see also 'pro-life' groups and violence
fetus,
  rights of, 155, 161, 163–4, 165, 166
  status of, 155, 161, 162, 163, 165
Firestone, S., 56, 127, 159
First Amendment to the American Constitution, 174, 176
Foreman, A., 22
Foucauldian, 39
Foucault, M., 37, 99–100, 202
Freely, M., 125–6
free speech, 173, 174, 176, 179
French, M., 23
Friedan, B., 11, 26, 60, 132
Frug, M., 83

G
gay men, 66, 69, 87, 208
gender,
  and disability, 50, 65–6
  identity, 38, 41, 49, 83, 88–9, 113–14, 134, 201, 200–2, 209, 221
  multiplicity of genders, 50, 87, 204
  as performance, 41, 42
  socially constructed, 30, 31, 41–2, 46–7, 83, 115, 202, 207–8, 215–16
  variable with class and race, 33, 49–50, 53, 114, 202
  see also biological bases of sex difference; femininity; masculinity; sex, classification by; sex/gender distinction
gender gap in voting, 105–9

  see also elections/electoral politics; vote
genderquake, 2
Gilligan, C., 81, 166
Gilman, C., 16
'glass ceiling', 137
Glass Ceiling Commission, 137
global feminism, 8
governance, 100
Grant, J., 41–2
Greater London Council (GLC), 103–4
Greenham Common peace camp, 69, 96, 102
Greer, G., 26

H
Habgood, J., 209
Hakim, C., 134, 139
Harding, S., 23
Harman, H., 137, 204
Harstock, N., 22–3
Hartmann, H., 19, 21
Hester, M., 198–9
heterosexuality
  and women's oppression, 7, 127, 189, 190–1, 192
  positive views of, 180, 192
heterosexual women, 148, 191, 192, 214–15
Hill, A., 68
Himmelweit, S., 162, 166
Hispanic people, 57
Hochschild, A., 147
Hoffman, J., 101
homeworkers, 138
homicide, 207
hooks, b., 32, 35, 64, 70
House of Commons, 117–18
  see also women members of parliament
housewives, 11, 22, 56–7, 60–1, 123, 130
  see also Wages for Housework
housework, see domestic and caring work; Wages for Housework
hours of work, 136, 137, 142, 143, 146, 147, 201

Human Fertilisation and Embryology Act, 151, 154

I
Iceland, 110
immigration laws, 129
indecent material, legal definition 181
India, 51
Indianapolis anti-pornography ordinance, 174–5
  see also Minneapolis ordinance
individual rights, 10–11
  collective/contextualised approaches to, 44, 156, 157, 158, 160, 170
  approach criticised, 12, 76, 149, 159–160, 160–4, 219–220
  see also liberal feminism; reproductive rights
infertility treatment, see fertility treatment
infibulation, 54, 70
International Monetary Fund, 207
in vitro fertilisation (IVF), 128, 153
  see also fertility treatment; reproductive technology
Israel, 53–4, 102, 118–19
Italy, 154
Itzin, C., 174

J
Jackson, S., 192
Jaggar, A., 5, 22, 140, 157
Jews, 51
  see also Israel
joy riders, 206
justice, 112, 196, 199, 213
  and the family, 127
  gendered nature of, 72, 81, 113, 166–7, 210

K
Karvonnen, L., 111
Kelly, L., 79
Kennedy, H., 73, 79, 80, 85

Index 261

King, C., 70
King, D., 61
Klein, R., 212
Kollontai, A., 16
Kostack, M., 180

L
Labour government policies, 131, 133, 136–7
Labour party,
  candidate selection, 116, 117
  and electoral reform, 118
  and local government, 103, 104
  women-only shortlists, 75, 117, 120–1
Lacan, J., 38
law,
  male bias, 72, 78, 81, 84, 85–6
  and patriarchy, 72, 82–3, 84, 178, 193
  as a site of struggle, 72, 83, 84
  see also abortion l.; criminal l.; employment l.; legal profession; pornography laws
League of Women Voters, 106
Lees, S., 79–80
legal profession,
  male domination, 72, 79
  women in, 72, 73–4, 81, 85
lesbian feminism, 8
lesbian publications and censorship, 175, 178, 183
lesbian separatism, 29
lesbians, lesbianism, 4, 28, 34, 54, 190, 215
  and abortion, 148
  and the family, 130
  and marriage, 87, 88, 128, 130
  and right to become mothers, 128, 148, 154, 170
  and sado-masochism, 183, 190
  and women's committees, 103, 104

Liberal Democratic party, 121
liberal feminism 8, 9–11, 15, 43, 220–1
  criticisms of, 12–15
  and employment, 12, 139–40, 144
  and the family 13, 125–6, 139
  and men, 11, 196–7, 198
  and politics and the state, 13–15, 90–1, 96, 97
  and pornography and sex, 176–7, 178, 179
  and reproductive rights, 11, 155–6, 160–1
  see also individual rights
'Linda Lovelace', 184
Lister, R.,132
local government, 100, 103–5
  see also municipal feminism
lone mothers, 74, 146
lone-parent families, 123, 124
  and employment, 131, 132, 138
  and underclass, 130
Longford, Lord, 173
Lovenduski, J., 113, 116, 122
Lyndon, N., 200

M
Mackay, F., 104–5
MacKinnon, C., 75, 77, 82–3, 158, 174, 179, 181–2, 184, 185, 187, 189, 190–1
MacKinnon–Dworkin Ordinances, 174–5, 182–3, 193
Maddock, D., 119
male norm, 12–13, 75, 200
  and anti-social behaviour, 206–8
  and citizenship, 94
  displacing, 213
  and employment, 75–6, 142–3, 143, 145
  and the law, 75–6, 78, 81, 82, 84

  and patriarchy, 200, 203–5
  and politics, 205
  man as a category, 215
  manslaughter and the law, 78–9
Marchiono, L., 184
marriage, 125, 204, 205
  financial resources within, 58, 124, 127, 140
  and lesbians, 12, 87, 128, 130
  positive views of, 127, 128
  and women's oppression, 127, 128, 130
Marsh, C., 145
Marx, K., 16, 22
Marxism, Marxist feminism, 17, 19–25, 38, 39, 55, 221
  and the family and domestic and caring work, 20–2, 56–7, 62, 63, 126, 130,
  and men, 197–8
  and politics and the state, 95, 98, 178
  and reproductive rights, 21–2, 157–8
  and sex and pornography, 21–2, 177, 178–9
  and women's employment, 20, 57–8, 140
  see also alienation; capitalism; class; socialism, socialist feminism; social reproduction
masculinity, 46, 47, 66, 197, 198, 202
  and crime, 206–8
  and domestic and caring work, 134
  non-oppressive forms, 203, 209, 209–10
  and politics, 42, 115–16
  problematised, 203, 205–8, 210, 211, 212
  see also gender

maternity leave, 1, 14, 47, 74–5, 76, 85, 97, 135, 136, 217
  in Britain, 75
  and sex discrimination, 74–5
  in United States, 74–5, 136
  see also family-friendly employment; parental leave
McDonagh, E., 165
McDonnell, K., 162
McGregor, S., 177
McIntosh, M., 125
Medicaid, 151
members of parliament, *see* women members of the House of Commons
Meese Pornography Commission, 174
men,
  beneficiaries of present system, 7, 21, 127, 198, 199, 199–200, 211, 213
  changing, 46, 134, 204–5, 209, 204, 213
  competing feminist perspectives on, 196–200, 202, 203–10, 214
  as the enemy, 7, 29, 195, 198–9, 201, 202, 213
  as feminists, 195, 196, 197–8, 198, 212, 213, 214
  gains from equality, 7, 17–18, 195, 196, 197, 198, 211, 213
  as oppressors, 7, 26, 27, 56, 195, 198, 213
  and patriarchy, 198, 199, 211
  and pornography, 182, 188, 192
  positive views of, 30, 68, 192, 195, 214
  sexist behaviour of left-wing men, 18, 19, 20, 26, 197
  and sexual violence, 185, 186–7, 188

  see also African-American men; black men; breadwinners, male; fathers; gay men; heterosexuality; male norm; man as a category; masculinity; oppression of men; oppression of some groups of men; white men; working-class men
men's groups, 198, 205, 206
  see also anti-sexist men; pro-feminist men
men's studies, 205–6, 210–11
merit, 14, 77, 85, 119, 142, 144
  see also affirmative action; equal opportunities policies
middle-class women, 15, 23, 33, 34, 204, 214–15
  and employment, 140
  and gender stereotypes, 50, 53
  and politics, 104, 114, 122
  see also feminism and elitism
military service, and women, 53, 74
Mill, J.S., 11, 73, 196, 204, 213
Millett, K., 27, 39, 62, 200
Million Man March, 70
Millns, S., 83
minimum wage, 8
Minneapolis anti-pornography ordinance, 174–5, 182–3
Mirza, H., 35–6, 40
Mitchell, H., 18
Moi, T., 211, 212
Moraga, C., 54
Moral Majority, 173
Morgan, R., 30–1, 62
Morris, J., 215
Morrison, T., 68
mothers, motherhood and mothering, 88

  in black families, 129, 133
  competing feminist perspectives on, 125–9
  and depression, 125
  and ethical thinking 48, 128, 210
  see also childbearing/women's reproductive role; disabled women, right to become mothers; ethic of care; lesbians, right to become mothers; 'womanly qualities'
municipal feminism, 102, 103–5
  see also local government
murder and the law, 78–9
Murray, L., 125
Muslim societies, 189

N
Nation of Islam, 70
National Association of Women's Organisations (NAWO), 109
National Health Service (NHS), 151
National Organisation for Women (NOW), 11, 97, 106, 196–7
nationalism,
  and gender, 52–4
Native Americans, 51
Netherlands, 152
networks, networking, 1, 73, 93, 94, 116, 122, 222
Neustatter, A., 162
new feminism, 8
'new man', 124, 211
New Left, 26
New Right, 13
non-hierarchical organisation, 95–6, 102, 103
Norris, P., 116
Norway, 77, 110
  see also Scandinavia

O

objectivity,
  as male perspective 39–40
  post-modernist critique of 37, 39
obscenity, obscenity laws, 174, 175, 176, 178, 180–1
  see also pornography
Okin, S., 127
oppression,
  based on
    class, 16, 26, 29, 35, 68
    disability, 65–6
    race, 29, 32, 35, 52, 68
    sexual orientation, 65
  hierarchical, 6, 27, 45, 61–5
  interconnected, 34–5, 61–5, 66–7, 68, 139, 214, 218, 219
  of men, 17, 200–2
  multiple, 34, 35, 61–5
  of some groups of men, 15, 35, 59, 203, 208
  see also capitalism and women's o.; childbearing/women's reproductive role and women's o.; heterosexuality and women's o.; marriage and women's o.; pornography and women's o.; religion and women's o.; sexuality and women's o.
Organisation of Women of Asian and Afro-Caribbean Descent (OWAAD), 67
Overall, C., 165

P

page three, Page Three Bill, 175, 181
paid employment, paid work *see* employment; women workers/women's employment
Pakistan, 51
Palestinian nationalism, 54
parental leave, 43, 85, 143, 146
  in Britain, 71, 77
  in Scandinavia, 76–7
  in Sweden, 136, 143, 146
  in United States, 76, 77, 136
  see also family-friendly employment; maternity leave, paternity leave
Parks, R., 70
part-time work, 136, 138, 139, 142
  and black women, 139
paternity leave, 85, 136, 137, 212
  see also family-friendly employment; parental leave
patriarchy, 20, 21, 27–31, 39, 40, 47, 50, 62
  changes over time, 30
  concept criticised, 29
  concept defended, 30, 218, 221
  defined, 200
  and the public/private distinction, 91–2, 141
  see also abortion and p.; capitalism and p.; education and p.; the family and p.; the law and p.; male norm and p.; men and p.; pornography and p.; rape and p.; sex, sexuality and p.; sexual harassment and p.; sexual violence and p.; state and p.; violence against women and p.; women workers/women's employment and p.
Pennsylvania University, 181
pensions 87, 131
personal is political, 27, 28, 30, 218
  see also public/private distinction
Petchesky, R., 156, 157, 161, 163–4
'phallic drift', 212, 215
Phillips, A., 92, 102, 114, 119–20, 142
political representation of women, 6, 90, 109–11, 112–21, 205, 218
  importance of, 112–14, 145
  under-representation of women, 4, 107, 114
    causes, 115–16
    solutions, 116–21
  see also elections/electoral politics; state politics,
  changing feminist attitudes to formal politics, 98–9, 101, 102, 105–6, 107–8, 109, 112, 122
  competing feminist perspectives on, 90–2
  see also elections/electoral p.; feminist p.; personal is political; political representation of women; state
Pollert, A., 62
Pollitt, K., 164
pornography,
  and black women, 184–5, 188
  child, 173–4, 182
  definitions, 172, 180–4, 189, 193, 194
  effect on sexuality, 184, 189, 190, 191–2, 193, 212
  feminist perspectives on, 174–9
  and harm to women, 178, 179, 180, 184–92, 193
  laws, 14, 174–5, 180–1, 182
  as outlet for male sexual needs, 176–7
  and patriarchy, 28, 82, 177–8, 189, 190, 218
  and sexual freedom, 172, 173, 190, 193
  and sexual violence, 7, 172, 180, 186

Index 263

depicted in pornography, 173, 174, 176, 182, 184, 202
caused by pornography, 178, 179, 183, 184, 187–9
and women's oppression 172, 179, 182, 184, 191, 192–3, 194
see also anti-censorship arguments and campaigns; anti-p. arguments and campaigns; censorship and p.; citizenship and p.
positive action, 110, 143–4
see also affirmative action; positive discrimination; quotas
positive discrimination, 85
see also affirmative action; discrimination against men; positive action
post-feminism, 5
post-modern feminism, 8, 9, 41–3
post-modernism, 23, 31, 36–9, 221
feminist criticisms, 40–1
and individual rights, 159–60
and the law, 42, 83, 86–9
and men, 202
and pornography 183–4, 194
and reproductive rights 159–60
and sex and gender, 47–8, 49, 114
and the state, 99–101
post-structuralism, 36–8
see also post-modernism
poverty, 206
in lone-parent families, 131, 144
within marriage, 124, 127
women's 3–4, 74, 124, 138, 140
power feminism, 8, 11
pregnancy, 163–4

abortion and women's experiences of pregnancy, 162, 163, 166, 167
and employment law, 74, 75, 83
'presenteeism', 146
see also hours of work
pro-feminist men, 211, 212
see also anti-sexist men; men and feminism
'pro-life' groups and violence, 150
see also fetal rights movement
proportional representation, 118–19
prostitution, 14, 177
psychoanalytic theory, 21, 38, 128
public/private distinction, 13, 90, 91–2, 99, 100, 126, 218, 219
see also personal is political
puritanical attitudes to sex, 173, 176, 180 182–3, 190

Q

quotas, 6
in employment, 144
in politics, 90, 108, 110–1, 119–21
see also affirmative action; positive action; women-only shortlists

R

race, 6, 27
and employment, 137–8
socially constructed, x, 50–2
terminology of, 50–1
see also oppression based on race; multiple oppressions; interconnected oppressions
racial hatred, laws against incitement, 176
racism, 23, 52, 93
and the police, 54, 67

and pornography, 184–5, 188, 193
see also feminism and racism
Radford, J., 79
radical feminism, 8, 9, 25–31, 39, 221
criticisms of, 28–30
and employment, 139–43
and the law, 82–3, 177–8
and men, 27, 29, 48, 198–200
and politics and the state, 26–8, 30–1, 90, 90–1, 95–7, 97–8, 102, 121–2
and pornography, sex and violence, 27, 158, 174–5, 176, 177–8, 179, 181–2, 184, 185–92
and reproductive rights, 28, 158–9
see also patriarchy
Ramazanoglu, C., 57
Randall, V., 93, 122
rape, 4, 28, 39, 88
definitions, 185–6, 191
false accusations of, 80, 201
and the law, 78, 79–80, 81, 86, 178
in marriage, 82
myths, 79, 80, 188
and patriarchy, 27, 187
and race, 60, 64
rate, 185
in war, 53
see also pornography and sexual violence; sexual violence
rape crisis centres, 122
Rawls, J., 127
Reagan, R., 106
Reagan–Bush years, 150
Reaganomics, 13
reason,
as basis for rights, 10, 46, 155
women's possession of, 10, 46
Reclaim the Nights marches, 60

Redstockings Manifesto,
  56, 198
religion, 71
  Christian, 71
  fundamentalist, 4, 71
  Islamic, 71
  and women's oppression,
    25, 27
reproductive rights, 2, 4,
  149–50, 217–18
  competing feminist
    perspectives, 11, 21,
    148–9, 155–60
reproductive technology, 2,
  21, 149, 152–4, 165
  and the law, 83, 154
  liberating potential, 56,
    155, 157, 159
  oppressive effects, 157,
    159
Republic of Ireland, 152
Republican party, 106, 163,
  169
Rich, A., 127
Richards, J., 127
rights language
  inappropriate, 158–9,
    159–60, 160–1, 164, 220
  see also abortion; birth
    control, coercive;
    citizenship and
    reproductive rights;
    contraception;
    individual rights;
    reproductive
    technology; surrogacy;
    'a woman's right to
    choose'
Roberts, Y., 214
Roe v. Wade, 150
Roiphe, K., 188
Romania, 54, 64, 152
Rubin, G., 32
Ruddick, S., 128, 210
Rumbold, A., 119

S
sado-masochism, 183, 190,
  193
Savage, W., 165–6
Scandinavia, 204, 205

family and employment,
  32, 133, 134, 145, 204,
  205, 76–7, 133
  politics, 102, 109–112,
    114, 120, 145
  welfare states, 14, 17,
    109
  see also Sweden
Scottish Assembly, 121
Segal, L., 128, 177, 189,
  192, 207
Seidler, V., 206, 211
self-employment, 138
self-help, 139
Selle, P., 111
separatism, 31, 71, 196,
  199, 215
  see also women-only
    organisations
sex–class, 56–7
  see also women as a class
sex, classification by, 49,
  72, 86–9, 130
sex, sexuality, 21–2, 53
  competing feminist
    perspectives 190–2
  male 207, 212, 208
  and oppression 25, 26,
    82–3, 177, 190–1
  and patriarchy 28, 82,
    158, 182, 190–1, 218
  sexual freedom 2, 172,
    173, 190, 193
  see also child abuse;
    heterosexuality;
    lesbians, lesbianism;
    pornography;
    puritanical attitudes to
    sex
sex education, 169
sex/gender distinction, 41,
  46–50
  see also biological bases
    of sex difference;
    gender
sexual attractiveness, 191,
  200, 215
sexual harassment, 43, 68,
  69, 106, 107, 185
  and patriarchy, 141–2
  and race, 68
sexual orientation, 7, 50,
  57, 66, 67, 71, 87, 89

sexual violence, 2, 7, 78,
  86, 122, 172
  extent of, 185–6, 187,
    189–90
  and patriarchy, 27, 186–7,
    199, 201
  and race, 60
  see also domestic
    violence; pornography
    and sexual violence;
    rape; sexual harassment
Short, C., 122, 175, 218,
  219
sisterhood, 27, 29, 35, 40,
  68–9, 222
slavery, 24, 32, 33, 53, 158,
  202
slaves, women compared to
  32, 73
Smart, C., 82–3, 86, 89
Smith, J., 121
'snuff' movies, 174
social democracy, 14, 16,
  110, 120
social reproduction, 21, 57,
  58, 63–4, 157, 178
socialism, socialist
  feminism, 8, 9, 16–18,
    103, 197, 221
  criticisms of, 18–19, 37
  and employment, 140
  and the family, 126,
    132–3
  and men, 17–18, 197–8
  and politics and the state,
    95, 103–4
  and reproductive rights,
    156, 157–8, 166
  and sex and pornography,
    177, 178–9
  see also Marxism,
    Marxist feminism
solidarity, 35, 42, 68, 71,
  114, 214, 222
Southall Black Sisters, 67
Soviet Union, 18
  see also communism,
    communist societies
Spender, D., 39
sperm donors, 154
  see also artificial
    insemination by donor

standpoint,
  black, 34, 35, 36
  disabled, 57
  feminist, 8, 22–3
  white, 52
Stanton, E., 11, 25, 32
state,
  competing feminist perspectives on, 97–101
  and patriarchy, 15, 27–8, 97–8, 100, 121, 122
  see also politics
sterilisation, forced, 54, 64, 148, 151, 158
  see also eugenics
Strossen, N., 176–7, 179, 182–3
suicide, male, 201, 202, 208
Supreme Court of the United States, 68, 75, 107
surrogacy, 58, 149, 153, 154, 157–8
  see also fertility treatment; reproductive technology
Sweden, 4, 110, 124, 138, 189
  parental leave 136, 143, 146
  see also Scandinavia

T
Taylor, B., 142
Taylor, H., 11
'test-tube babies', 153
  see also fertility treatment; reproductive technology
Thatcher, M., 14, 47
Thatcherism, 13
therapy, 28, 30, 211
Thomas, C., 68
Thomas, D., 200
Thompson, J., 165
Thompson, W., 16
time, 111, 115
  see also hours of work
trade unions, 14, 69, 120, 140–1, 144–5
transsexuals, 49, 87, 88
transvestism, 42
Truth, S., 33

U
Uganda, 51
'underclass', 130, 151
United States, 11, 16
  Abortion and reproductive issues, 53, 54, 149–51, 153, 163–4, 166, 168, 169
  culture of individualism, 12, 17, 111, 120, 160
    see also individual rights; liberal individualism
  family, 124
  law, legal system, 73, 74–5, 76
  politics, 97, 105–8, 110, 114–15, 116, 117, 118
  pornography debates, industry and legislation, 173–4, 174–5, 176, 180–1, 182, 188
  women's employment, 74–5, 76, 77, 136, 137, 138, 139, 144, 146–7

V
victim feminism, 8, 11, 29
violence against women, 2–3, 4, 64, 218
  and citizenship, 95
  effect on employment, 186–7
  and patriarchy, 27
  see also domestic violence; rape; sexual violence
vote, 25, 26
  feminist campaigns for, 25–6, 59, 105
  women's right to, 9, 11, 72
  women's voting power, 145
  see also elections/ electoral politics; gender gap in voting

W
Wages for Housework campaign, 20, 130
Warren, M., 155
Whelehan, I., 15
white as a category, 52
Whitehouse, M., 173
white men, 75
  and rape 60, 64, 80
  voters 105
white women
  and pornography 185
  racial identity of 52
  voters 105, 106
  see also feminism and racism
Williams Committee, 174
Williams, S., 113
Wolf, N., 2, 11, 29–30, 162–3, 192, 214
Wolf-Devine, C., 167
Wollstonecraft, M., 10
woman as a category, 40–1, 42, 86–9, 112–13, 215
woman-friendly state, 102, 109
'womanly qualities'/ 'womanly values', 12, 26, 48, 81, 91, 102, 113, 128, 142, 160, 167
  see also femininity; ethic of care
'a woman's right to choose', 6, 11, 149, 159, 162, 163
  see also abortion rights; reproductive rights
women,
  as a class, 55, 56–9, 198
  voters, 102, 105, 106, 145
  see also African-American w.; Afro-Caribbean w.; Asian w. in Britain; black w.; woman as a category; w. of colour; mothers, motherhood and mothering
Women Against Fundamentalism, 71
Women Against Pit Closures, 69
women members of the House of Commons, numbers, 110, 115, 117, 121

behaviour/qualities, 42, 113, 114–15
women members of Scandinavian parliaments,
  numbers, 109–10
  behaviour/qualities, 111–12, 114
women members of United States Congress,
  numbers, 107, 110, 115
  behaviour, 114–15
women of colour, 32, 33, 34, 35, 59, 70, 158
  term discussed, 51
  see also African-American w.; Afro-Caribbean w.; Asian w.; black w.
Women of the Waterfront, 70
women-only organisations, 1, 18, 21, 69, 96–7, 195, 196–7, 213, 215
  see also separatism
women-only shortlists, 75, 117, 120–1
  see also quotas
women's refuges, 1, 28, 40, 82, 122, 201
women's committees, 103–4
Women's Institute (WI), 93, 95, 109
women's movement 1, 11, 22, 26, 31, 32, 42, 59, 106, 122
  see also feminist politics
women's studies, 3, 33, 61
women workers/women's employment, 2, 135–47, 205
  competing feminist perspectives on 139–43
  low pay 3, 74, 136, 137, 138, 141, 144, 201, 218
  and patriarchy, 140, 141, 143
  see also employment; part-time work

Wood, E., 62–3
work, *see* domestic and caring work; employment; women workers/women's work
working-class men, 18, 19, 45, 60, 70, 104
working-class women, 23, 33, 34, 50, 98
  and employment 74
  political activity, 59, 69–70, 92–4, 103
World Health Organisation (WHO), 152

Y
Young, I., 112

Z
Zero Tolerance Campaign, 104–5
Zetkin, C., 16